THE BOYS OF SUMMER

THE BOYS OF SUMMER

or 'THERE'S AN ELEPHANT IN THE ROOM!'

A TALE OF CUDDLY CHARACTERS, PROUD CARAVAN OWNERS
AND A ROCK AND ROLL BAND

by

DAVE BARTRAM

fantom
publishing

First published in hardback in 2012 by Fantom Films
fantomfilms.co.uk
Paperback edition (with additional chapter) published 2013

A catalogue record for this book is available from the British Library.

Paperback edition ISBN: 978-1-78196-098-1

Typeset by Phil Reynolds Media Services, Leamington Spa
Printed and bound in the UK by ImprintDigital.com

Cover design by Robert Hammond

To Cathy – My shining light

THREE ANCIENT LANDS, FIVE MIGHTY OCEANS AND THIRTY-THREE SORTIES INTO UNCHARTED TERRITORY

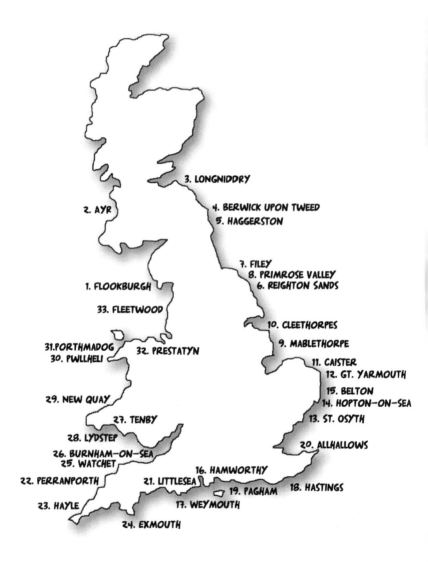

3. LONGNIDDRY

2. AYR

4. BERWICK UPON TWEED
5. HAGGERSTON

7. FILEY
8. PRIMROSE VALLEY
6. REIGHTON SANDS

1. FLOOKBURGH

33. FLEETWOOD

10. CLEETHORPES
9. MABLETHORPE

31. PORTHMADOG
30. PWLLHELI

32. PRESTATYN

11. CAISTER
12. GT. YARMOUTH

15. BELTON
14. HOPTON—ON—SEA

29. NEW QUAY

13. ST. OSYTH

27. TENBY

28. LYDSTEP

20. ALLHALLOWS

26. BURNHAM—ON—SEA
25. WATCHET

16. HAMWORTHY

22. PERRANPORTH

21. LITTLESEA

19. PAGHAM

18. HASTINGS

23. HAYLE

17. WEYMOUTH

24. EXMOUTH

CONTENTS

'Surely the venues can't be that bad, and the chalets and caravans they would provide us with would be more than adequate – wouldn't they??'

FOREWORD

WHEN I WAS a schoolgirl, just like most of my friends my bedroom wall was adorned with colour centre-spreads taken from the girlie publications of the day such as *Patches* magazine.

As opposed to David Soul, John Travolta and the other cheesy heart-throbs of the 1970s, my pin-up was the lovely Showaddywaddy singer Dave Bartram.

Dave's cheeky smile and unique charisma set him apart from the pack and never failed to put a smile on my face as he strutted around in his shocking-pink stage suit belting out *Under the Moon of Love*, *You Got What it Takes* and a host of other hits I'd happily jig around the room to.

Each Thursday night as *Top of the Pops* came onto the TV, I'd wait in anticipation hoping the band would appear so that I could rush up and kiss the screen, believing he would know I was close up and could feel my heart pounding on the other side.

I look back with incredible fondness to those late-seventies days and my infatuation with Dave, and though I was very young I always liked a man in a flashy suit! Still do! So I was really touched when he contacted me to 'cheekily' ask if I would be willing to write a foreword for his debut as a writer.

After a long and fruitful career Dave has some amazing tales to tell of his life on the road, including the hilarious hell on earth tour featured here in *The Boys of Summer*.

I wish this genuinely nice guy every success in his new vocation.

Amanda Holden
November 2012

INTRODUCTION

READY TEDDY
(LITTLE RICHARD/BUDDY HOLLY/ELVIS PRESLEY)

PERHAPS YOU COULD say I'm blowing my own trumpet when I tell you my band had a run of chart success unparalleled by any other artist(s) during the decade that spanned the 1970s, but it's a fact of which I'm immensely proud.

It was my mug shot that mostly characterised Showaddywaddy, and graced the covers of teen magazines like *Jackie*, and more sparingly the so-called 'respected' music rags such as *New Musical Express*, *Melody Maker* and *Sounds*.

In all honesty it was a privilege (though on the odd occasion misfortune) to be the band's front man and 'pin-up' from its inception in 1973, and in retrospect it's hard to believe I'm still in one piece after a rollercoaster ride that has endured for the best part of forty years.

There have indeed been many unprecedented ups and downs along the way, none more so than the ten-week period described in this 'warts and all' account, which by some quirk of fate I diarised for the first time ever after thirty-two years of touring.

By 2005 I'd been handling the band's managerial affairs for over twenty years and, with the main source of motivation being to make a moderately good living, accepted a run of thirty-three holiday-camp dates, which stretched the length and breadth of Great Britain's bucket-and-spade resorts.

What I'd failed to take on board was that, even as seasoned performers, we would be entering into uncharted territory; and from experiencing 'life in the fast lane', the band were about to undergo 'a breakdown on the hard shoulder.'

This is the story of a tour to end all tours – ten weeks that strained every sinew and emotion virtually to the limits of human endurance.

TOUR PROGRAMME – SUMMER 2005

JULY

Monday 18th	Flookburgh, Cumbria, England
Tuesday 19th	Ayr, Ayrshire, Scotland
Wednesday 20th	Longniddry, East Lothian, Scotland
Thursday 21st	Berwick Upon Tweed, Northumberland, England
Friday 22nd	Haggerstone, Northumberland, England
Monday 25th	Reighton Sands, Yorkshire, England
Tuesday 26th	Filey, Yorkshire, England
Wednesday 27th	Primrose Valley, Yorkshire, England
Thursday 28th	Mablethorpe, Lincolnshire, England
Friday 29th	Cleethorpes, Lincolnshire, England

AUGUST

Tuesday 2nd	Caister, Norfolk, England
Wednesday 3rd	Great Yarmouth, Norfolk, England
Thursday 4th	Saint Osyth, Essex, England
Friday 5th	Hopton-on-Sea, Norfolk, England
Saturday 6th	Belton, Norfolk, England
Tuesday 9th	Hamworthy, Dorset, England
Wednesday 10th	Preston, near Weymouth, Dorset, England
Thursday 11th	Hastings, East Sussex, England
Friday 12th	Pagham, West Sussex, England

Saturday 13th	Allhallows, Kent, England
Thursday 18th	Littlesea, Dorset, England
Friday 19th	Perranporth, Cornwall, England
Saturday 20th	Hayle, Cornwall, England
Sunday 21st	Exmouth, Devon, England
Tuesday 23rd	Watchet, Somerset, England
Wednesday 24th	Burnham-on-Sea, Somerset, England
Thursday 25th	Tenby, Pembrokeshire, Wales
Friday 26th	Lydstep, Pembrokeshire, Wales
Saturday 27th	New Quay, Cardiganshire, Wales
Tuesday 30th	Pwllheli, Gwynedd, Wales
Wednesday 31st	Porthmadog, Gwynedd, Wales

SEPTEMBER

Thursday 1st	Prestatyn, Denbighshire, Wales
Friday 2nd	Fleetwood, Lancashire, England

SHOWADDYWADDY BAND PROFILES

Name	Romeo Challenger
Instruments played	Drums, percussion
Place/date of birth	Antigua, West Indies
	May 19th 1950
Hobbies	TV addict, chess, teaching drums to children
Favourite band/artist(s)	Led Zeppelin
Favourite food	Cumberland sausage
Favourite TV show(s)	*The Wire*, *24*, *Lost*
Dislikes	Harry Hill, Cheri Blair

Name	Rod Deas
Instruments played	Bass guitar
Place/date of birth	Scarborough, Yorkshire
	February 13th 1948
Hobbies	Golf, snooker
Favourite band/artist(s)	Bob Marley, Stanley Clarke
Favourite food	Indian, French
Favourite TV show(s)	*Top Gear*, *The Osbournes*
Dislikes	Bad manners (not the band!)

Name	Trevor Oakes
Instruments played	Rhythm guitar
Place/date of birth	Leicester
	September 9th 1946
Hobbies	Football, being a nuisance
Favourite band/artist(s)	The Who
Favourite food	Indian, 'advocado pears' (nb), ketchup
Favourite TV show(s)	*Lovejoy*, *Countdown*, *Footballers' Wives*
Dislikes	Hairdressers, discipline

Name	Jeff Betts (aka Al James)
Instruments played	Bass guitar, vocals
Place/date of birth	Billesdon, Leicestershire
	January 13th 1946
Hobbies	Crosswords, shooting, circuit training
	(around the local pubs)
Favourite band/artist(s)	Led Zeppelin, Green Day, Ron Jeremy
Favourite food	Traditional English
Favourite TV show(s)	*The Osbournes, Anatomy for Beginners*
Dislikes	Egotists, early closing times

Name	Danny Willson
Instruments played	Lead guitar, vocals
Place/date of birth	Leicester
	November 14th 1957
Hobbies	Decorating, walking, photography
Favourite band/artist(s)	XTC, Wishbone Ash, The Thorns
Favourite food	Fish and chips
Favourite TV show(s)	*The Office, Alan Partridge*
Dislikes	Rhythm guitarists, Graham Norton

Name	Dave Bartram
Instruments played	Lead vocals, guitar, piano, harmonica
Place/date of birth	Lutterworth, Leicestershire
	March 23rd 1952
Hobbies	Football, cricket, reading, running
Favourite band/artist(s)	Ryan Adams, Ray Charles,
	Bruce Springsteen
Favourite food	Roast beef and Yorkshire pudding, Indian
Favourite TV show(s)	*Shameless, Bleak House*
Dislikes	Shrink-wrapping, flash gits,
	Gordon Brown's mouth (God forbid
	he ever becomes Prime Minister)

THE BOYS OF SUMMER

(All of the above profiles are based on preferences from the summer of 2005.)

With thanks to the hard-working crew:

Steve Beale – sound co-ordinator
Stefan Radymski – back line technician

1

SUMMERTIME BLUES
(EDDIE COCHRAN)

I TOOK THE first call in early November 2004. The agent explained what a potentially lucrative business opportunity this was, and just how fortunate we were to be in the frame, when many other artists were clamouring to be considered for the gig.

He described the venues as 'popular holiday parks', and though perhaps not quite as upmarket as the rival Butlin's camps, the in-house facilities would be more than adequate to stage a suitably adept performance by the band. Smiling to myself, my initial reaction was, 'Butlin's! Upmarket! Now there's an oxymoron, pull the other one!'

The gist of the conversation soon unfolded. This would be two months' hard graft for an adequately healthy pay-cheque at the end of it. I'd also perspicaciously taken into account that the agent would be in receipt of a fat commission should he persuade me to agree.

'They've upped the budget for this year's summer season, and want some bigger names to give the parks more credibility,' he rambled on.

After being involved in music management for twenty-two years, I'd developed a kind of sixth sense as to when things are likely – perhaps – to come unstuck, and somewhat inauspiciously by the end of that initial conversation became blighted by a contagious dose of 'bad vibes'.

The music business has always attracted a cunning breed of entertainment agents and guileful promoters who, shall we say, can be economical with the truth, and from experience I was well aware of the pitfalls of what was flippantly known in the trade as 'a bank raid'. However, this time my arm was being firmly twisted from the outset, in that the immediate months ahead were worryingly quiet compared to previous years; and with summer fast approaching the thought of a healthy bank balance accumulated from a few weeks by the sea became ever more appealing by the minute.

To make the package even more attractive, the leisure company we were dealing with would throw in accommodation to boot, which would prudently trim down on the expenses. The temptation was there: and I remember thinking at the time, 'Surely the venues can't be that bad, and the chalets and caravans that they would provide us with would be more than adequate – wouldn't they??' This had to be worth a punt!

♫

On the back of three or four weeks of technical specifications, riders, rooming lists etc. toing and froing from one party to the next, we were just about there. Everything was more or less covered contractually, and we were confident that any unforeseen problems would be dealt with in a helpful and professional manner; and perhaps more importantly the band ourselves were prepared to get out there and give the knotted-hanky brigade a great night out at every fun-packed resort. The rabbinical obstacles had been negotiated without as much as a blip on the radar, and it was time to hit the holiday trail.

Long regarded as rock-and-roll stalwarts, Showaddywaddy had been successfully touring for more than three decades. The rip-roaring days of teeny-bop stardom during the late seventies were just ego-massaging memories, but we still had a great following, looked upon ourselves as being good pros, and could give most bands a run for their money when it came to live performances. But what lurked beneath the surface during those mid-noughties summer months would serve to numb every nerve, muscle and bone within our rock-wearied carcasses.

For a number of years the band had been a little up against it when we toured, largely down to the fact that the crew manager we employed in 2005 could not be described as a people person, and most certainly didn't suffer fools gladly. Come to think of it dear old Steve didn't suffer anyone gladly. Basically he was a born curmudgeon, and pretty much considered everyone he met as a bonehead, apart from the odd but rare occasions when he could somehow be won over, generally by a man's man (though there would more than likely be plentiful free beverages involved for this to happen!).

Steve first began working with the band in the pre-digital mid-seventies as a lighting designer, which when abbreviated (as is most technical jargon) meant he was our LD, but little did he know that in more deprecating terms his employers cruelly jested it also stood for lorry-driver, though needless to say no one was about to let him in on the joke.

His appearance was initially intimidating, regularly sporting a Che Guevara revolutionary green cap, and a long beard that would have been the envy of any ZZ Top member or devotee.

To strangers his vocabulary was largely monosyllabic, which rubbed up the staff of many a show hall the wrong way. He simply didn't react favourably to over-the-top warm welcomes or inane chit-chat, and his laconic approach to his would-be new friend was more along the lines of 'where d'ya want the fucking gear?'

I did on the odd occasion spend some social time with Steve, and in fairness he could be surprisingly knowledgeable and good company. Indeed we once travelled together on a twenty-four-hour trip from Hong Kong (when it still belonged to the Brits) into Guangzhou, China, and throughout my time with him felt I got to know a far-and-away gentler human being during what was a rewarding and fascinating day out for the pair of us.

That said, when it came to work his cantankerous side came very much to the fore. So the next few weeks would not be easy, as I realised that prior to my own arrival at any of the camps I would have to bear the brunt of Steve's (and his opposite number's) wrath by mobile phone; and furthermore I would be forced into making apologies and excuses to the staff on site he'd rubbed up the wrong way during the load-in, when the band attended the sound-check a little later in the day.

Steve stubbornly still believed that the days of huge articulated trucks, multi-stacked PAs and lavish lighting gantries were just around the corner (I for one have never forgotten the impression that three mammoth articulated trucks carrying Emerson Lake & Palmer's gear had on me, where each truck was emblazoned with a band member's giant initial, i.e. E, L and P!) but regrettably, and in reality, the budget and facilities on offer for this tour felt to him like a betrayal, and as very much a downturn in fortunes.

It wasn't as if we hadn't performed at any holiday camps before. Indeed a few years back we'd played twenty-six consecutive Sundays at venues that weren't dissimilar at all, many of which had been great gigs; and the travelling, although tiresome, must have helped toughen us up for what lay ahead in the coming weeks. Steve's premonitions, however, were by no means unfounded, as many of the gaily coated brigades that worked these camps had serious attitude problems, often brought about by excessive working hours, particularly when it came to crew members to whom they considered themselves vastly superior. Were this to habitually prove the case it would not be well received by our infamous road manager, and would undoubtedly cause major difficulties.

On the plus side, there was actually some cause for optimism, as we'd already played at a couple of the parks on this circuit during the close season, effectively as prototype gigs. Happily there had been no problems reported whatsoever, and Steve, realising any issues may prove costly, had been on his very best behaviour. So now it really was time to knuckle down and literally get the show on the road.

I'd pre-warned the grumpy crew boss that we would simply have to grit our teeth for two-and-a-half months and get on with it, and that perhaps we could laugh about it over a beer when the tour was over; but he typically remained stony-faced as ever, and blew a deep, gruff sigh.

The sun was in the sky, the temperatures had soared to twenty-one degrees Celsius. Summer had arrived, and the first gig was fast approaching.

2

SHAKE RATTLE & ROLL
(BIG JOE TURNER/BILL HALEY & THE COMETS)

Monday 18th July 2005

As a kid I had many memorable family holidays in Norfolk, and certainly did not look down my nose at British holiday resorts or the innumerable stretches of caravan parks perched, sometimes rather precariously, towards the cliff-top ledges.

We'd set off at the beginning of the August fortnight break, in my Dad's motorbike and sidecar, with what seemed like all our worldly goods crammed inside underneath the waterproof canopy along with my well-insulated, but excited, big brother and me.

Mum would ride pillion, with a haversack on her back, arms wrapped around Dad's stomach, clinging on for dear life. That was until little sister Patricia came along, and the family were forced to invest in a small car, the make and model of which has slipped my mind. This too would be loaded up to the gunnels, as we hiccupped and backfired our way along the bumpy old A47 trunk road to the genial Mr Leake's caravan site in East Runton, near Cromer.

In something of an ambitious project, my father and his brother-in-law – known as Uncle Ken – actually constructed a huge six-berth caravan entirely from scratch, at the bottom of the garden of our home in the Leicestershire village in which I was brought up. This was to prove an arduous and prolonged project of two years or more, but upon completion, and with a fearful maiden voyage to the Norfolk coast in the bag, provided us all with a seaside retreat that the whole family embraced and grew to love dearly.

So there I was, under no illusions from travelling the world and staying in five-star luxury hotels, and armed with the knowledge that the facilities in the twenty-first century had to be far superior to those of the antediluvian late fifties and early sixties. I'd simply be undertaking a nostalgic return to my roots.

♫

In readiness and in an effort to appear organised, tour itineraries had been prepared for the whole company, and – Steve apart – the fearless body of men were as ready as they'd ever be, leaving few doubts they would enter into this new adventure with alacrity.

The first show and overnight stay was to be on the craggy Cumbrian coast, not far from the renowned Lake District in a tucked-away resort called Grange-over-Sands. With the Lakes' reputation as one of the UK's loveliest areas preceding it, the expedition seemed destined to kick off in a very positive mode, which I suppose in retrospect to a degree it probably did!

In a business-like attempt to be prudent, the overall running costs had been stripped down almost to the bone; which, on top of indicating there would be little money to play with, also meant that the amount of gear to be lugged into the venue upon the crew's arrival was way less than the guys were accustomed to.

The band showed up a little later to discover that everything had happily gone according to plan. As per technical requirements a number of able-bodied humpers had been waiting on site to assist the crew. Steve had instructed them efficiently, and been on his best behaviour, and the modest rig had been set up with a minimum of fuss.

We were handed keys and a haphazardly complicated map of the park, which after ineptly fathoming it out finally led us to our accommodation. The party would be spending the night in four caravans, and although we were expected to bunk up together, there were two bedrooms in each caravan, so the only thing we'd really have to share was a bathroom.

The brightly attired rep who'd handed me the keys had melodramatically emphasised that these were not just caravans, but were Prestige class! 'There's only Platinum class that are superior to these,' he'd added.

'Oooh!' I'd reacted in a girly falsetto voice, before animatedly returning to the boys, smiling to myself, and putting into question everyone's reservations, and in my optimism imagining that things really wouldn't be so bad after all.

I wandered back to the reception area, as prior to the gig I'd received a phone call from the duty manager, who'd said he was looking forward to meeting me and asked if I'd pop in to say hello upon arrival. Behind the front desk was an anorexic-looking girl who informed me that he was on a call, but wouldn't be long, if I'd be so good as to take a seat.

My eyes were immediately drawn to the pallid woman, who clearly had an aversion to the fare they served up at the camp, if not to anything nutritious in general.

There's something eerie about very skinny people that gives me the creeps: perhaps it's the angular bones that jut from beneath a thin sack of skin that renders their appearance as almost deathly. But whatever it may have been, rather than engage in a conversation about her daily dietary requirements I took the option of perusing the notice board, which listed some quite fascinating forthcoming attractions.

The new 'higher budget' kids on the block weren't exactly in esteemed company, with the colourful blurb advertising acts such as 'The Immaculate Deception – A tribute to Madonna' and 'The Cool Crooner, featuring the music of Sinatra, Dean Martin and Andy Williams' who was on the following night. Coming soon was a Hogwarts tribute featuring Harry, Ron and Hermione lookalikes; and the next Sunday they had a Madness tribute called 'Badness', which on the poster looked more akin to a seventies glam-rock band.

It was difficult not to notice that the programme consisted of tribute after tribute. The Beatles, Elvis, the Eagles, Kate Bush (amusingly called 'Fake Bush'), Queen, Abba – they were all represented here. The list went on and on right into September through the entire season.

The impending arrival that particularly caught my attention was boldly displayed on a garishly designed poster, featuring three rather rotund guys who hilariously went by the name of 'The Gastric Band'. The blurb read: 'A comic tribute to the Three Tenors,' and chuckling away I pondered whether this may be a play on words, and was more of a reference to the thirty quid they may be getting paid!

Ben, the duty manager, hand outstretched, came from his dugout to greet me and, although cordial, seemed a little nervous about the stacks of equipment that had been loaded into the concert room.

'I didn't realise your set-up is similar to that of a proper rock band,' he said.

'Well, we're not a tribute band, that's for sure,' I answered.

'Funny you should say that: we've already had your tribute here, the one featuring Freddy Rock,' he informed me.

I'd been made well aware that there was a band called Showmaddymaddy who were out on the circuit paying homage to our good selves, but in all my experience I'd never yet come across the legendary Freddy Rock!

'Was he any good?' I questioned.

'Mmm, that's a matter of opinion; I sincerely hope the real thing is a lot better,' he said diplomatically.

The pleasantries out of the way, I explained to Ben that the excessive gear was really nothing to worry about, and after I'd succeeded in reassuring him he kindly thanked me, wishing us all a great night, before I strolled back to my makeshift homestead.

Lead guitarist Danny, bass player Rod and myself were the band's lovers of the great outdoors, so once everything was smoothly in place and our minds at rest we decided to take a pre-sound-check stroll and sample our first blast of sea air. The weather was inescapably bracing for the time of year, but the threatened downpour had failed to materialise as we breathed in the stimulating briny flurries of fresh ozone.

'Are we somewhere near to that nuclear power plant that's up this way?' asked Danny.

'You mean Windscale?' I chipped in, but was quickly corrected by Rod:

'I think you'll find it's called Sellafield!'

It was agreed it was one or the other, but apparently it was some miles north of this stretch of sand; and, happily reassured there was nothing whatever toxic in the atmosphere, the invigorated trio trudged back across the stones towards the entertainment complex in readiness for the daily run-through.

The stage area was a lot smaller than we were used to, and didn't fully comply with the technical specifications that had been prearranged; but, that said, we'd played the odd worse gig and I was desperate not to rock the boat on the opening night of the tour.

The main headache was that a troupe of dancing girls would be using the same area shortly before the band's allotted performance time, the likes of whom had left a number of fluffy props strewn around that formed part of their routine. Happily it was agreed with the rather effeminate stage-manager that these items would be swiftly removed prior to the bill-toppers taking to the stage, and another potentially contentious issue had been competently side-stepped.

Plates of chunky sandwiches, sausage rolls and large pots of tea and coffee were generously provided as we wound up our shakedown, and spirits were optimistically high. After what had already been a long day, it was now time for a pre-gig chillout in front of the television in our prestigious caravans.

♪

Though the park had appeared to be pretty deserted during daylight hours, the Show-Bar where we were set to perform was absolutely packed to the rafters. Where on earth had everybody suddenly surfaced from? It was something of a mystery; but every performer loves a full house, and the ensemble's nerves soon settled in anticipation of a wild night before a well-oiled and enthusiastic crowd.

What was most bewildering during the early part of the show was the number of small kids who were to be seen running amok beween the rows of seating, with no sign of them tiring well after eleven p.m. Still, this was the silly season and a time for the family, in spite of the fact it was immediately apparent that the dads were situated at the rear bar area of the room, whilst the majority of the mums were seated to the forefront of the stage, chauvinistically expected to keep an eye on the sprogs, whilst dreaming of their teenage years.

Come to think of it a sizeable proportion of these mothers were probably still in their teens, and may never even have heard of the band, but undeterred we played a tight seventy-minute set before a perspiring but appreciative crowd and scurried off to our house trailers to raid the fridge and take an early-ish night.

♪

Three weeks prior to that first gig I was sceptical at the likelihood of being away from home for any extended period of time, as my dear old Mum was hospitalised after the most serious of a number of recent falls.

I'd visited her every day that I could, and can still to this day picture her face lighting up each time I strode into the ward where she'd be propped up against a tilted-up bed and a pile of pillows.

She'd been in and out of hospital for some years now, with various age-related problems, but the whole family deep down knew that this time was different. She'd become tearful and unhappy and was eating precious little, and the family visits that lit up her day were just about the only thing keeping her going.

Notwithstanding, the road awaited and Mum would have been furious had I as much as contemplated a change of plans that would selfishly involve letting anyone down.

Being in a band is in many respects similar to being part of a family, in that each member bears a responsibility to the others to get on with things, generally whatever the circumstances.

Our bags were packed and it was heads down, full throttle into thirty-three undiscovered two-wheel townships.

3

GREAT BALLS OF FIRE
(JERRY LEE LEWIS)

Tuesday 19th July 2005

The opening night had been well received and encouragingly had boosted everyone's confidence. The caravans had been comfortable enough, and with no complaints of a sleepless night – other than Trevor carping over a couple of noisy kids outside his window at first light – there was just cause for optimism prior to venturing further north into bonny Scotland to the coastal town of Ayr.

We'd long possessed a fondness for the Scots, and had played many wonderful concerts spanning thirty years at some incredibly atmospheric venues throughout the untamed but hospitable land. The 'haggis-bashers', as we jokingly referred to them, would invariably afford an exuberant welcome, and loved their rock and roll with a passion; in my experience, and at the risk of sounding patronising, the Scots have to be amongst the most receptive of all audiences the world over.

Going back to the seventies we performed a number of concerts at the legendary Glasgow Apollo (which was sadly later demolished), and I'd previously gone on record as saying it was my favourite gig on the planet. Watching the packed top balcony literally vibrate and throb to the rhythm of the loud music and the crowd's exaggerated exertions still makes my nerve ends tingle to this day.

So surely even at a holiday park the Scots would be their ever ebullient, fun-loving selves: after all they were on holiday! Following an acceptable fry-up we made a reasonably early start (for a band) of ten-thirtyish, and navigated north for *Braveheart* country.

We'd actually played the Ayr venue some years before, when it was an all-singing and dancing holiday centre, with high-tech facilities, and a generous entertainment programme budget that brought in some big names. During the low-season winter months these camps regularly held themed weekends, and we would often get roped into the seventies or occasionally eighties bracket. Bands would play around the clock, whilst the party animals went seriously 'on the lash' and shagged themselves silly for the best part of seventy-two hours, before returning home, burnt out, to their unknowing spouses and partners.

By 2005 the camp was almost unrecognisable from its former glory days, and probably hadn't seen a lick of paint in ten years or more. The public buildings had become shabby, discoloured and depressingly drab, and the whole place was sorely in need of a makeover. Even the stuccoed chalets designed to shelter the paying guests were in a serious state of disrepair, with chunks of plaster missing from the walls and bare breezeblocks showing through. On a turbulent, chilly July day that felt more like November there was an air of discontentment and dampness all around, which – combined with the aroma of stale chip-fat lingering in the wind – made for a depressing backdrop.

The onsite eateries didn't look particularly tempting either, with a cluster of downmarket pizza parlours and copy McDonald's joints on offer that I was adamant I wouldn't be frequenting for the entire duration of the tour.

During the weeks building up to the stint my caring wife Cathy had put me on a healthy food regimen. She was familiar with my rock-and-roll tales describing the rigours of the road, and had come to realise I'd more than likely be indulging myself in excessive portions of fast food throughout the trip; and thus responded by serving up innumerable greens and high-fibre rations as part of my new and disciplined diet. It was lentils and haricot beans with everything, and after around ten days of the stuff the sounds emanating from my rear end simulated that of a light aircraft.

I persevered along an avenue of moribund stores selling cheap souvenirs and candy floss in search of the Spar supermarket I'd been led to believe was on the same thoroughfare.

I'd been punishing my body by running and exercising most days in preparation, as I'd been found wanting during a couple of backbreaking tours over the years, when the onstage physicalities and constant late-night socialising began to take their toll. So I was acutely aware of how draining living out of a suitcase could be. The travelling alone was debilitating, and with the band all being in our fifties there were regular grumblings of back pain, arthritis, cramp and sciatica.

I've often said that a guy knows he's approaching old age when he wakes up in the morning and everything's stiff apart from his cock! During one's twenties it's quite the reverse! But regardless of the gags, I had to make every effort to stay in reasonable nick.

The orderly tending the supermarket was absent from his post at the till, but impatiently I looked along one of the aisles and spotted him neatly replenishing the baked-beans shelf. His ruddy, zit-covered face – which he clearly had a passion for tampering with – was at first off-putting, but as one of a captive multitude I had little choice but to try and attract his attention.

There was no cheery 'good morning' or even 'kiss my arse!' He simply shrugged his shoulders grudgingly, and reluctantly lifted up his slovenly frame before trudging back to his little domain behind the counter.

I enquired: 'Do you have a loaf of bread?'

He pointed towards the rear of the shop and wearily advised me, 'On the back wall mate.'

There were around half a dozen starchy thick-sliced white loaves, and a few loose crusty rolls, which were not quite what I had in mind. I walked back to the till, and asked if he may have a wholemeal sliced in stock, to which he quizzically replied: 'Does that mean brown bread?'

'Spot on,' I giggled.

'No call for it mate, they don't like all those bits in it round 'ere,' he muttered.

This was clearly going to be an uphill battle, but undaunted I asked if the store stocked fruit.

'There are some pineapple chunks over there next to the baked beans,' he acknowledged.

'Not a can – fresh fruit. Oranges, apples, pears, anything like that,' I urged.

The predictable response wasn't long in coming: 'No call for it mate!'

Disappointed in my unfulfilment I wound up buying a bottle of Lucozade and a gooey pink frosted doughnut. The health kick was on the slippery slope already, but being kind to myself it was the only thing in the shop that looked even semi-appetising.

'Are you sure you want that doughnut? It's yesterday's you know,' remarked Zit Boy, making it obvious he'd had his eye on the same sweet delicacy to be consumed during his tea break.

'I'm perfectly sure thanks,' I answered curtly, and slightly bemused left him to feast his eyes on an alternative afternoon treat, ahead of continuing my stroll along 'The Strip'.

♫

Our daily wanderlust fulfilled, Danny, Rod and I ventured forth into the Lounge Bar Café, which in reality was just a posh name for the canteen.

I sampled an appalling imitation of a chilli con carne, which with its lack of spice tasted just like an insipid bowl of beef stew with a few added tomatoes, and was bland and full of gristle. What's more it hadn't even been cheap; but with no desire to wind myself up, and in an effort to distract my taste buds from the flavourless slop, I sat and counted a total of three red kidney beans in the entire sorry concoction.

Already, with thirty-one camps ahead of us, I had begun fantasising about a succulent rack-of-lamb dinner, or a traditional home-cooked Sunday roast, whilst pondering how prison food would compare to the unsavoury swill before me.

Sound-check came and went in the pretentiously named Atlantic Show-Bar, which may well have sounded glitzy, but in reality bore no relation to the trappings and opulence of its infamous Las Vegas sound-alike: just the reek of stale alcohol and a well-worn tartan carpet that squelched underfoot with every tentative step. Nevertheless, the stage area was spatial and there were no fluffy hindrances or indeed any other obstacles to encumber the evening's performance.

♫

The gig itself was going swimmingly well, although every now and then the lights seemed to flicker and dim, almost as if the grid were close to overload as the power intermittently surged and faded. Then, twenty minutes into the set, a screeching, whining high-pitched tone was heard that gradually increased in volume and began to drown out our own cacophony of sound.

Within seconds several brightly coated members of staff were on hand, basically disappearing up their own backsides and waving their arms in a disorderly flap, urging the punters to leave the building with immediate effect through the clearly marked fire exits.

Another orange-faced odd-job man suddenly wrestled my microphone from me and screamed into it, 'Fire alarm, everybody to the exits, and that means everyone!'

This signalled an almighty stampede towards the rear entrance of the building, and in no time we found ourselves outside on the pavement, surrounded by a group of exuberant, lobster-faced holiday-makers, who audibly were fast losing the power of speech!

The month undeniably was July, but the bitter brass-monkey weather came as a huge shock to the system, feeling much colder now that our perspiratory glands had opened up from the exertions of the first twenty minutes of the set.

Stood in a close-knit circle, the boys slapped their shoulders and arms in a bid to mollify the rising goosebumps, until after what had seemed an eternity we were finally goaded to re-enter the stage door, back into the dressing room, where a maintenance man informed everyone that the kitchen's electrical system was playing up and had tripped the venue's over-sensitive alarm mechanism.

The band now faced an uphill task, in that the loud and impactive introduction to our show had been seen and done, and with no contingency plans should any discontinuance or *force majeure* come into play, we were left with something of a dilemma. With the boisterous crowd back in the room it was decided to simply get back out there without delay and launch into something punchy which would smack 'em right between the eyes and doubtless restore the good-humoured temper with immediate effect.

We were sadly mistaken. It seemed as if our rekindled overture had fallen flat on its backside, and that the happy campers were more concerned with ordering large rounds of drinks, as insurance against any further interruptions. To make matters worse, a mass void had developed between the stage and the packed bar areas to the rear of the complex, and the mood had become strangely muted, as we now played second fiddle to the headlining bartenders.

'After a while we did great (grate),' quipped one of the guys, with an apt *double entendre*, at the show's close; but in fairness we'd stuck at it and eventually had managed to rouse some of the crowd, who'd been up and dancing. But that apart the earlier buoyant ambience had most definitely been soured, and in all honesty the final hour had been toilsome.

Following an encore that felt fraudulent and burdensome, we disconsolately changed and disappeared to the sanctuary of our dilapidated chalets.

4

ROCK & ROLL I GAVE YOU THE BEST YEARS OF MY LIFE (KEVIN JOHNSON)

I'D KNOWN TREVOR, our rhythm guitarist, for a number of years before I was ever in a band with him. He was very much an individual, who always liked to do things his own way, whether right or wrong.

Suffice to say, Trev, in a sense, bore the responsibility of actually discovering me at the ripe old age of seventeen, when I sang and played guitar in a semi-pro band with the awful name of 'Buttercup Jelly' (clearly influenced by the late-sixties flower-power movement!).

Two years later and there he was on the blower asking me to join his band 'Choise', who excitingly were a fully professional outfit with a big following, and were well respected in the Midlands area in particular. It was flattering to be given the opportunity to fulfil my life's ambition of making music for a living; and, after dealing with the politics of giving up a steady day-job with future prospects, at which I'd not long completed a successful three-year apprenticeship, I leapt at the chance and took the plunge. Although my parents were never a hundred per cent happy with the decision, deep down they realised where my ambitions truly lay, and notwithstanding their initial disappointment were resolutely supportive in every way.

Those early Choise days proved to be a wonderful introduction to the mechanics of a rock-and-roll career, and were arguably one of the most creative periods of all. As songwriters, Trevor and I at the time were nothing short of prolific, and many of the compositions born of that era later saw the light of day as Showaddywaddy recordings.

In spite of this I'd long suspected that Trevor never quite possessed the same passion for SWW as he did for Choise, and freely admit that when the band were stuck in a rut of covering oldie after oldie during the late seventies, our creativity – particularly as writers – became to some extent stifled. To this day I firmly believe that dear old Trev never forgave the band for that!

By 2005 it was clear he was not the happiest of people, but perhaps the ordeal we'd taken on would prove a welcome distraction from any personal issues. He'd always possessed a keen eye for the opposite sex (no matter what they looked like), but sadly this had eventually cost him his marriage to his childhood sweetheart, Sue.

There was something palpably different about him when these dates began. For sure the whole party had their misgivings that this could be a downward step in our careers, and consequently a taxing experience. But right from the very first night away, I had a feeling that Trev's mind was not really focused on the task. Even his voracious appetite for chatting up the available totty had diminished, and his body language had become downcast. The situation was undoubtedly disquieting.

Next morning's breakfast saw the band and crew gathered together inside a highly disinfected café, which had overtly been used as a bar the night before. Upon entering, the acrid germicidal smell almost made your eyes water, but undeterred and famished I ordered the biggest fry-up on the menu and pulled over a rickety wooden chair from an adjoining table before parking my backside to join the happy throng.

I was greeted by a sullen-looking Trevor who mumbled, 'Fucking beans are cold.'

'Well, send 'em back,' I countered.

'Already have done once,' he exclaimed, followed by, 'What a fucking shithole,' as he promptly rose and slumped off.

My earlier suspicions were already being put to the test: Trev was never one to swear gratuitously, and was manifestly upset about something far more serious than a plateful of tepid food. The tour was becoming more onerous by the minute, and his fractiousness was of deep concern.

'Oaksie' as we affectionately nicknamed him (in truth he was bestowed with more bynames than anyone I've ever known) was often the butt of many a private joke within the band, but these were nothing more than childish pranks, and never in any way malicious; plus we frivolously rather enjoyed his lugubrious retorts. He was, as already mentioned, a talented songsmith, but for all his fervour never a naturally gifted musician. Trev quite simply liked it loud and brash; and, of the umpteen pseudonyms he accrued as a result, 'Iron-fist', 'the Six-Million-Watt Man' and 'Glove-hand' are perhaps three of our enduring favourites.

The maverick guitarist was also thornily in denial over his accelerating hair-loss, which led to further derogatory comments not only from ourselves but from every man jack. Visibly he saw this as a personal affront, one which bothered him deeply when ironically it was hoped that the mockery would nudge him into 'owning up' to his trichological problems.

In an age where celebrities were unashamedly opening up to their new-fangled hair transplants in an effort to regain their dissolving youthful looks, Trev unwisely opted for a cheap and nasty alternative, which was daubed over the thinning areas, ostensibly to conceal the offending bald patches. Distressingly (pardon the pun) the results were easily detected by the naked eye; and by 2005 with further deterioration he was effectively painting his head, and looked like a downmarket imitation of the licentious ex-Italian president Silvio Berlusconi.

We'd all had our moments when it came to vanity, but Trevor remained unmoved by any quiet-but-friendly words of advice, and by and large ignored the jibes.

On a lighter note Trev's vocabulary was, to put it bluntly, the most extraordinary word stock imaginable. In a uniquely engaging fashion he would comically substitute his own audible sound-alikes in place of their literary equivalents. These bywords or short phrases were affectionately dubbed by his bandmates 'Trevisms'. A miscellany of these aberrant definitions can be found on the next page.

The plan was to hit the road for Longniddry in East Lothian at eleven-thirty a.m., in the hope that by then 'Young Mr Grace' (another of Trev's epithets) would be full of beans, and of a far more cheerful disposition.

TREVISMS

Original Showaddywaddy member Trevor Oakes was blessed with a language that was singularly his own. Over many years this jargon developed into a kind of quirky and endearing trait. These flagrant misusages of the English language were designated as 'Trevisms'. Here are a few examples:

Advocado pear	A pear-shaped fruit sometimes used in sallids!
Albun	A collection of songs on CD (or vinyl) by an artist
Autonomous	Autumn-like
Beearmaz	The Bahama Islands
Binana	A nutritious yellow fruit
Birmingum and **Nottingum**	Two large Midlands cities
Cold slaw	A dish of shredded cabbage with dressing
Cuntabin	A truncated version of 'couldn't have been'!
Dint (1)	An indentation
Dint (2)	Didn't

Eggnore	Pay no attention to
Eggzit	A way out
Elbone	A joint in the human body
Epceptional	Something very impressive
Esculator	A moving staircase
Fella gorge	A feeler gauge
Goyn	Going
Laxadaisickle	Lazy or sloppy
Loave	Batch, granary etc. (of bread)
Mungrel	A dog of mixed breed
Norridge	The county town of Norfolk
Nothink	Zero
Optical delusion	An object causing a false visual impression
Ostridge	A long-legged wild bird
Rio de Janerio	A city in Brazil
Sallid	A healthy, leafy dish, green or mixed!
Shaint	She isn't
Skellington	A framework of bones, often kept in one's closet!
Soldiering iron	A pointed tool for making electrical joints etc.
Terradactile	A prehistoric flying bird
Trumbone	A brass musical instrument
Undisciplined	Badly behaved
Unedible	That cannot be eaten

Some notable celebrities:

Barbara Strizeland	A famous US female diva/actress
Richard Branston	The Virgin entrepreneur
Sean Conry	Scottish actor
Christopher Columbo	Italian explorer
Englebert Humpledink	A veteran crooner (from the band's hometown)

Kelvin Klein	Fashion designer/brand
Merrill Street	A gifted American actress
Herb Albert	The *Tijuana Taxi* trumpeter
Fidel Castrol	The oily Cuban revolutionary and premier
Peter Cushion	The *Hammer House of Horrors* actor
Eureka Jonsson	Swedish ex weather girl
Illy Mustazie	Legendary male tennis star
Martina Navraticova	Legendary female (though there were doubts) tennis star
Robbie Willyums	Singer
Dame Judi Tench	Acclaimed British actress

5

FORTY MILES OF BAD ROAD[*]
(DUANE EDDY)

Wednesday 20th July 2005

A regular on-the-road occurrence was an indulgence known as a 'sweetie stop', where the troupe would take a break to refuel and load up with sustenance, newspapers, magazines and high-calorie goodies for the journey that lay ahead. Today was no different in spite of the fact that we only had around seventy-five miles to travel.

Heading in a north-easterly direction into unknown, rugged Caledonian territory, we soon pulled into a roadside refuge where we could fill up the people-carrier and eagerly satisfy our cravings. The busload of men were relieved to be well away from the inauspicious surroundings we'd put up with in Ayr, on top of which we'd heard that the camp supermarket didn't carry broadsheet newspapers. I smiled to myself as I could just hear my zit-covered pal chuntering, 'No call for it mate.'

Our drummer Romeo (there were rumours the Beckhams named their third son after him?) liked to peruse *The Times*, while I enjoyed pitting my wits against the *Daily Telegraph* crossword to pass the time. Jeff, our second bass player, was also a keen cruciverbalist but preferred the puzzle in the *Daily Mail*, which led to supercilious taunts from my good self that it was child's play. Trevor, perhaps predictably, would normally plump for the tabloids such as the *Sport*

---

[*] It was actually more like eighty miles!

or *Daily Star* (or anything that featured big knockers), whilst Dan and Rod had a wider selection by simply browsing through everyone else's.

Well provided for like mollycoddled kids, we continued on our merry way through undulating countryside on a peaceful highway as we ventured towards the Firth of Forth coast, only to meet with a curious obstacle in the road that proved difficult to overtake. A pair of local yokels on a battered motorcycle were transporting a ladder, amusingly not alongside the bike, but crosswise taking up the entire carriageway. The boys creased up at their mischievous, bucolic expressions and waved, as we finally managed to find a stretch of open road where we could narrowly squeeze past them.

The works bus (as we fondly referred to our trusty wheels) had started playing up. It was only around a year old, but had begun to have fits of coughing and spluttering, which with thirty-one resorts left to visit was the last thing we needed. The only course of action available was to again pull over and take a look. Danny knew a little bit about the mechanics of a car – largely as he'd had his share of 'bangers' in his time – but appeared from underneath the bonnet scratching his head. The problem was a worry, but the most important thing was to somehow make it to the next camp.

The bus obligingly restarted and it was decided to at least try and get to the nearest settlement to seek professional help; but hearteningly a couple of miles down the track the troublesome chariot appeared to have corrected itself, thus allowing us to continue onward through the small town of Muirkirk in the hope of reaching our destination without further ado.

Infuriatingly we'd spoken much too soon. Fifteen or so miles into the middle of nowhere the ailing bus indulged itself in a further bout of coughing. There simply was nothing else for it but to draw to a grinding halt.

Expletives now filled the air, and the general atmosphere of discontentment failed to improve one iota when the thing we'd really been dreading happened. The damn vehicle wouldn't restart!

Danny, chipper as ever, had a brainwave that the malfunction was down to the alternator, with which we'd had similar difficulties with our previous mode of transport, a bus of a similar model and make.

A surprisingly lively Jeff piped up from the back seat: 'Give the starter motor a good whack.'

'What the bloody hell for?' came Trevor's retort. (Jeff and Trevor were the band's very own grumpy old men, and indulged in these testy altercations on a regular basis, rather reminiscent of Statler & Waldorf from the Muppets!)

'Because it worked on one of those old Ford Granadas we had years ago,' stated Jeff.

Dan chirped up: 'Well I'm up for giving it worth a go,' and promptly jumped from the driver's seat in search of any wooden implement he could find, followed by myself and Rod.

By happy chance a sturdy tree-branch lay at the roadside which Rod picked up and claimed: 'This baby should do the trick.' To the astonishment and amusement of the passing motorists, each of the guys took it in turns to lean beneath the raised bonnet and literally knock the crap out of the poor defenceless starter-motor, but when Dan turned the ignition miraculously the afflicted engine burst back into life. The stick of salvation had inexpertly come to the rescue, and was stowed safely into the overcrowded boot.

The sweet sound of contentment had been restored as confectionery wrappers rustled throughout the interior, and the engine softly purred. We were back in business.

My mobile rang. It was crew boss Steve. He'd already arrived at today's port of call, Longniddry, but was in no way enthusing over his new surroundings.

'What a shithole this is,' he complained, which I'd come to know didn't necessarily mean the gig wasn't up to scratch, as virtually every venue we visited that posed even the most minor of problems was looked upon by the ever low-spirited Steve as a 'shithole'!

'Why, what's up?' I asked.

'Well to start with there's no fucking three-phase, the stage is about the size of a postage stamp, there's no humpers, and the manager is a complete twat,' he ranted on, followed by, 'Shall we just piss off?'

Instantly niggled at the thought, I flipped, and launched into a diatribe of abuse along the lines of, 'The only fucking reason we are doing these gigs is to stop you from sitting on your fat, miserable arse – you knew this tour wouldn't be easy!'

I somehow managed to quickly compose myself. 'Just grit your teeth and get on with it. We've still thirty more to go, and I don't need this shit every day,' I lectured him; but this time he didn't respond. 'We talked about these venues being potentially difficult; for God's sake get on with it,' I rambled on.

Unimpressed, he mumbled dolefully: 'Huh, what time will you be here?'

'I'd reckon on around half an hour,' I replied.

'Okay, I'll let you sort it out; shall we start loading the gear in?' asked Steve.

'Yeah, go for it – and get the kettle on while you're at it,' I said trying to lighten the mood.

'No fucking chance of that, this arsehole wouldn't give you the drippings off his nose,' he forlornly replied.

'Oh, I'll see you in a bit,' was my parting shot as his phone abruptly clicked off.

♫

With a much longer journey than anticipated behind us, we finally arrived at the camp, to be confronted by a long red and white barrier to the side of which stood a kiosk where an obese, ruddy-faced fellow was seated playing with his walkie-talkie. The man sported an outsized blazer along with a pair of elasticated tracksuit bottoms and an ill-fitting baseball cap that was perched uneasily on the very top of his head. Realising his presence was now required he blew a huge sigh and uncomfortably squeezed his blubbery frame out of the chair, before stepping out of the cage and waddling over towards the vehicle.

Unsurprisingly there was no cheery greeting or 'Good afternoon gentlemen', simply a brusque 'What?'

'Hello mate, we're Showaddywaddy, here for tonight's show,' Dan affably announced.

'Shoddyshoddy who?' he jested, smugly thinking his retort to be both clever and funny.

The unexpectedly tedious journey had frayed a few nerves and the inane wisecrack was not best received. There were cries of, 'Who's the fucking comedian, Chubby Brown?' But more earnestly: 'Never mind that crap, just lift the barrier, you fat twat!'

Right from our *Top of the Pops* days, trying in vain to enter the BBC studio complex past the overzealous gatemen, we'd been ever consistent over the years in not suffering jobsworths gladly. Fortunately the catalogue of insults aimed at the dolt soon stirred him into action, and after muttering something incoherently into his radio-set he finally wobbled across and manually raised the offending obstruction.

Steve was – for a change – spot on with his vituperative assessment of the entertainments manager, who in no time came across as an unhelpful, jumped-up, self-important drama-queen. Considering myself to be more of a people person than the charming, gregarious crew-manager, I tried on a little soft-soaping that somehow did the trick and seemed to diffuse the uncomfortably developing situation with immediate effect.

The limp-wristed handshake didn't impress me at all, but with the go-ahead for the load-in approved, things arguably could have been worse. I followed Steve outside and said: 'Okay, I'll leave you to it – any more problems let me know and I'll deal with the shirt-lifter.'

'I tell you what, that bender was lucky not to get twatted, I ain't being spoken to like that,' Steve belatedly threw in.

It wasn't until later in the day when I discovered it wasn't really my communication skills at all that had in any way influenced the entertainments manager into being more cooperative, but rather that he'd taken a fancy to Stefan, our young crew-assistant. Realising this further substantiated the reasons behind self-confessed homophobe Steve's utter dislike of the disingenuous affected individual. I'd have to keep a watchful eye and make every effort to ensure they didn't lock horns again.

Over thirty-two years we'd performed a stack of concerts in Scotland's impressive first city Edinburgh, and had long enjoyed our soirées into the auld capital. Longniddry is a neighbouring resort around fifteen miles from the medieval old town, but felt like another world when we'd earlier idled along the main street in search of the camp. The place had clearly once been a small, quaint fishing village, but had pleasingly retained much of its briny character in spite of a handful of misleadingly idyllic-sounding caravan parks situated beside the southerly road out of town. Tantrums over (for the time being) it was time to stretch the legs and explore, and maybe even grab a late bite of lunch.

The unspoilt little honeypot proved the perfect respite from the histrionics back at the camp, but seemed to be plagued with more than its fair share of voracious seagulls, which dangerously hovered above us. Happily avoiding any unwanted souvenirs, the daily jaunt turned into a more than welcome diversion as we came across a charming, olde-worlde café that was still busy serving food at three in the afternoon. Feeling undernourished after two days of unhealthy fare and scraps, it was rejuvenating to sit and relax with a wholesome and appetising tuna bake, and once again feel at peace with the world. That was until my mobile chirped into life and I took another call from an even more irate Steve.

'We're nowhere near finished setting up and that jumped-up arsehole wants us out 'cause there's a kids' show in the same room at five p.m.,' he moaned.

'Well, sod off out then,' I angrily snapped. 'Go and get something to eat, chill out, use a bit of common sense and go back at five,' I urged.

'For fuck's sake,' was all I heard as his phone once again clicked off.

In all fairness on this occasion I did sympathise with the crew's predicament, as it was clear that the odious entertainments manager was going out of his way to make life difficult for the guys, a situation which was further exacerbated when the unhelpful buffoon attempted to put his arm around the youthful Stefan, only to receive an abusive and unbending rebuff.

Stefan was at the time a nineteen-year-old aspiring bass-player; and had the looks of a teenage Robert Redford, that would've earned him a place in any up-and-coming boy-band. The girls (and also it would appear some of the boys) flocked to him given the feeblest of excuses, making him the envy of his disgruntled elders (in particular Trevor). In reality he was a good, honest hard-working lad, and it was felt that a back-to-back run of dates such as this would do him no harm at all, and could only serve to be beneficial in his future vocation.

His method of dealing with the irksome stickler had actually been pretty impressive, as when I arrived back at the camp the situation had improved tenfold and things on the surface seemed to be amazingly calm. Most of the preparatory work had now been completed, and the flustered hands were perched on stools at the bar sharing a well-earned pint.

Contrary to the cordiality we'd chanced upon in the town, this camp was very much the opposite, with a menacing air of discontentment that manifested itself throughout the ranks. Two further months of this and we'd all be at each other's throats too. So I was fiercely determined to 'nip this in the bud' without delay, and in pursuit of the keys to our accommodation for the night decided to act as a peacemaker.

I marched over to the esteemed top man's office in my role as mediator, only to eavesdrop on what was emanating through the door, which was slightly ajar: 'I don't know who they think they are, bunch of fucking has-beens,' followed swiftly by, 'They want this, want that, well I'll fucking show them!'

Already today had been trying at best, but this was not what I wanted to hear, particularly as the band hadn't yet come into contact with this person. Not knowing quite what to expect I lightly rapped at the door.

'Who's there?' came the effeminate semi-lisp.

I entered and calmly introduced myself, asking for the keys and directions to our sleeping quarters, before I said: 'If there are any further concerns on your part about anything whatever to do with my band's performance, then please just give me a tinkle on my mobile, and I'll do my very best to be co-operative.' I handed him a business card, and noticed for some reason he was sneering, as was his butch, moustached female assistant, who passed over two large envelopes bearing the company logo. The 'camp' representative then arrogantly remonstrated:

'By the way you're on at ten-thirty p.m., but you can't use the dressing rooms until thirty minutes before, as the other performers will be changing in them.'

This time I bit my lip and thought, 'I've no hope of ever pacifying this petulant little prick,' and promptly left, forgetting my manners in the process, and slamming the door shut.

Simmering inside I tramped off, grumbling to myself, 'If I had to spend six months in this place perhaps I'd become an ill-mannered asshole too!'

We drove the short distance to the boondocks of the camp, where two shabby-looking trailers lay in wait well away from the more upmarket rented models occupied by the paying customers. I held four keys in my possession but it soon became blatantly obvious that there were two sets for each of these ramshackle carts.

Upon entering the first one it resembled the opening scene to an episode of TV's *A Life of Grime*. Not surprisingly the air turned blue: overnight the touring company had become trailer-trash, with the inside enclosure resembling a tip that had not been cleaned or disinfected in ages.

'This is hell, it's disgusting and unacceptable,' was the consensus, which indeed it was; and even more cause for concern was that we were expected to sleep four to each revolting hovel, with just three filthy mattresses and a manky sofa-bed. The beds themselves were more akin to cots, and the bedclothes badly stained; and there were filthy cups and glasses lined up on the draining board and more soiled dishes in the sink. Ketchup-stained cartons full of Southern Fried Chicken bones, cold moulding chips and other grubby polystyrene fast-food containers littered the blotchy floor. It was squalid and unfit for pigs!

Now I was spitting blood. This was palpably an act of retribution on the part of our unmanly new acquaintance, and with no time to lose legged it purposefully through row after row of yucky cream-and-green-coloured holiday homes for approaching half a mile until I arrived back at the incendiary's office.

The door again was slightly open, but this time I impolitely barged straight in and, in a 'no more Mr Nice Guy' tone, growled, 'Those caravans are absolutely disgusting and totally unacceptable!'

'Well, they are the ones we earmark for our visiting entertainers,' he defiantly shot back.

'You're not listening,' I said firmly, beginning to raise my voice, and throwing the sets of keys onto his desk. 'In my contract it stipulates that each member of our touring party will be allocated suitable, clean sleeping accommodation with fully working washing and showering facilities. I reiterate these shit-heaps you've given us are filthy and simply not good enough!'

He bitchily countered: 'Well, they're all I've got, and I'm not used to being spoken to in that tone of voice!'

He'd struck a nerve. 'Well, you'd better fucking get used to it. I have it in writing that you must provide suitable and adequate accommodation that guarantees each person in my party a comfortable night's sleep. Get it sorted now!' I demanded.

'Who the hell do you think you are?' he whimpered anxiously, realising at long last he was fighting a losing battle.

'I'll tell you exactly who I am: I'm someone who has a contract with the company that employs sick morons like you, and if you don't rectify this shambles immediately I will call your head office and explain what an unhelpful twat you've been from the moment we arrived, and then it will be your sorry, well-worn arse that is on the line!' I insultingly exclaimed, in an angry tirade.

He'd begun to tremble as if he were about to burst into tears, but amazingly still took a further pop: 'I can't believe this – you're so up yourself!'

'That's as may be, but if you want a show on here tonight you'd better get your finger out and get things sorted,' I countered aggressively as he cowered behind his desk. The pleasantries of a mouth-watering lunch, just a mile up the road, all at once seemed a thing of the distant past. 'You've got fifteen minutes to come up with something, or I promise I'll lock my crew manager in this room with you for half an hour,' I threatened, and stormed out.

In desperate need of the fresh air I was breathing in, I checked my watch and did everything in my power to compose myself as I nervously paced the adjoining yard. Fifteen minutes later I was back inside, only to be greeted by the overweight gateman who was wearing a forced smile.

'Jamie's had a hard day and is feeling a little peaky; he's gone for a lie down,' he said, handing me four more packages of caravan keys.

Blowing a heavy sigh, I queried facetiously: 'Aren't you deserting your post at the entrance?'

'Ha ha, not at all, my oppo is down there now,' he chucked. 'I don't just work the gate you know, I have many other duties around here,' he self-importantly declared, picking up a carrier bag full of goodies.

'Including stuffing your ugly fat face,' I whispered under my breath, snickering as I strolled back to find the team.

True to form the new accommodation wasn't much better, but at least we had a bed and the heavily starched sheets were relatively clean. This was as good as it would get on this day.

♫

Right from the 'sweetie stop' much earlier in the day, Jeff's concentration had been focused solely on the *Daily Mail* crossword, which he was still busy puzzling over some five hours later when I visited the caravan he was sharing with Trevor. I inquired, 'Are you struggling ba?' (the endearing term being an old south-Leicestershire rural adage for boy.)

'I've hit a brick wall ba,' he replied, tossing the paper over into my lap. It had been a fraught day and feeling utterly brain-dead I couldn't even be bothered to have a stab at it. After a quick cuppa I returned to my own salubrious surroundings to take forty winks prior to showering and preparing for the show.

As I reclined on the coffee-stained sofa my eyes became heavy and soon I was transported back to the late 1960s and the rowdy pub gigs I'd played, where from the stage all eyes would be glued to the door, conducting a rough head-count to determine the rewards we may – or may not – net at the end of the night. As the final forty-five-minute set drew to a close the drunken punters would empty out onto the vomit-spattered streets looking to end their evening's entertainment on a high with an almighty punch-up, as the band packed away the gear and waited nervously in the hope of obtaining a fair night's pay for their endeavours from the proceeds of the door take.

I'd imagined those days to be long gone, but our new flaky acquaintance had awakened those forgotten nerves and a sense of insecurity that hadn't been prevalent in aeons. In a kind of stupor I stirred, my head spinning as I brought to mind the wistful reverie: thinking that, if this lowlife had been on a crusade to bring the band down a peg or two, he'd well and truly succeeded.

Notwithstanding any planned retribution on the part of the entertainments manager, we remained positive that the evening's performance would be well accepted, despite the miniature box-stage and the venue's technical limitations; but what of the show's aftermath? The belief was implanted in our minds that this cretin had it in for us, and would most likely find fault in the most dramatic fashion possible. We simply could not allow even the most infinitesimal cause for complaint. It was time to grit our teeth and get our act together; after all we were seasoned pros! Showered, coiffured and garbed in a rainbow of coloured outfits, we clambered back into the Previa and in trepidation made our way to the Show-Bar for more fun and games.

Fuelled by anger and fierce determination the adrenaline pumped effusively throughout the band's seventy-minute set. Ironically we'd been at the top of our game in every quarter, and left the stage to passionate cries of 'Encore, encore, more, more!' as drinking glasses were hammered down onto the tables in mass appreciation. We had unequivocally stormed the place!

The following morning neither crew nor band had the pleasure of renewing our acquaintance with the rabble-rousing drama queen, as he'd conveniently taken the morning off to go into Edinburgh. Romeo quipped: 'He's probably gone to have his highlights redone!'

Relieved and triumphant, the self-satisfied troupe motored south in the direction of the ancient border town of Berwick-upon-Tweed.

6

WHAT A DIFFERENCE A DAY MAKES
(DINAH WASHINGTON/ESTHER PHILLIPS)

Thursday 21st July 2005

We'd bypassed Berwick on a number of occasions whilst heading north towards Edinburgh on the old winding A1 trunk road, but had never actually visited the archaic place. So it came as a pleasant surprise to arrive in an historic walled town of quaint cafés, individual shops and characterful pubs.

The camp was situated on the town's outskirts, and tricky to find, being oddly accessed through a large housing estate. Finally after passing through a rustic post-and-rail entrance gate, the weary band of men made our way into an impressively smart wood-panelled reception area, hoping above hope there would be no repeat of the previous day's shenanigans when it came to the comfort provided in our overnight sleeping accommodation.

'The caravans are in the process of being cleaned as we speak,' the friendly receptionist informed us upon arrival, as we were politely ushered into the neighbouring Show-Bar where within minutes, almost miraculously, pots of tea and coffee along with plates of sandwiches and biscuits were kindly laid on.

A hirsute, chubby, smiling fellow walked across, introducing himself with an outstretched hand as, gobsmacked, I stood and happily reciprocated, grasping his sweaty mitt and acquainting the cordial host with the rest of the party.

'Welcome to Berwick; we're all really looking forward to tonight,' he said amiably. 'There'll be a full house too!' he exclaimed, raising his eyebrows as – a little taken aback and almost speechless – I feebly managed to squeeze out, 'That's terrific, we'll be out there giving it our best shot.'

'I'll see you all later; if there's anything you need just give me a shout – your vans should be ready in around fifteen minutes,' he continued, before scurrying off to go about his business.

The immediate change in the band's body language was something to behold, and as we bid him goodbye Trevor looked at me and surmised: 'What a lovely bloke!'

The caravans were positively luxurious compared to anything else we'd dossed in thus far. The floors were carpeted and freshly vacuumed, instead of the usual cheap regulation linoleum we'd figured was standard. There was even a bath, complete with a selection of toiletries, and everything was pristine and spotless.

With a few hours to kill before the gear would be set up, Danny, Rod and I took a walk along a rustic footpath to a nearby pebble beach, where we exerted ourselves by skimming stones across the grey water's surface; but as boredom began to set in it was time to check out the town. Observant as ever, Dan, map in hand, pointed out a marked tourist route that scaled the ancient walls, so following his lead the intrepid trio briskly took it upon ourselves to circumnavigate the age-old well-trodden trail.

Borrowing the informative directions, I bookishly shouted to the guys, 'Hey, listen to this: "The historic ramparts were constructed at a cost of £128,648 after being given the go-ahead by Elizabeth the First in 1558;" bloody hell, what would that equate to now?' But all I received were raised hands and glum expressions.

Matchstick-man artist L. S. Lowry had spent much of his time in Berwick, and was apparently inspired by the unique character of the place, where it was said he completed some of his finest works; and there is no doubting the town possesses a certain warmth, with an arty, laid-back kind of appeal that makes it easy to understand why old masters and other creative types would seek out the place as a backdrop to their masterpieces.

Back at the camp everything in the garden was rosy. It was a beautiful sunny day, with people lounging in deckchairs everywhere, exposing their pale paunches by their caravans. Romeo and Trevor were watching TV with their window wide open so that all and sundry could enjoy the running commentary, as Jeff studiously buried his nose into yet another crossword. Stefan had his shirt off in an effort to get some colour onto his pale, slender torso, and even Steve looked happy with life, sporting a paisley bandana to protect his hairless pate.

'What a difference a day makes,' said Danny, swiftly removing his T-shirt as we surveyed the scene, soon followed by Rod, as in the distance a cry was heard from Romeo who humorously shouted, 'Put that ugly body away!' from the steps to his caravan doorway.

Rod had been gifted with the most unfortunate of nicknames a few years prior, i.e. 'The freckly bastard!' He'd had this title bestowed on him during a one-off boys' break in Tenerife with Trevor and Jeff in the early nineties. As the story goes, the three of them were relaxing sunbathing at the poolside of a friend's private house, when Jeff was paid a visit by a Gary Glitter tribute act he'd got to know on a previous trip to the island, with his wife in tow.

The tribute artist's good lady was famed locally for her acerbic wit, which after cordial introductions to Jeff and Trev was immediately put to the test. Looking over at the prostrate Rod, she blurted: 'And who's this freckly bastard?' to groans of hysterical laughter from everyone on the terrace. A further cringeworthy quip of the tongue soon followed, as she spouted, 'You look like you've been sunbathing underneath a colander,' which cruelly caused more hilarity, though poor Rod was not a bit amused.

I did actually meet the lady in question a few years later when the band were booked to play two shows on the island. Although I was prepared for the worst she greeted me most politely, but there was a glint in her eye and it was easy to see that she was something of a character.

Another tale of her scathing repartee came from a post-gig night out with her other half when, drinking at the bar of a local nightspot, husband Dorian excused himself to take a leak, only to find her upon his return in a passionate embrace with her tongue down a rather large blond German guy's throat. Agog, Dorian exclaimed, 'I go for a piss and come back to find you sucking on a bloody foreigner's lips!'

The sardonic reply was not long in coming: 'Just think yourself lucky you only went for a piss!'

The odd but happy couple were in attendance at our public performance in Playa de Las Americas some years later (the second show had been for a private building company's new property launch) by which time the revelations of Glitter's disgusting indiscretions had been made public and were well documented throughout Europe, if not the world. When questioned about the disgraced star's abhorrent behaviour, looking for sympathy Dorian replied: 'That perverted bastard has fucked up my career good and proper!'

Jeff had kept in touch, and explained that Dorian later changed his onstage format to a glam-rock tribute show, and happily business had picked up again.

♫

The sound-check rescued the sun-worshippers from an overdose of ultra-violet rays, and on entering the concert room we found that yet more refreshments had been lavishly provided. Conceivably Longniddry would go down as 'a bad day at the office', but then again Ayr had not exactly been our finest hour. Soon both would be nothing more than distant memories, and with the sun beating down spirits were on a high and at long last there some cause for optimism.

Not unexpectedly the crowd-pleasing band were in good form that night, and although the audience were arguably a little more reserved than north of the border, their sun-kissed, happy faces exuded a perceptible warmth, which throughout the day had manifested itself in all quarters.

At breakfast, other than the staff Trevor was the only person in the small canteen. I'd turned in, as had Romeo, at the fairly early hour of one a.m. leaving the rest of the gang to enjoy a well-earned *apres*-gig bevvy to put the lid on a satisfying day.

'How were your beans this morning?' I tentatively posed, pulling up a chair.

'Bloody lovely, black pudding 'n' all, the best yet,' Trev cheerfully explained, mopping up the remaining juices from his plate with a piece of fried bread. Almost as soon as the final mouthful entered his cakehole, ill-manneredly he was up and gone.

The boys were still in slumber, so I took a short stroll to the mini-mart, ambitiously in pursuit of a daily dose of vitamin C in the form of some fresh fruit. The lady assistant was chipper and polite, and revealed in a broad Scouse accent: 'I caught the last twenty minutes of your show last night, blimey that brought back some memories!'

'Happy ones I hope?' I said.

'Oh yeah it were luvlee ta. Is there anything I can do you for darlin'?' she queried.

'Have you got any fresh fruit?' I enquired hopefully.

'We used to 'ave it, but it was all goin' rotten,' she filled me in, before continuing as if reading from the script: 'Not much call for it round 'ere I'm afraid!'

'Ah well, just a bottle of Evian will have to do then,' I replied, puzzling as to why they stocked pricey top-of-the-range French water.

'Just help yourself from outta the cooler,' she advised, followed by: 'Bit different from your mate, the one wearing the wig – he was here at eight-thirty on the dot waiting outside for me to open.'

'Ah, I bet he bought a newspaper; you haven't got a *Telegraph* have you?' I asked.

'Afraid not,' she conveyed, mischievously gossiping on: 'He bought a bottle of Smirnoff and a copy of the *Sun*, very rock-and-roll!'

I felt a tinge of sympathy for my old mate and in his defence countered: 'He doesn't wear a wig at all: he uses dry shampoo to fill it out a little.'

'Well, it looks like a proper Woollies special to me,' she joked, as I smiled along with her, offered my thanks and went on my merry way.

The alarm bells started ringing inside my head as I contemplated the news that Trev was back on the sauce. He'd had his share of problems with the dreaded stuff a few years prior, but had battled manfully to kick the habit and had remained teetotal for a long time now. Sure, he'd been oddly on edge and kept himself to himself since the tour began, but he was in good shape for his age and must've learned a hard lesson from his previous experience.

I decided to keep it to myself for the time being, not wishing to rock the boat as it was still early on in the tour; but it was deeply disconcerting. 'The joys of being a bandleader,' I mused, walking the damp path back to pack my stuff.

It was just seven miles to the next camp, which was located in a place called Haggerston not far south of Berwick. The plan was to leave at eleven-thirty a.m., to allow the piss-artists the chance of a late breakfast.

7

SMOKE ON THE WATER
(DEEP PURPLE)

Friday 22nd July 2005

The breaking news on the radio was full of the story of an alleged 7/7 terrorist that a unit of armed police had shot at Stockwell tube station on the London Underground. The details – the bulletin reported – were still unclear, other than that the unfortunate guy had been hit a staggering seven times; but this didn't stop us from entering into an in-depth conversation as to how we failed to get our heads around what all this destruction to the West baloney was all about, and furthermore what exactly had the people of the western hemisphere personally done to upset some long-grey-bearded fanatic from Saudi Arabia?

Little did we know at the time that the luckless Brazilian pumped full of lead was nothing other than an innocent victim, and that the cops had got it badly wrong, which had we known would no doubt have provoked further debate.

The malevolent world outside our bubble once again filled the headlines, and the tribulations of a travelling rock-and-roll band soon paled into insignificance as we considered ourselves fortunate to be part of a profession that essentially brought pleasure to those around you.

Lead guitarist Danny Willson (two l's, he'd constantly remind you!) was the new kid on the block, and also the baby of the troupe. He'd joined the band ten years previously in 1995, at a point in our careers when things had become uninspired and a little stale. The consensus had been that some new blood was required to inject a bit of life into the worryingly unmotivated throng, and Dan's cheery, sanguine personality proved just the ticket; notwithstanding that he was a fine guitar player, with a strong voice to match.

Our newest recruit was never one to let things get on top of him and in spite of going through a draining, albeit amicable, divorce around the time of the tour he remained buoyant and positive throughout. On the rare occasions he needed time to mull things over, instead of stepping out with myself and Rod he'd wander off alone to brood, but would rarely be gone for any length of time, always returning revitalised and in good spirits.

We'd discovered him in a rough, small-town Leicestershire pub one winter's night, after being tipped off that not only would he be an asset to the band, but would also be a pleasure to work with, which as luck would have it had proved to be sound advice. 'Two Coats', as he was initially nicknamed, leapt at the chance to become a Waddy, and soon downed tools from his day job as a painter and decorator when it became clear he was the right man for the job. Auspiciously he slotted in seamlessly, and in no time at all had brought a much needed sense of urgency into the camp that was soon to lead the band back into the studio to record a collection of new material for the first time in many years.

Paradoxically the one and only thing that ever appeared to ruffle Dan's feathers was the over-loud and undisciplined playing of his fellow guitarist Trevor, which palpably frustrated the hell out of him and proved a stumbling block when it came to developing a genuine musical understanding with his partner. This lack of affinity often led to Dan feeling the need to 'clear the air' during rehearsals when occasionally things reached boiling point, but incredibly within minutes he'd see the funny side and be back to the upbeat character we'd grown to love.

This run of dates, however, would prove to be a different kettle of onions and – though at the time we were oblivious – would put each and every member's good-naturedness to the sternest of tests.

♫

The long leafy drive into the Haggerston camp led directly to the rear doors of the venue, where Stef was lazily sitting crashed out in a deckchair. Upon hearing our familiar voices, a little startled he awoke and pushed open the fire doors which allowed us into the empty gig.

The next set of trailer homes had not yet been serviced, and with the load-in time for the gear not until much later at three p.m. we had plenty of time on our hands to become acquainted with our new surroundings, with the choice of an early lunch or perhaps a spot of sightseeing.

'What've you been up to, you dirty little git? You look knackered,' I grilled the yawning lad.

'I got shacked up with a right nympho last night, bit of a slag but well fit,' he boasted. Not yet five days into the tour, Stefan was attracting the attention of young girls everywhere we went, and had already become what's known in the trade as a 'fanny magnet'. In truth it mattered little; after all he was young and well-proportioned, but what of it – all the boys had received more than our fair share of female idolatry at a similar age in years gone by. (Trev liked to think he still did!) So if Stef desired to make the most of his on-the-road opportunities, he did so with our blessing.

'If you keep going on like this your knob will have dropped off by the end of the tour,' I kidded him.

'Ah well, I'll risk it for a biscuit,' he replied, smirking from ear to ear.

Danny was leaning by the open Previa door with a map spread out over the front seat, and called over, 'How about a little outing to Lindisfarne, it's not far from here?'

Looking over at Rod's reaction, who nodded his assent, I shouted back, 'Yeah, c'mon let's go for it!'

Holy Island, more popularly known as Lindisfarne (a great Geordie band I befriended some years ago took their name from the Isle), covers an area of just four square miles. There's precious little there other than some castle ruins, a disused monastery – founded in AD 635 – and a smattering of small guesthouses, which accommodate birdwatchers and ramblers seeking a modicum of tranquillity away from the hustle and bustle of the nearby mainland. The only way to get there is via a mile-long causeway; but importantly the journey must be timed to perfection, as the sea that stretches around the atoll is tidal.

As we approached the narrow thoroughfare a phalanx of motor vehicles had begun making the short crossing; but rather than tag along behind, and opting to wait for a hole in the traffic, we parked up for a nose around the souvenir shop, and to take in a warming cuppa at the adjoining café. Ten minutes later, refreshed and ready to roll, it seemed our timing was spot on as we climbed back into the bus with but two cars ahead of us making for the monastic site.

Roughly half way over, the guy in front (who was clearly a twitcher) pulled up, leapt avidly from his vehicle and shouted: 'Sorry, won't be a sec, I just spotted a pale-bellied Brent goose, they're pretty rare you know!' But for all we knew it could've been an alien invasion.

Rod had observed that the water at the roadside had begun lapping far more aggressively; and, slightly concerned, yelled from the open window to Twitchy Eyes: 'Pardon me mate, but how long before the tide comes in?'

'Oh, probably an hour or so,' he loudly called, his hands cupped over his mouth.

'So how long before we could get back after that?' cried Danny over the howling wind.

'Oh, six or seven hours,' the birdwatcher said.

Looking at each other with mouths agape we bellowed in unison: '*SHIT!*'

There was now a procession of onrushing vehicles heading in the opposite direction, leaving little or no room to attempt a three-point turn; but remaining on the isle for seven or more hours was plainly not an option. The need to return to the camp was our top priority, and with sound-checks and other prep work to be done the decision to head back was a no-brainer.

The Birdman of Lindisfarne finally returned to his car and put his telescope back into the boot, before immediately putting his toe to the board and speeding towards the Island. Two further vehicles to our rear surveyed the potential deluge with extreme trepidation, the oncoming traffic virtually aquaplaning across the surface as the water began gushing over the causeway. Noticing a gap had opened up in the constant flow of cars, Danny accelerated forward, only to be halted by an idiot behind who saw fit to hit the throttle and overtake the entire queue, which uproariously caused a cascade of filthy seawater to come soaring over the people-carrier's roof and in through the open driver's-side window.

Soaked to the skin and cursing loudly Danny angrily jerked the bus forward again, but frighteningly the temperamental four-wheeler stalled. A subsequent frantic twist of the ignition key to turn the engine over met with nothing but a dull thunk, and things were getting out of hand with the cars bringing up the rear manoeuvring and zigzagging in all directions amongst a feeling of mounting chaos.

Dan frenetically tried the ignition again, but the dogged wagon was as dead as a dodo. At one point we even, disturbingly, talked of abandoning the poor bus and legging it back to safety, but remained calm and conceived it must be the dodgy alternator problem rearing its ugly head yet again.

Paddling out to open the tailgate in waterlogged shoes, Danny retrieved the stick of salvation from its cubbyhole, as I released the bonnet catch for him to mercilessly knock seven bells out of the afflicted starter-motor. I quickly leaned over and once again turned the ignition key to hear a hopeful gurgling sound, followed by a cloud of smoke as the constipated bucket of bolts coughed and spluttered, like an eighty-a-day man, responsively back into life.

Slamming down the hood, Dan leapt athletically back into the driver's seat and in a flash spun the vehicle round on a sixpence, as if fleeing from a bank robbery, as we hysterically ploughed through the spray and sped back to dry land.

'Holy smoke!' wisecracked Rod as we eventually reached the shore, gathered ourselves, and hastened back to the safe haven of the camp.

♫

By the time we made it back to the park the other members of the gang had oddly disappeared, but the helpful Geordie assistant in the cramped little entertainments office handed out key pouches and a wallet of colourful directions to our temporary abodes within the labyrinth of caravan-lined avenues. These models were pretty basic, which for a change wasn't so much of an issue as we would later be travelling back to the luxury of the creature comforts in our own homes, so only really needed facilities for washing and changing.

Saturday is what's known in many of these establishments as change-over day, when it's very much out with the old and in with the new as vacationers from the previous week make way for screaming hordes of animated johnny-come-latelies, who pretty much begin celebrating their new-found freedom with immediate effect. Each and every bar is soon sussed out and paid an inaugural visit, followed by the arcades, casinos and amusement park facilities that become packed to the rafters within the first few hours of the holiday.

Consequently, the main programme of entertainment is put temporarily on hold, which allows the staff some much needed downtime, and visiting artists such as ourselves a little respite for a day or two.

The fatigued soldiers of fortune were looking forward to the familiar surroundings of a weekend at home, and I was desperate to see Mum. However, there was still the matter of one final hurrah before we'd be gleefully homeward bound, like kids on the final day of term.

The gig was by no means one of our better performances, which we put down to the exertions and anxiety of the previous five days taking its toll. The venue wasn't the best either and was no different from the afternoon sound-check when we'd observed how spartan and devoid of atmosphere the room was. In the final vestiges of their hard-earned summer break, the largely disinterested rabble drank themselves into a stupor, and would doubtless return home with thumping hangovers to accompany a sackload of holiday memories.

Feeling a little surplus to requirements the band dispassionately went through our stage routine, with the pumping adrenaline of the preceding nights, brought on by the crowd's enthusiasm, sadly lacking. A sprinkling of punters, who perhaps were staying on, let their hair down, but it was one of those nights a performer is glad to see the back of.

The bus, thankfully, fired up straight away and pulled away from the camp at just after midnight for a testing three-hour trek back, but regardless we'd later be sleeping in our own beds, hardly anyone uttered a word during the entire trip.

8

RIP IT UP
(BILL HALEY & THE COMETS/LITTLE RICHARD)

Monday 25th July 2005

As one of the senior members of the band Rod had begun planning for the future, and had invested a few quid in an express courier service. With the band loaded up and heading north to the East Yorkshire resort of Filey on the Monday following the weekend sabbatical, he'd assumed responsibility for the company's telephones, which had been diverted to his ever-chirping mobile.

Clearly business was buoyant, as for a large part of the journey up he frequently pronounced into his headset: 'Route One,' followed by a line of well-rehearsed sales patter and the odd quotation. In the light of the previous week's exploits I reflected, 'Maybe he's got it right,' with the band's rock-and-roll career plummeting to new depths playing ill-equipped caravan parks.

The next three performances were all within ten miles of one another, close to the long expanse of sand that stretches for miles across Filey Bay. We'd been up this way on the same littoral a number of years ago, little more than a stone's throw along the coast in Bridlington; but this sojourn was to be an introduction to its northerly neighbour. The place was to leave an indelible mark on my soul, far more so than I could ever have imagined!

I'd visited my Mum on the morning of our departure. She was motionless and had become painfully thin. All her life she'd been a strong-willed, obdurate soul; and, coming from a war-torn generation when they built them of stern stuff, wasn't going anywhere without putting up a fight.

Holding her frail hand I drew the faintest of smiles as I joked about taking her along with me as the band's cook, but soon it was time to leave as I kissed her on the forehead and said: 'See you in a few days.'

Steve had arrived at the camp good and early, and was soon on the blower to inform me that word had been passed on to the in-house staff that the band were, as he put it, 'a right bunch of *prima donnas!*' This was inexplicable and difficult to take on board, as none of the guys in the band had as yet (the hermaphrodite in Longniddry apart) come into contact with any members of staff. What the hell was wrong with these people? The constant bitching was becoming an enormous source of irritation, which was further inflamed when I was informed that the concert room was – dare I say it – 'a shithole' with yet another poky stage, half of which was occupied by the resident DJ's state-of-the-art console.

'Then it'll have to be moved,' I said.

'They're telling me it's fixed to the stage,' Steve moaned.

'Well, tell them back that this *prima donna* is about to call their head office to discuss technical specifications they agreed to,' I beefed.

'I suppose we should get the gear in first, and you'll probably be here by the time we're done,' Steve answered, passing the buck, and unwilling to bear the responsibility for any further unpleasantness.

I was now nearing the end of my tether, and figured it really was time for a call to the company HQ to lodge an official complaint, as without the intervention of someone in authority these niggling daily problems would remain ongoing. My best unfortunately was not good enough as, despite handling the call as diplomatically as I possibly could, after listening to five minutes of blather I came away from the phone flabbergasted and bewildered. The office mouthpiece haughtily emphasised that it had been made perfectly clear prior to the issuing of contracts that not all of the venues could comply with the band's demands, and that should the facilities be deemed unsuitable in terms of staging a competent performance, we would be within our rights to cancel forthwith and move directly on to the next centre... although the small matter of remuneration would be suspended for any annulled shows.

This was not what I wanted to hear, as first and foremost we were only doing this tour for the relatively healthy purse that lay at the end of it; and as the anger welled in the pit of my stomach I blurted out to the boys: 'This contract is an absolute joke; I may as well wipe my arse with it, or better still just rip it up!'

'Great title for a song,' chirped Trev inanely.

'What? *Wipe My Arse*!' I fractiously struck back, failing miserably to see any kind of funny side.

The only way around this now was to attempt to turn on the charm when my fellow egomaniacs and I reached the camp.

The entertainments manager was a lady called Jenny Whittle, and boy did she live up to her name! She garrulously blabbed on about this and that, and then the other, much that had little to do with our scheduled performance later on, and oddly when she did finally pause for breath to let me get a word in edgeways, there was no eye contact which I found awkward and disconcerting as she looked off to my side with a kind of cross-eyed squint.

Perturbingly we were allotted three 'entertainer's' caravans as I pleaded for a fourth, but alas to no avail. The truth was there wasn't a single caravan available, as the camp, in Ms Whittle's words, was 'bursting at the seams'. On this occasion there was little choice: we'd just have to turn a blind eye and rough it, with three persons sharing each of two vans, and two in the other.

Thankfully there was freshly laundered bed-linen this time around, and clean towels! 'What a luxury,' Rod remarked as he kindly offered me the marital suite, which consisted purportedly of a double bed (it was in fact a large single) only to find that his own cubicle was scarcely two feet wide and would have had trouble sleeping a small child. Later that night after a few sleep-inducing post-gig beers, the cot was abandoned when the tipsy bass-player staggered in and dragged over the bedclothes from the tiny room before curling up on the sofa and snoring his silvery-maned head off.

The DJ's set-up had pleasingly been relocated – much to his annoyance – to a raised platform at the rear of the stage which helped matters considerably. Jenny whittled on with me hardly listening, until I suddenly cottoned on that dinner had been organised for our party in the Lounge-Café at six p.m. This was indeed a first: whatever next – perhaps a blue-riband caravan, or maybe a fully sized stage, or even courteous staff? It was beyond belief and I could hardly wait to tell the boys.

I was feeling bloated but satisfied after a passable steak-and-kidney pie (much to vegetarian Steve's displeasure) when Ms Whittle came a tap-tap-tapping on the caravan door to ask if we could be ready to go on an hour earlier than originally planned. The woman truly did have the gift of the gab; but there was something endearing about her efficient, hands-on approach to her daily routine, and more importantly there were no high jinks as she dexterously just got on with her job.

What should have taken two minutes took ten, as she explained that after a hot and humid day the heaving Show-Bar was like a furnace, and with no air-conditioning in the building it would be most helpful if we could oblige.

The only real stumbling block was that the rescheduled onstage time was barely an hour away and there may be something of a scramble to get changed and ready; but what the hell, it was a balmy night and an early start would give us the added incentive of an extended post-show binge.

♫

The clammy heat in the room was insufferable, with six hundred perspiring bodies packed together like sardines in a can. The semi-circular stage would have been better suited to a revue bar, but still provided ample space for us to trip the light fantastic in our own inimitable style to the delight of the appreciative crowd, who seemed unconcerned by the excessive humidity as they clamoured for more.

With another one safely under the belt the exhausted but contented ensemble gathered beneath a full moon in the starry sky outside the Lounge-Bar in a bid to rehydrate with a few well-earned beers, and naturally to massage our celebrated egos. But as the conversation turned and became critical of the camps, and the midges grew bothersome, I made my excuses and cleared off to hit the hay.

9

LIKE I'VE NEVER BEEN GONE*
(BILLY FURY)

Tuesday 26th July 2005

I awoke to a glorious morning, and trooped off to the breakfast area for the regular daily intake of carbohydrate. The daily fry-up had long been something of a ritual when we stayed away; yet curiously enough none of the guys ever indulged themselves in a 'full English' whilst under their partners' noses at home. Most of the gang were already busy tucking into their mini-feasts, but Trevor was conspicuous by his absence.

'Where's Trev?' I asked Dan.

'Oh, he's been and gone for quite a while. He came knocking on my caravan door at eight a.m. asking for the Previa keys. I'd only been awake a couple of minutes,' Dan explained.

'Where's he gone?' I laconically queried.

'He said he was off to visit a friend who lives nearby, but he didn't say where. Why, did you want to drive out somewhere?' Dan asked.

Sheepishly I leaned across the table so as not to be heard by the other lads, and whispered: 'I hate to say it but I think he's back on the sauce!'

'Oh shit! What makes you say that?' Dan inquired a little bewildered, but then added, 'You know, I thought he was being very secretive; oh well, hopefully he'll be back before too long.'

---

* The first single I ever bought with my own hard-earned cash from a newspaper round.

'I only hope he's not had a drop this morning!' I huffed.

'Mm, me too. Do you fancy walking that plateful of fat off when you've done? There's a lovely stretch of beach over yonder,' the guitar man chirped.

'Sounds like a good idea; okay, see you in ten. I'll tell you how I know then.'

'Hey, hang on for me,' Rod nodded over, intimating he'd be joining us, as he stuffed a large piece of burnt sausage into his freckly face.

♫

The sated trinity strolled manfully along a pebbly coastal path that ran by a beach known as Reighton Sands, and scaled some fairly hefty dunes, getting sand in our shoes as we descended on the far side. The sun was already in its element in a cloudless sky, and pretty soon three pale bodies were revealed as our T-shirts were removed. Danny and I looked at each other mischievously, and staring at Rod's mottled torso voiced boldly in unison: 'You freckly bastard!'

He shrugged, wearing a resigned grin, but wasn't bothered at all by the insult. We marched on, youthfully chortling and, as the heat tingled on our skin, surmised that perhaps the tour wouldn't be such a bind after all. After a forty-five-minute potter we moseyed back to base, glowing and refreshed by the light sea-breeze, expecting to collect our kit and make the short hop barely five miles further along the coast to the opposite side of Filey.

As we arrived back in the courtyard there was still no sign of the people-carrier, and consequently neither hide nor hair of Trevor. Arrangements had been made to leave at midday, so clearly there'd been a breakdown in communication; but what had happened to him?

Two hours later and he still hadn't returned. The wind was getting up into a mini sandstorm, and people were rushing everywhere seeking shelter away from the swirling grit, which included Rod, Dan and yours truly.

The open-plan fun bar that put a roof over our heads was full of kids, who seemed far more interested in picking their noses than paying attention to the various life-size cuddly characters who were attempting to entertain them. Bizarrely fascinated we looked on, sympathising with the poor members of staff inside the furry outfits on such a stifling hot day who would surely be just skin and bones by the end of the season.

The hours ticked by, but awkwardly the cleaning staff had courteously requested that we vacate our caravans for them to be sanitised as tonight's star turn – a Russian dance troupe – would soon be arriving. In no rush whatever to leave, the guys casually gathered their stuff together, including Trevor's crumpled stage clothes (that looked as if he'd washed his car with them), all of which was loaded onto a trolley and wheeled to a storage room in the lobby by an elderly but jovial porter.

'Look at the state of his stage gear, typical bloody Oaksie, the man's just got no pride!' uttered Jeff cantankerously as he followed the trolley's progress. But in all seriousness he did have a point, as the rags in question patently hadn't seen the insides of a dry-cleaner's in ages.

The gusting wind abated as – bored out of our skulls, twiddling our thumbs and chatting aimlessly – we waited agitatedly for the band's ever-discordant nonconformist.

He finally made it back at four-thirty p.m., some four-and-a-half hours late, not surprisingly to ironic cheers and mickey-taking. 'Where the hell have you been?' Rod demanded.

'I've been to see somebody I know who lives near Manchester,' he chuntered, as if nothing had happened.

'I thought you said it was just up the road!' Dan said.

'That's a round trip of two hundred miles,' I chipped in, aghast.

'Yeah, it was a bit further than I thought; anyway, why all the fuss? I thought we were playing in the same place, so what's it matter?' he questioned defensively.

'The same town, not the same bloody camp you idiot!' I cried in despair.

'Well nobody told me,' muttered Trev.

This had been his stock excuse since the band's inception when things in any way went awry, and was enormously irritating.

'The problem is you never fucking listen,' Rod said in frustration, but Trev simply shrugged his shoulders and wandered off, completely unperturbed, as we sauntered back to retrieve the trolley, forlornly shaking our heads.

♫

The less-than-exotic-sounding Gristhorpe Bay was the next point of disembarkation, but situated just to the north of Filey it wasn't the easiest of places to find, even for the wizardry of the new sat-nav. There appeared to be a plethora of caravan parks in this parish, many with outlandish tropical names; trapped in the maze, we stopped an affluent-looking lady to ask for directions.

Affixed to her blue-rinsed head was the biggest sun-visor I'd ever seen, which created a shadow over her wizened features, no doubt to protect the extensive plastic-surgery work she would've paid a small fortune to have carried out. The lady was certainly no spring chicken, but clearly took pride in her appearance and bore a cultured air of sophistication, as she gesticulated with her wrinkled hands, amusingly pointing across the road before probing rather affectedly, 'That's the rear entrance right there; are you tradesmen?'

'I suppose, in a manner of speaking, yes,' I answered.

'Well, just pull in there and go to the bottom of the drive and I'm sure Big Don will sort you out,' she pompously articulated.

Doing a three-point turn I heard Jeff quip from the back seat: 'I bet Big Don's been sorting her rear entrance out for years,' to which the guys all cackled laddishly as she waved goodbye from the other side of the road.

Maddeningly we'd missed the sound-check, and further vented our fury in Trevor's direction before taking some time out to get a taste of the early-evening cabaret performance that was under way in the same room.

In the narrow corridor by the cooped-up dressing rooms, Jeff chatted to a magician who formed part of the show, while in the background a couple of the boys stood mocking, as the poor guy seemed to have a mild bout of Parkinson's Disease, which wouldn't really be well suited to any sleight-of-hand tricks!

The comedian on stage wasn't helping matters either, as – sporting a schoolboy cap – he went through a very unfunny old-time music-hall kind of routine that seemed sadly out of place here in the twenty-first century and which was dying on its backside.

Steve had diligently gone about his work, without any dramas whatsoever, and during our absence had efficiently carried out what's known as a 'line check'* after I'd called to say we were running late.

The rest of the day gladly passed without incident, apart from a slightly awkward moment on stage when a drunkard sporting huge grey and ginger sideburns grabbed my temporarily unemployed microphone to perform an impromptu duet with Jeff, who was taking the vocals on our rendition of the Elvis Presley classic *Jailhouse Rock*.

The biggest problem was that our uninvited guest seemed to be crooning a different song, which I detected as being his take on *Blue Suede Shoes*; but whatever it was it sounded awful, as the bibulous crowd derisively egged him on for their own amusement, until he was manhandled from the stage by two muscular, sinister-looking security guards.

'What did you think of the Elvis impersonator?' I cried out at the end of the song, to which the baying mob responded unanimously:

'Rubbish!'

I only hoped they hadn't meant Jeff, as I took hold of the microphone and acknowledged: 'Ah well, as the saying goes, that's rock and roll!'

---

* A line check is the testing of each instrument's channel on the sound-desk without the aid of the performer.

10

BLUE BAYOU
(ROY ORBISON)

Wednesday 27th July 2005

Bridlington encapsulates the ethos of a quintessential English coastal town, and is the perfect place for a day trip. The intrepid trio had persuaded the other boys to leave earlier than usual at ten a.m. to allow a full programme of sightseeing on what had turned out to be another beautiful start to the day. The next camp was but a handful of miles away, and once we were ensconced in two scruffy little bungalows tucked away in a quiet cul-de-sac (we were heading home after the gig) we quickly donned our shorts and it was time for the three amigos to revisit the popular East Riding town for the first time in many years.

Once a small fishing port, Bridlington opened its arms to tourism in the early 1800s and has never looked back. It boasts beautiful beaches, and apparently has won numerous awards for its meticulously maintained gardens and promenades.

As we reached the town a signpost pointed to a public pay-and-display car park; and, upon finding a space, we headed in the direction of the nearby quay area to satisfy Danny's obsession with fishing and to check out what a few of the old sea dogs were dragging in.

Noon was still around an hour away and the front was crawling with tourists and day-trippers, whilst the nearby beach was packed with sun-seekers whose kids playfully ran in and out of the ocean whilst their parents paddled at the water's edge, or lazed in deckchairs protected by candy-striped windbreaks.

The hot spell had sustained with the day set fair, and an engaging hubbub reverberated around the place. Weatherbeaten fishermen dangled their lengthy rods from the harbour ramparts. Overweight families slouched along the promenade, no doubt in search of sustenance. Cocky, bronze-coloured jack-the-lads offered bumpy (and pricey) speedboat rides from the quay out to sea. Ice-cream salesmen were snowed under, and fish-and-chip restaurants were already filling up for lunch. The buzz surrounding the resort was quite remarkable, proving it really is hard to beat a good old-fashioned, no-nonsense British seaside resort on a lovely summer's day.

Caught up in the radiant briny atmosphere we ambled jauntily around the harbour and prom, concocting whimsical little ditties about 'Speedy Boat Rides' and 'The Candy Floss Kid', and playfully amused ourselves by doing a spot of people-watching.

By the time our stomachs began to rumble the quay area was literally teeming with bodies, and the place had become uncomfortably crowded, so reluctantly we returned to the Previa and set off to discover the historical old town.

The main street that runs through Burlington, as the settlement was once called, is a rambling, higgledy-piggledy cordon of endearing and well-maintained Georgian buildings. The area was in complete contrast to the harbour, and appeared to cater to a more discerning type of tourist with tiny vegetarian restaurants, juice bars and charming tea-houses lining the pretty street.

Fortuitously we chanced upon a quaint-looking little bistro that offered on a blackboard outside: 'Home country cooking with fresh local products.'

Two well-bred ladies served up pots of Yorkshire tea with real bone-china and a conversation piece which intriguingly was a strainer, accompanied by thick wedges of oven-baked, healthy granary bread and butter, followed by a delightful, wholesome light lunch.

Shopping has never been one of my favourite pastimes, so I was ambivalent when it came to browsing among the many small outlets adorning the attractive avenue, but happy to go along with Dan and Rod's wishes it was good to find a sprinkling of quirky individual little stores, one of which oddly stocked the brothel-creeper shoes that formed part of our stage regalia. This served as a stark reminder that there was work to be done, and it was fast approaching the time for us to head back to the idyllic-sounding Primrose Bay to prepare for the evening's show.

Amazingly the venue had a conventional theatre-style stage, with backdrops and wings, and once more back in our comfort zone we immediately felt at home. To improve matters even more the entertainments team went out of their way to be helpful, and the stage was set for a rousing performance.

The oppressive heat had evaporated and gone out of the day, and a tad spent from the day's mystery tour we returned to the secluded blind alley, away from the incessant bustle of the caravan complex, to put our feet up, get the kettle on and slouch in front of the TV.

I walked outside to call home, as the signal inside the shack was weak, and was scrolling down through my contacts list when the phone vibrated and made me jump as it rang in my hand. The call was from my brother Jim, from whom I immediately detected a tremor in his voice as he gave me the news I'd been long dreading.

'We're at the hospital; Mum passed away five minutes ago.'

They say you can never prepare for something like this, and that it often takes a while for it to sink in; the impact of his words hit me like a ton of bricks. I was instantly distraught and completely disoriented, as I stuttered and briefly arranged to meet up with the family the next day.

I slumped back to the bungalow almost in a trance, and gave Rod and Dan my sad news. Choked, I needed to go back outside for a moment's peace.

As the dusk closed in I stood alone atop a large boulder, arms outstretched, eyes awash with tears that welled over and cascaded in small rivulets down my cheeks.

I perceived a presence in the air around me, in the tree's shade, and filtering through the emerging moonlight.

Inconsolable, I gazed out at the firmament that unfolded before me. The sea was tranquil and a fading, heavenly blue.

The sandy expanse of Filey Bay stretched alluringly for miles.

I had connected with this place, and inhaled the untainted air in deep breaths.

I whispered softly, 'You need the rest Mum, the kind denied to those who live on in this frantic world.'

I uttered a quiet prayer, gathering myself; and jumped down to go back to the bungalow to the comforting presence of my friends.

The show that night was surreal, and an unmitigated blur. The only real recollection I have is that I was more or less on autopilot for the entire performance. It helped hugely that the surroundings were more familiar in a theatrical sense, as I could go through the motions and just rattle off song after song without really thinking.

The crowd reaction, too, was other-worldly, but as if in a vision strangely uplifting. By the final bars of the encore I was physically and emotionally drained, and restlessly nodded off for much of the homeward journey.

11

DEVIL IN DISGUISE
(ELVIS PRESLEY)

Thursday 28th July 2005

The band had performed at the next venue in the cheap and cheerful Lincolnshire resort of Mablethorpe earlier in the year, as part of a trio of essentially 'blueprint' gigs which had proven a useful and practical exercise and helped prepare both parties as to the wherefores and pitfalls that lay ahead during the summer months.

It had been this particular venue that had caused me a few sleepless nights, as by then contracts had been signed and sealed for the thirty-three shows between July and September.

The 'entertainments executive' (as she was pretentiously labelled on her badge) was a dreadful woman. She'd put the crew through hell back in May, which left everyone sceptical about the future dates. Michelle was, to put it mildly, a tyrant! A born misandrist and a totalitarian control freak, the park's staff were terrified of her, and humorously but unflatteringly dubbed the woman 'the camp commandant'. She resembled a more butch and humourless Dawn French, and permanently sauntered around with her nose in the air wearing a hateful expression.

Little did she know that three months down the line she would paradoxically be doing me an enormous favour!

The crew had arrived as per normal at lunchtime, and were instructed that the show would puzzlingly be held in a different venue to that of our last visit. Upon inspection the two-man crew were confronted by a towering six-flight fire escape, which with the stack of heavy gear would be an impossible task for Steve and Stef to negotiate alone. It was a no-brainer and imperative they received some assistance.

The Gorgon (as she'd been nicknamed on the initial visit) was summoned, while the boys were tryingly made to wait another thirty minutes before being reacquainted with the hard-nosed woman; but, knowing I had other things to occupy my mind, Steve admirably stepped up to the plate to take on the mighty Michelle (or Medusa as was her new handle) and to stand his ground and perform a magnificent job.

The conversation went along the lines of:

Steve: What was the point of doing the show in May if you're gonna put it on in another venue?

Medusa: I decide where the show will take place and you have no right to question my decision which is final!

Steve: I'm just trying to be practical as the last show went really well.

Medusa: You are again questioning my authority – are you deaf? I want to speak with your manager.

Steve: He won't be here until later, so you'll have to sort it out with me. We'll need six humpers to help with the load-in if the gear's got to go up that fire escape.

Medusa: That's impossible and out of the question. I will not bow to your demands!

Steve: Well, how the fuck do we get the gear in then?

Medusa: You will not address me in that abusive fashion. I demand the contact number of your manager. I will not speak to the oil-rag when I can discuss this with the mechanic!

Beneath Steve's stubborn facade there lurked a big heart and staunch loyalty, and he was fiercely determined I would be allowed to grieve without interruption from this monster.

The altercation continued:

Steve: Well he's not available due to a family bereavement, and has asked me to deal with any problems as I see fit. So like it or lump it: if there are no bodies on hand to help with the load-in you'll have to take responsibility for the show not going ahead! I've never met anyone so fucking unhelpful in my life!

Medusa: What kind of amateurish organisation is this to allow the likes of you to make abusive demands on me?

Steve: Demands? It's just common sense, and anyway all this was agreed months ago!

Medusa: Well, I will not allow my staff to lug heavy pieces of equipment up those stairs. They may suffer industrial injury, and I'm sure a shabby set-up like yours will not be adequately covered by insurance should they do so!

Steve: Wrong! We have full liability insurance, I've even got the documents in the truck!

She cynically exclaimed 'Huh!' and began to storm off, as Steve bravely chastened her:

'I need to know *now* if you're gonna provide some humpers; is this show on or off?'

The camp commandant turned back towards the crew-man, apoplectic with rage, and in the heat of the moment yelped for all and sundry to hear: '*OFF!*' Followed rudely by, 'Go and crawl back to where you came from!'

Steve had boxed very cleverly, and proved that behind the usual mulish façade lay a man of steel and principle.

He called me immediately and apologised profusely for interrupting the family matters I was attending to with my brother and sister. Speaking uncharacteristically calmly he said, 'I'm really sorry to bother you mate, but we've had a nightmare at this place and I've had to pull the plug on tonight's gig. It ain't going ahead!'

'What's the story?' I asked, a little confused.

'That bitch of a manageress has called it off,' he replied, before filling me in with the details of their shouting match. The tone of his voice said it all, and it became patently clear that the abrupt cancellation had been no fault of his own. More importantly, the woman's rush of blood to the head had led her to make a rash and foolish decision, which contractually meant that the holiday company would have no choice but to compensate us fully for their employee's recklessness and intransigence.

I turned to my brother and said: 'My show tonight's been cancelled.'

'Oh really, why's that?' he asked.

My mind frazzled, and reluctant to go into detail, I told a little white lie.

'On compassionate grounds, of course; well, it's only fair!'

12

BOOM BOOM OUT GO THE LIGHTS
(LITTLE WALTER)

Friday 29th July 2005

At the risk of offending its local inhabitants, Cleethorpes is not exactly my idea of an attractive seaside getaway. The town sits on the Humber estuary and at low tide a huge expanse of mud forms between the beach and the water's edge, literally causing an unsightly blot on the seascape.

In recent years large amounts of money have been ploughed into an extensive redevelopment programme in a bid to lure back the holiday hordes of years gone by, but alas the old township still retains a tumbledown image, together with a serious litter problem.

The weather had taken a severe turn for the worse, and there was no sign of any let-up as we arrived at the park with the incessant rain still bucketing it down. As the bus passed through the Colditz-style camp gates, we could only look on and admire the grim determination of the poncho-clad vacationers to make merry whatever the circumstances. British holidaymakers are indeed a rare breed, and fully appreciating that hopping off abroad is not everybody's idea of utopia, a day like this could be instrumental in swaying even the most jingoistic of hearts.

It was abjectly wretched! The lashing downpour gushed into the overworked drains, while empty chip-trays performed aerobatics on the squalling wind. Kids excitedly splashed in puddles as their cussing elders looked daggers at them, and members of staff carrying blue and yellow umbrellas frantically darted to all corners of the park seemingly disappearing up their own backsides.

♫

The ever-suffering road crew had endured yet another problematical load-in, but Steve was cautiously biting his lip and going easy on me, realising I was understandably a little down in the mouth.

The raging storm apart, this place was dreadful; but it was change-over day tomorrow so gladly we weren't staying over, and as opposed to caravans had been allotted a couple of store-rooms for changing. The stooping band sprinted from the bus, loaded up with stuff, as on the way in I failed to spot one happy face. Fair to say my current demeanour wasn't helping, but whatever the circumstances this place could only be described as utterly depressing.

The claustrophobic rooms remarkably had tea-making facilities, but somewhat typically it was impossible to brew up as the wall sockets were blackened and had fused.

Trevor hated heavy rain with a passion, and was dolefully slumped on a moth-eaten old sofa in the corner, as Romeo sat happily studying the broadsheets. Those left trudged off in search of a warming cuppa, two to each umbrella, passing a Burger King on the way that was full to bursting with people who resembled drowned rats.

Things encouragingly picked up a little as we took shelter in the lounge bar with a bowl apiece of hearty Scotch broth and a half-decent pot of tea for four; but despite the change for the better it was unanimously agreed that the three hours we were to spend in this rat-hole would be more than sufficient.

During the build-up to the tour I'd spent a fair amount of time online researching the camps, and oddly enough this one had caught my eye as one of the more attractive destinations. Sadly though it bore no resemblance to the beautifully landscaped, unspoilt beach retreat portrayed in the internet blurb that I'd printed off to show to the guys, much to their wry astonishment.

'What kind of bullshit is this? They shouldn't be allowed to get away with it,' declared Romeo. But whatever gobbledegook the paying public had swallowed, we were here to do a job of work, and it was time to get tuned up, togged up and ready to rock and roll!

A member of staff arrived on the scene and dished out bright yellow ponchos before leading us all to a room the size of a brush-cupboard situated to the side of the stage. The relentless rain hammered on the flat roof and was creeping underneath the door, as I paced on the spot, running up and down some vocal scales in readiness for our grand opening in five minutes or so.

All of a sudden there was a loud clunk, and the whole place was plunged into darkness. The audience screamed and whoop-whooped through the blackness, amidst the sound of tumbling glasses smashing to the floor. 'Another day, another camp, another catastrophe,' I mused; but it was a fact, as chaos perpetually seemed the order of the day in these places.

Jeff pulled the bar to open the door, attempting to illuminate the airless, agoraphobic den, but looking outside it appeared there was no emergency lighting whatever throughout the entire camp, just a pitch-black moonless gloom.

Ten minutes later and only yards from us in the concert room a huge cheer erupted as the fluorescent tube on the ceiling above us stuttered into life, followed almost immediately by a further blackout, to loud groans of discontentment from the agitated patrons.

Silhouetted in my peripheral vision was Trevor, whose gormless expression for some inexplicable reason had tickled my senses and sent me into a fit of the giggles. 'What?' he glumly exclaimed, sitting bolt upright, as I continued sniggering and replied helplessly 'Nothing,' which seemed to trigger off everyone else in the room, and by the time the power was finally restored the whole entourage were sitting watery-eyed in hysterics.

The gig was crazy. During the first twenty minutes every time there was eye contact across the stage another member burst out laughing, provoking further merriment elsewhere, and although musically it must have sounded appalling, in a way the distraction acted as a kind of release, which perhaps had been on the cards for a long time.

It is extraordinary in these situations how the punters in an audience often want in on a private joke, and the rain certainly hadn't dampened this crowd's spirits, where a large proportion of them seemed to be laughing along with us.

That was until a table tipped over and two burly, scarred roughnecks engaged in some fisticuffs, which the pusillanimous security staff wanted no part in, standing to one side as the well-hard lads tore into each other.

It was left to an elderly, crouching lady to intervene, brandishing a rather large leather handbag with protruding buckles as she brutally laid into the pair, bringing the brawl to a swift conclusion with her spirited attack and leaving the relieved bouncers to escort the offending dunderheads outside to cool off and privately settle their differences.

I was later informed by a steward that the pugilists had turned out to be brothers. 'Really? Well, there's nothing like a bit of brotherly love,' said Dan upon finding out, followed by Romeo's quip: 'And that was nothing like a bit of brotherly love!'

The gig had been bearable and pretty well-received, despite the infantile behaviour and brief altercation, and the camp dynamos had ultimately sorted out the erratic electricity supply. The laughter had bizarrely given us all a lift, though – other than Trev's expression – quite what kick-started it still remains a mystery.

It was time to once again rev up and **** *** (go home), and embark on a treacherous expedition from the deep, dark depths of Lincolnshire back to our electrified Leicestershire homes.

13

SHAKIN' ALL OVER
(JOHNNY KIDD & THE PIRATES)

Tuesday 2nd August 2005

I'd been to Caister with my aunt and her family when I was a young kid and it was there that I took to the skies for the very first time, along with my cousin and brother. Quite why this experience failed to give me a fear of flying I'll never know as the company, viz. Caister Pleasure Flights, went out of business a month later after a fatal crash that took the lives of everyone on board. Even so my childhood memories of the place had remained fond ones, so perhaps this would be a chance to rekindle a few youthful reminiscences.

'Here we fucking go again,' was the disdainful cry from the rear seats, as the works bus skidded away from the meeting point after the day had begun at various rendezvous points where we safely parked our personal vehicles before clambering aboard the wagon for the journey ahead.

It seemed already that everyone was adopting a 'Steve'-type mentality of talking the gigs down well before we'd even set foot in the camps, but we were human and it was understandable on the back of the events of the tour's first ten dates.

Traversing the twisting and turning carriageways of the A47, a service station beckoned thirty miles into the journey, which signalled the obligatory 'sweetie stop' and thankfully brought a temporary end to the bickering.

The infamous crew-manager's ears must've been burning as my mobile chirped into life and it was, speak of the devil, Steve.

'The pissin' truck's broken down,' he groaned. 'We're waiting for the rental company to bring out a replacement so we're gonna be late; can you let the people at the gig know?' he added.

'Where are you?' I queried.

'Wisebeck,' was the puzzling reply.

'Where?' I asked, screwing up my face in wonder.

'That was what Tony Hayes used to call it,' he joked, guffawing throatily. (Tony had been the band's tour manager many years before and had a peculiar aversion to the correct pronunciation of place names.)

'Oh… Wisbech,' I cottoned on.

'You got it! They're supposed to be bringing a truck from Peterborough, but knowing them wankers they'll take their time; I'll keep you posted,' he grumbled before signing off.

The prospect of idling around slothfully clicking my heels at yet another fast-food haven suddenly seemed rather unappealing. I yelled to the guys across the garage forecourt: 'Hang on a mo – the crew are running late… why don't we check out a country pub for lunch!'

We soon came across a side-road hostelry in the Cambridgeshire village of Parson Drove, which was pretty much in the middle of nowhere, surrounded by hectares of dusty flat fenland, but nonetheless displayed a Les Routiers sign advertising 'Award-Winning Cuisine'.

'This'll do,' said Rod, turning into the large car-park.

The place looked deserted as we entered to find an old man slouched in a chair, wearing a time-worn Barbour jacket, a tatty old trilby hat and a pair of wellington boots. Lying beside him on the floor was a slobbering but faithful old black Labrador.

The cherry-faced landlord (he clearly had blood-pressure issues) emerged from the adjoining bar and greeted us affably: 'Good afternoon, gents; are you having lunch?', followed surprisingly by, 'Hello Jeff!'

'How are you, Ron?' Jeff replied, obviously caught unawares to see an old acquaintance.

Teeheeing in the background like schoolkids we looked on, tickled pink by the reunion, as it soon became obvious Jeff knew the man well – as undeniably he did countless pub landlords the world over who it seemed formed a large part of his Christmas-card list.

Indeed, years before when the band had travelled to the Falkland Islands to entertain the troops and entered a small tavern on a backstreet in the island's only town of Port Stanley, Jeff had received a similar greeting, astonishingly some seven thousand seven hundred miles from home.

The stalwart bass-player had a reputation for enjoying a tipple now and again, and it was often said that he was the band's answer to Keith Richards (of the Rolling Stones), as there was no doubting he'd been 'a bit of a lad' in his time. He was however, vehemently opposed to drug abuse, which was where the similarity ended.

When the band first became successful in 1974, the majority of the boys used their newly found wealth wisely, by investing in property and savings bonds, but not Jeff! Shortly after passing his driving test in 1975 he typically showed up at the band's next soirée in a gleaming Rolls Royce Silver Shadow; and whether or not his profligacy could be perceived as foolhardy, it was impossible not to admire the man's sense of style!

Around the same time he was still occupying a council house with first wife Maureen in a rural Leicestershire community, where the parked Roller on the street outside rubbed many of the local residents up the wrong way, causing havoc as letters of complaint flooded into the local council offices.

I sat in a pub with him one night as he read out a notice of eviction he'd received from the powers that be, together with a covering letter that included the line: 'It would appear that your financial circumstances have improved by some measure.' This was one hard-luck story I found it difficult to sympathise with, and had me almost wetting myself by the end of the night when I staggered home short of breath, my bones aching from an overdose of merriment.

With a reputation that preceded him, Jeff's post-gig binges had become almost legendary, especially amongst our music-business friends and a number of not-so-familiar acquaintances who just happened to be around when he was in full flow. Not entirely undeserved, this celebrity status was born of an endearing but caustic wit and a remarkable staying power, which more often than not was hugely entertaining – as was most definitely the case at an after-show session in a Weston-Super-Mare hotel in the mid eighties.

The gauntlet had been firmly laid down by our Geordie merchandiser Ronnie, who had boasted he could drink Jeff under the table. Naturally the challenge was accepted with relish, and with crew boss Steve also willing to participate, the contest began in earnest. Multiple pints of real ale and lager were chased by Jack Daniel's, vodka, brandy, Jägermeister shots, in fact you name it... they drank it!

The spectators, which included myself, observed gobsmacked whilst taking a few refreshing bevvies on board in a far more relaxed and moderate fashion. Steve dropped out early doors, perhaps realising that he'd need to be up ahead of everyone else the following morning, which left Jeff and Ronnie to battle it out to the bitter end, as weird and wonderful cocktails were concocted by the South African hotel-manager, who other than being fascinated by the combatants' powers of consumption was further impressed at the way his projected bar-takings had been boosted tenfold.

Eventually at four a.m.-ish Ronnie collapsed into a chair and the drinking Olympics were finally over. Chairs of differing heights were dragged into place as the onlookers proceeded to assist the contestants into gold, silver and bronze positions in readiness for the medal ceremony, which as you may well imagine was not the simplest of tasks. But after much ado, and with a little support, they stood almost upright as the bystanders formed into a circle to hum the National Anthem.

With the tournament at an end we all turned in at roughly five a.m., but only a few minutes later there was a light knocking at my room door. It was the night manager, who in his broad Afrikaans accent asked: 'I'm not sure if you can help, but the gold medallist can't seem to find his room and what's more he can't even remember his name, so I haven't a clue as to which key to give him.'

Dragging my jeans back on I looked at my rooming list (compiled at check-in for reasons such as this) and followed the Boer to reception to retrieve Jeff's room key and help try and get him to his bed. The minute we entered the chamber he collapsed in a rubbery heap onto the mattress and was unconscious in seconds, as I pulled a sheet over him and left without a sound, thinking to myself, 'What a night!'

The following day the band were booked to play at a private event for Westland Helicopters, located just thirty miles away close to the city of Bristol. But at the midday chucking-out time Jeff was still sound asleep in his room. Repeated calls to his bedside telephone came up short, so it was left to a chambermaid to force entry by means of a pass-key, and an hour later he shuffled into reception to ironic applause shaking like a leaf and clearly suffering a nasty bout of the DTs. Looking wan and like death warmed up he anxiously revealed, 'I can't feel my hands!'

His wet nurses reassured him that the anaesthetic would wear off as the day progressed, and helped carry his baggage out to the bus; but unknowingly we were all mistaken as, when the jaded band sound-checked the same evening, he was still very much immobilised.

We somehow struggled through the night's performance, but the excesses of the marathon session had physically got the better of one and all, with Steve nodding off at the sound-desk, and the band's onstage efforts blunted, and frankly way below par!

♫

The Caister camp was not the best either, equipped with another postage-stamp stage, tatty caravans, and a general downmarket feel. The whole set-up was badly run down and in need of a major facelift, which begged the question: 'Why would anyone wish to spend their hard-earned pay on a summer holiday in this place?'

The thing that immediately struck me was the average size of the park's inhabitants, as I disparagingly imagined there may be a statutory weight requirement to allow entry to the site. I could just picture the would-be newcomers mounting a human weighbridge at the park gates to ensure they could meet the necessary criteria, as the malnourished few left disconsolately after receiving their marching orders from the burly gatemen. But back in the real world it was in truth pretty startling.

I decided to abandon my fruit-finding mission for the day, as this unwholesome environment would surely fail to come up trumps, and drifted aimlessly in my solitude, seeking a little inspiration for the eulogy I'd be reciting at Mum's funeral the following Monday. Muttering to myself and jotting down a few notes, I became completely distracted by yet more galumphing hordes of acutely obese in-dwellers, and pondered whether this may be the UK headquarters of one of those 'fat farms' I'd seen on TV, as people trundled around in outsize shorts and T-shirts, legs rubbing together and blubber quaking with every thunderous step.

I did though feel a twinge of sympathy for a large proportion (no pun intended) of them, as it truly must have been a drudge carting around a superabundance of flab, especially in the warm seventy-degree temperatures we were currently experiencing.

On the rare occasions thus far that we'd dined within the camps' walls, everyone had made a mental note as to the size of the portions some families consumed, and with arguably too much time on my hands I began to compile a list of the eating habits of a cross-section of these insatiable holiday-makers. The boredom factor was ever increasing on the Richter scale, and subsequently I was egged on by my colleagues, who it appeared were also in dire need of a diversion from the daily grind.

For the next few days I was inundated with the band and crew coming to me saying, 'I just saw a bloke eating this, a woman eating that, a kid tucking into a bucket of Southern Fried chicken all on his own;' the record was endless, but it really was gobsmacking the amount of grub some of these people could put away.

So, based on these witnessed accounts, a menu was compiled (purely for fun) based on what may have been the daily intake of, shall we say a slightly over-indulgent family man.

The survey was conducted by a newly founded and unofficial institution called the IBM.

YE OLDE ASSOCIATION OF BRITISH CARAVANNERS RECOMMENDED DAILY INTAKE

BREAKFAST

1 cup of instant coffee with full fat milk & 3 sugars
2 rashers of streaky bacon
2 pork sausages
2 fried eggs with extra grease
1 large portion of baked beans
2 slices of black pudding
3 slices of fried bread
lashings of tomato ketchup
1 pint of lager

ELEVENSES

1 large slice of Victoria sponge cake
1 mug of tea with 3 sugars
1 large sausage roll
2 chunky Kit-Kat bars
1 pint of lager
1 can of Strongbow cider

LUNCH

1 quarter-pounder with cheese
12 chicken nuggets
2 cans of Diet Coke
1 chocolate milkshake
2 apple turnovers
2 pints of lager

AFTERNOON TEA

1 mug of tea with 3 sugars
1 packet of Jaffa cakes
1 jumbo hot dog
1 can of Diet Coke
3 scoops of ice cream
2 pints of lager

DINNER

1 supersized portion of fish & chips
1 portion mushy peas
1 portion curry sauce
2 doorstep slices of thick buttered white bread, vinegar, salt
1 pickled onion (large)/mayonnaise/tomato ketchup
1 deep-fried Mars bar

2 banana fritters with golden syrup
2 bottles of Lambrusco
2 pints of Strongbow cider
2 pints of lager

SUPPER

2 chip butties & ketchup
1 Pukka pie
2 pints of lager

MIDNIGHT FEAST

1 doner kebab
1 portion of chips with ketchup
2 bottles of Budweiser

Research conducted at twelve random holiday centres across the UK during Summer 2005 on behalf of the IBM (Institute of Band Members).

Ironically that evening our pre-gig feast consisted of junk food, largely because there was little else available either in the small town or at the camp. There is something wickedly unruly about chomping on a whopping cheeseburger or KFC with chips, ketchup and the obligatory fizzy drink, and we gluttonously devoured every delicacy in sight with aplomb; and, thoroughly bloated, felt the need to walk off a smattering of calories before reluctantly returning to our frugal caravans to prepare for the night ahead.

♬

Following seventy minutes of getting in each other's way on the tiny podium, we needed some time to unwind, and returned to the bar adjacent to the venue for a couple of beers before turning in.

As I waited to order a round, I was jostled by a worse-for-wear, red-faced and gaunt-looking guy, who shoved in and stumbled to the bar, disconcertingly eyeballing me and causing me to move a yard or two to my right to avoid an unwanted confrontation. He, however, had other ideas, and slid along the polished rail to remain in close proximity. This dubious character then proceeded to kick off in a hostile Northern Irish drawl, saying insultingly, 'Your band are shite!'

'I beg your pardon, was it me you were talking to or the rubbish bin over there?' I barked.

'It was ye – I said ye were shite!' he gutturally repeated.

'Oh, you've been in to see the show next door, have you? How kind of you to say,' I said sarcastically.

'No, I wouldn't have been seen dead in there; I could hear yous in here and ye were shite,' he slurred, almost incoherently.

I turned away, ignoring him as my irritation began to grow; but if nothing else he was persistent and rambled on: 'Ye were shite in the sixties and you're still shite now!'

My dander was up as I turned aggressively towards him and spat out in retaliation, 'We weren't even together in the sixties – we didn't form until seventy-three, you ignorant prick!'

Unbelievably the nuisance brought the conversation to a close by saying, 'Well, you were still shite whenever it was you formed,' before collapsing onto the floor, without the need of any help that may have been on its way.

At that moment the barman asked, 'What can I get you?'

'A one-way ticket out of here,' I answered before spinning on my heels and scurrying off to the relative sanity of my caravan.

At four-thirty a.m. I awoke to sunlight streaming in through the gaps in the unlined curtains. All I could hear were birds tweeting and the more unpleasant sound of Rod's sonorous snoring. I tried turning over to get some more kip, but gave up after a couple of minutes and rose to put the kettle on. As the water gurgled Rod grunted and woke up, and we chatted quietly, as he told me that after I left there had been problems with some drunken punters, who were also unimpressed with the surroundings and were looking to take it out on some poor unsuspecting soul. Bouncers had intervened but had been equally hostile towards Rod and Danny, so they'd given up the ghost and made a speedy departure.

This attitude of resentment had been in evidence since the tour began, and we were utterly flummoxed as to what the hell it was all about; but there was no doubt it was discomfiting and the only thing to do was learn to grin and bear it!

The pair of us fortunately managed to get a little more shut-eye, and after a rushed breakfast, packed and briskly made our exit from what could best be described as an antagonistic hell-hole.

14

QUARTER TO THREE
(GARY U.S. BONDS)

Wednesday 3rd August 2005

North Denes, just outside of Great Yarmouth, is best known for its airfield, which for many years doubled as a heliport for services out to the southern end of the North Sea gas platforms but is now facing closure with all operations set to move to nearby Norwich airport.

The bus idled by as we indulged ourselves in a little plane-spotting on the short drive along the A149 to the next encampment, when I reflected aloud: 'Wouldn't it be great to just fly off into the sunset, and not have to play any more of these dives?'

The statement provoked an instant response from Trev who exclaimed: 'Tenerife'll do me; I wonder if there are flights from there?' which emphasised a peculiar obsession he had with the much visited Canary island, where he holidayed just about every year (though he did once travel all the way to the Bahamas* at great expense, only to spend the entire fortnight on the beach, without experiencing anything of the local culture!).

Tutting to himself, Rod chipped in with, 'The only difference between Great Yarmouth and Tenerife is the sunny weather,' but Romeo soon brought any fantasising to an abrupt halt with: 'We ain't even halfway through these gigs yet, so dream on motherfuckers!'

---

* *Beearmaz* – see 'Trevisms'.

There was a depressing similarity to each of these parks, and every new day was becoming like Groundhog Day with the same fast-food chains, broken-down amusements, limited concert facilities, and even cuddly characters which bore identical names in every single fun-packed venue. Perhaps we were going stir-crazy; and considering this I made a mental note to try and spend a little more time away from the camps, if only for my sanity.

Stefan came rushing over in my direction full of eagerness as we arrived at the North Denes park. 'You'll never guess what I saw last night when I went back to check the dressing room,' he said excitedly.

'Go on then, fill me in,' I urged.

'You know those two security wankers, the pair of twats giving everyone a hard time?'

'Tweedledum and Tweedledee,' Steve interjected.

'Yeah, the pair who pissed off Rod and Dan,' I interposed.

'That's them; well, I opened the door, and Tweedledum was on his knees giving his mate a blow job! I've never seen anything so disgusting, it was fucking horrible!' the lad added, sticking two fingers towards his throat.

'Did they say anything?' I asked curiously.

'Oh yeah, he said, "Fuck off or you'll get hurt, you little prick;" but I managed to get one in: "It's you with the little prick, you bloody pervert," and then got my arse out of there as quickly as I could.'

I laughed out loud as he recounted the tale, and said, 'That's obviously why they were so desperate to get the bar area cleared, the dirty bastards!'

Steve indicated that he'd like a word, as he tore a long strip from a giant roll of gaffer tape. 'Tomorrow's gonna be my worst nightmare – the bloke from St Osyth (the next park) rang to say there's fucking wrestling on in the same venue as us until four p.m., and that means a late load-in.'

'I suppose that'll be the sound-check down the pan,' I surmised.

'Maybe, but whatever there's not much point you lot getting there too early; anyway, I'll see you later,' he signed off, climbing onto the stage.

I stopped and took a look around at the day's venue. The place was full of drab-looking, damaged leather seats situated at different levels, and a lengthy bar area that stretched from wall to wall. The room stank of stale beer and the previous night's dried-up vomit. Decorators hadn't seen the insides of this place in over twenty years, and the overall effect was depressingly dark and dingy.

After a few minutes I was badly in need of some daylight, and better still a burst of refreshing sea air, and beckoned Dan and Rod to join me; but Dan pointed out that there was a small fishing lake just to the rear of the caravans and that he was keen to take some time out trying his luck over there, as his unemployed tackle had been packed in the bus for some two weeks now.

Rod and I walked along the beachside path until we came across a raised area of shingle, where we parked our pale bodies in the warm sunshine. Within a few minutes Rod had dropped into a deep death rattle, and sounded like an old sow.

Back at the camp all hell had let loose, as a heavily tattooed lady's little boy had gone missing. The main cause of her apoplectic flap was that a member of staff had spotted a distressed child being forced into a battered Ford Escort by, as she put it, 'a ruffian' barely an hour before. An announcement had been made over the camp's antediluvian military-tannoy system, to the extent that virtually everyone left on campus was searching for the missing infant.

By the time Rod and I got back, the place was crawling with police cars bearing the logo of the Norfolk Constabulary, whose officers were busy interviewing the branded mother in the Show-Bar. She was clearly coiled up like a spring, as she uttered expletives in every sentence that passed her lips. It eventually transpired that there had been a domestic dispute between the lady and her now estranged husband, shortly before they were due to leave for their holiday. The angry father had refused to make the North Denes trip, but was belatedly missing the company of his little son, and as a result had driven to the camp in an attempt to take custody of the boy, ostensibly to allow Mum some quality time to herself to do some thinking.

The unsavoury episode had plainly ruined her holiday, as she informed the bewildered rozzers that it was time to pack her things and, in her own words, 'piss off out of this khazi!'

♫

The band were on top form that night, and for a second encore played a version of the Isley Brothers' (or Beatles') *Twist and Shout*, which we hadn't done in many a year. Second encores were a rarity these days and were generally reserved for the most persistent of crowds, which was very much the case here as they tirelessly chanted for more. There was a real summer party going on, with many audience members sporting swimwear beneath their T-shirt tops. Even the – dare I say – friendly camp staff were invited to join us up on stage to display a few of their nifty moves; and all in all it had probably been the tour's best gig thus far, despite the crumbling backdrop.

I was still in need of some time alone, and went back to the caravan for a moment's peace to add the final touches to Mum's eulogy, as the funeral was now just a few days away.

It's incredible how a good gig can lift a performer's spirits, and with the pillows stacked behind me as I sat up in bed the words began to flow. I made heartfelt references to her strength of character and good humour, and topped and tailed the piece in double quick time. Feeling a beatific sense of contentment I stretched my arms, yawning, and pulled the threadbare ceiling cord to switch off the light before dropping off in no time at all.

I awoke to a sudden ballyhoo and in a daze quickly groped for the cord, only for it to break off in my hand without providing any light whatsoever. Stumbling out of bed and opening the door stark naked I expected to find Rod clattering around in a drunken stupor, but instead I found a tall, sweaty man and a heavily made-up woman who looked like a gangster's moll. She instantly shrieked, 'Bob, he's got nowt on, who the fuck is he?'

I hurriedly reached for the bedclothes in an attempt to preserve my modesty, but Bob – who was clearly off his face – had other ideas, and swung a looping right-hander in the direction of my skull, shouting angrily, 'You fuckin' perv!' in a terribly slurred Northern accent.

Ducking swiftly I managed to avoid the intended blow as the uncoordinated Bob keeled over, nastily crashing into the furniture and onto the floor as his good lady continued her foul-mouthed diatribe at his expense.

From the frontage outside I heard another raised female voice that blurted out, 'Mam, Dad, you pair of dickheads, that ain't our fucking caravan!'

Still on the deck, Bob was having great difficulty articulating, but his ever-vituperative wife simply said, 'Fuck me,' to which I drolly replied: 'I don't think he's capable tonight love!'

The best she could muster up was, 'Ha ha, very funny,' followed by, 'Gerrup Bob, you fuckin' lard arse,' as she descended the steps with no hint of an apology, no 'Sorry to have woken you,' just nothing!

Deeply unimpressed I hopped back into bed and could still hear Bob and co. continuing their heated argument from across the way; but thankfully the din soon died down, before Rod arrived back shortly afterwards, peeping his head into my cabin to see if I was still awake. Feigning sleep with my eyes closed I thought I heard him say, 'Goodnigh'... see you in the morson,' not exactly possessing the power of clear speech himself.

The morning after the night before, Rod looked awful but was determined to indulge himself with yet another fatty fry-up, as he dressed while I opened the caravan door and stepped into the morning sunshine to inhale some much needed fresh air.

I looked across to the noisy neighbours, and must have blushed as I saw Mrs Bob's recognition kick in. She shouted over, pointing:

'Fuckin' hell, I've seen Showaddywaddy's lead singer stark bollock naked!'

Rod appeared, by now fully clothed, and we strutted away purposefully.

'What was that all about?' he asked, frowning.

'Oh nothing, nothing at all,' was my reply.

15

DUELLING BANJOS
(ERIC WEISSBERG & STEVE MANDELL)

Thursday 4th August 2005

I studied the roadmap on my lap as we passed through a backwater that looked almost like hillbilly country. We drove by a strange brown and yellow barn-cum-farm building shaped something like a gigantic batch loaf; perched on the fence by the open gate was a glum, spotty-faced interbred-looking youth, who I half expected to reach down for his banjo and begin entertaining us with some intricate finger-picking.

'This is just like a scene from the movie *Deliverance*,' I pointed out to the guys.

'Which one of us is gonna get buggered?' enquired Romeo.

'The only people that I know of recently getting rogered are a pair of prickly security guards,' I jokingly responded.

The journey had frustratingly taken two-and-a-half hours to drive under fifty miles along the coast to this remote corner of England, and the first impressions weren't good, as we came upon the kind of place that exuded bleakness, even in mid summer.

'The locals pronounce St Osyth as "Toosey",' I discovered on asking for guidance in the local post office; but when I asked why, the rather snooty lady put me in my place saying, 'We just do!'

As I made a couple of small purchases she seemed to change and became chatty, informing me that the village had the lowest recorded rainfall (five hundred and thirteen millimetres per annum) in the entire UK. Looking outside to see the rain sweeping across the headland on a blustery wind that felt more akin to early March, I cheekily enquired: 'What went wrong today?'

'It's only spitting, that's all it ever does around here,' she assured me.

The postmistress's directions led us down to the beach area, where we were confronted by literally thousands of drab-looking caravans, which made sense when I later found out from the camp boffin that the local population down here is swelled during the summer months by a staggering seven thousand people.

To add to the feeling of desolation, the walking encyclopedia I chatted to insisted on giving me a history lesson as to the number of tragic deaths during 'The Great Flood of 1953'.

'If this place is so jinxed then why do so many folk take their holidays here?' I curiously asked.

He effeminately replied, 'God knows; I can't wait for October to arrive, when I'll be off to Ibiza with my pals!'

♪

The show-hall was occupied by a large group of long-haired, muscular journeymen who proudly flaunted scars, cauliflower ears and rippling biceps in abundance, which I assumed were the wrestling fraternity that Steve had pre-warned me would be in attendance. In complete contrast to the six-pack-loaded modern generation of athletes, there were no strict fitness or dietary regimes involved here, as the old warriors gorged themselves on cartons of fast food, indifferent to any aspersions that the contents may affect their cardiovascular performance.

Whilst observing our pugnacious co-stars we became a little intrigued, and sociably enquired as to when the bouts would get under way. A huge barrel-chested guy with an extraordinarily long neck and 'Ivan The Terrorist Cooper' emblazoned on his sweatshirt turned towards our party to gruffly inform us that his first fight was at three p.m., and theatrically asserted that he was ready to 'kick ass!'

Clearly unimpressed by the brawler's claim, Steve cynically surmised, 'I heard that most wrestling matches are bloody fixed;' but the wily Ivan, though initially taken aback, looked over wearing a crooked smile and simply winked.

The action kick-started at two-thirty when two stocky opponents covered in oil clambered into the ring followed by an ageing emcee who was garbed in a dinner suit that had evidently once belonged to someone else twice his size. His baggy trousers concertinaed onto his grubby scuffed shoes, and I dreaded to think of the pittance he'd be receiving for his duties.

The bell sounded and the macho contenders laid into each other with an excess of grunts and manufactured groans, making it plain for all to see that this was a put-up job.

Four rounds later the grappler named 'Grizzly Bear' stood egotistically with his arm held aloft by the bedraggled emcee (who we'd already nicknamed 'creeping paralysis') as his feigning rival complained bitterly: but he was to suffer no more. Neither it seemed would the sparse crowd, many of whom, clearly unimpressed, rose from their seats and headed for the exit doors, oddly enough with ourselves following in their wake.

Back on the outside in the persistent drizzle we passed by the camp supermarket that looked surprisingly well-stocked. 'This is it!' I exclaimed to Rod and Dan. 'It has to be mission accomplished in there!'

'What the bloody hell are you on about?' queried Dan.

'That place is like an Aladdin's cave – they must have some fresh fruit in there,' I vociferated.

Dan nodded and agreed, 'You know, you may just be right,' sharing my excitement.

Striding through the door, high on expectation, I wandered up and down the aisles until we found a small greengrocery section. The stock consisted of potatoes, carrots and onions, but dismayingly not one single item of fruit.

Sometimes in life the most trivial of things can get on top of you and in a way I felt betrayed that after a glimmer of hope my aspirations had yet again been thwarted, as alas there were no fresh crunchy apples, juicy pears or oranges, just a few manky vegetables that even pigs would've turned their noses up at. Head bowed and chuntering like grumpy old fool, I once more headed straight for the door, followed closely by my prickly pair of friends.

♫

Dan wanted to take a look at a nearby ancient priory, but I wasn't so keen and left the two of them to their monastical treat before wandering back to the caravan where the TV was blaring out from next door. I guessed it must be Romeo – who is a TV addict – and peeped through the window to see him lying prostrate on the sofa, engrossed in some low-budget afternoon magazine programme.

Romeo was born on the beautiful Caribbean island of Antigua, and migrated with his family to the UK in the post-Windrush mid fifties, eventually settling in the suburbs of my home town, Leicester.

Always a powerful and hard-working drummer, he had a sniff of the big time in the late sixties with a band named Black Widow, who specialised in satanic worship and black magic. Their biggest claim to fame was an appearance on the bill at the now legendary 1970 Isle of Wight music festival, which featured a much publicised performance from the iconic genius Jimi Hendrix when the great man closed his set by bursting into flames.

That memorable event apart, Romeo ultimately satisfied his curiosity with the occult and moved on to join forces with Trevor, Jeff and my good self in Showaddywaddy's predecessors, Choise. Not unlike Trevor, his ambitions were initially far more focused towards the progressive direction that Choise were taking, which upon the merging of the two bands during the embryonic SWW period led to a comment that was to haunt him for years:

'If you want me to be part of that fucking rock-and-roll circus, you've got another think coming!'

However, as things progressed his mind was soon to change, and he remained a loyal member of the band to the present day.

Romeo is the only person I've ever known, or for that matter heard of, that purchased a Rolls Royce before even possessing a driving licence; and often during the mid to late seventies his silhouette could be made out through the car's tinted windows, sporting an expensive fur coat and smart trilby hat, whilst being chauffeur-driven through the city streets. Manifestly he liked to do things in style, which was very much what the seventies were all about.

In keeping with a more mature outlook, in recent years he took it upon himself to attend college to study a bookkeeping course; and more latterly began teaching drums to budding youngsters at a Leicestershire secondary school during the band's rest periods.

Never one to rush things (other than the occasional drum-roll!) he finally married Dawn, the love of his life, in his birthplace Antigua during the summer of 2010, after a mind-boggling thirty-five-year engagement.

♫

During the late eighties the band performed a series of concerts in the Republic of Ireland, which for financial reasons (on the promoter's part) included a couple of substandard provincial gigs that had slipped through the net, and which were scheduled for the two rest days.

Carrying the full theatre production, the crew loaded masses of gear into one of these 'lesser' venues, with cumbersome boxes stacked everywhere in what was nothing more than an ill-equipped village hall. The hastily erected stage area was basically made up of large sheets of plyboard nailed together in something of a bodge job, with an access corridor to the rear of the crude platform where further trunks and equipment flight cases were stored. The stacked amplifiers and drum kit were squeezed tightly into a confined space, making for a shambolic, topsy-turvy set-up that was not at all what the band were accustomed to.

Undeterred, we took to the stage to be welcomed by an unusual mixed bag of an audience that included country yokels in muddy wellies, scantily clad teenage girls (whom the crew and Trevor were observing closely) and the odd city-slicker, who had probably dashed up from Dublin (around sixty miles away) to witness the one-off spectacle.

In defiance of the venue's limitations we rocked into our repertoire in a hot but electric atmosphere, and with the crowd lapping it up there was a good vibe about the place.

Suddenly the booming drums came to an abrupt stop, with alarmingly no sound at all coming forth from the rear of the stage; and, as the band craned our necks to look behind us, to our horror there was no Romeo. He'd simply disappeared into thin air.

For a moment it entered my mind that his old satanic influences had eerily intervened to indulge in a spot of body-snatching and had whisked him away to subject him to a sacrificial ritual!

The crowd were as flummoxed as we were, as the crew frantically rushed up and down the backstage passageway in total disarray, until as the noise died down a faint, strangulated cry and thumping sound became audible, and the heavy flight-case directly behind the drum kit crashingly flew open.

Inside, back from the depths in a state of utter confusion, was Romeo clutching his stool and sticks; and, as he comically sat up, it quickly dawned on everybody just what had happened as we all bellowed into loud fits of laughter. His precariously positioned drum-stool had vibrated its way to the edge of the stage, and his body had tumbled backwards right into the jaws of the open case, which – in a scene straight out of a Charlie Chaplin movie – had closed on top of him upon impact.

The lively Irish audience saw the funny side when I explained the calamity, as the crew shunted the kit forward and secured it to the stage to prevent a repeat of the mishap, whilst Romeo, happily undaunted, shook himself down and carried on as normal in what turned out to be an extraordinarily enjoyable gig; but needless to say he was ribbed about the incident for weeks afterwards.

Fortunately there were no similar upheavals during the band's performance in 'Toosey' that night, other than a fierce battle against the elements as we made our way through the gusting wind and spitting wet stuff back to our accommodation, happy in the knowledge that yet another one was chalked up on the board.

The following morning as the troops assembled in the canteen, Trev pre-warned us that breakfast had been 'unedible',* though it didn't appear to be bothering Ivan the Terrorist and his grappling chums, who tucked into the ultra-greasy fare with great gusto.

Dan and I decided for once to give it a miss and walk to the Spar shop to sample a breakfast patty, which we'd spotted on the previous recce; but irritatingly this also turned out be spectacularly unappetising, and soon had me reaching for the Rennies.

Yet again the weather in the driest part of Britain was inclement as the continual drizzle refused to let up; and thirty minutes later the bus was cram-packed with our belongings, with no one wishing to overstay their welcome, as the tireless wheels rolled back towards Norfolk and the small resort of Hopton-on-Sea.

---

* See 'Trevisms'.

16

POSTCARDS FROM PARADISE
(FLESH FOR LULU)

Friday August 5th 2005

I first met Bill Williams in the lush surroundings of the Hong Kong Country Club, where the band had been booked to do an outdoor show in the exotic gardens during the summer of 1989.

Bill had popped his head into the band's dressing-room and politely asked if I would join his party at their table after our performance, as I'd been his wife Pam's pin-up during the late seventies and he wanted, by and large, to embarrass her in front of their friends. His likeable, infectious personality instantly conveyed he wasn't the bothersome type, so I was more than happy to oblige and hit it off with him from the word go.

The first question that anyone asked Bill was: 'Is your name really William Williams?' to which he chuckled and explained that he'd been christened with the mortifying name of Wilberforce after his grandfather but assumed the name Bill at an early age, largely due to his mother's preference for the abridged and less pompous tag.

After a couple of thirst-quenchers – as he put it 'purely for medicinal purposes' – the tongues loosened, and I soon came to realise that not only was he 'a good egg', but also an erudite and most fascinating man. Bill started his working life, after leaving school at fifteen, in the pits close to the Welsh mining town of Ebbw Vale where he was brought up. He loathed the job from day one and at nineteen quit to be recruited as a trainee policeman in the valley community of Merthyr Tydfil.

He subsequently worked his way through the ranks to become Sergeant at the tender age of twenty-five, which was unheard of in those parts, and within a year applied for a transfer after meeting local girl Pam whilst on a family holiday in Norfolk. The couple were married in 1982 and became the proud parents to daughter Melissa eighteen months later.

In 1987 he attended an interview in London for the plum job of Commissioner in the Hong Kong Police, and to his amazement he was offered the post. Considering the opportunity to be too good to pass up in spite of relocation headaches, here he was, as he put it: 'Playing cops and robbers in South East Asia.'

The pair of us got on like a house on fire that night, and as a result arranged to meet up for lunch close to the infamous Nathan Road a couple of days later, before our stint was over and we departed for the UK.

Walking through the seedy backstreets we came to the busiest restaurant imaginable, where it seemed two hundred or more chattering people were clinking chopsticks together and shovelling some unwonted delicacies into their gaping mouths. We were the only Europeans in there (you needed local knowledge to find this place) but my new pal was *au fait* with the local cuisine and ordered up some different but tasty-looking platters (one, he later told me, was snake) which I stuffed inside my gullet regardless.

Bill explained that he and Pam missed the UK desperately, and despite having a good social life in the colony the plan was to see through his tenure in Hong Kong until he reached the age of fifty-five in 2002, by which time he'd still have a few years of good health and a bountiful nest-egg with which to enjoy the rest of his days. When Melissa flew the nest he would take Pam to every corner of the planet she desired and someday wind up back in Norfolk, overlooking the Constable country they both shared a passion for.

We exchanged contact details and vowed to keep in touch, initially by sending postcards from any exotic or interesting places we visited throughout the world. We stood, shook hands and parted with a robust man-hug.

For almost three years the globetrotting twosome mailed glossy cards from various interesting and unexciting destinations we visited. The ice-breaker from Bill came from the Indonesian island of Bali, where they were spoiling themselves on a tropical beach holiday. I returned a postcard from Hell, which is, believe it or not, the name of a tiny village on the Caribbean island of Grand Cayman.

The list of out-of-the-way places grew and grew; and to add a little humour we began signing the cards with the names of famous world dignitaries and celebrities. I received greetings from Nelson Mandela, Mao Tse-tung, Ranulph Fiennes, Michael Jackson and many more. He in turn was to receive 'wish you were here' messages from the likes of Abraham Lincoln, Bishop Desmond Tutu, and Marco Polo to name but a few.

It was great fun while it lasted, but after a Christmas card in 1992, sadly the correspondence finally dried up.

Twelve-and-a-half years later a redirected airmail envelope popped through the letterbox of my new address. The letter read:

Dear Dave

Long time no see, hear, write etc!

I hope this letter finds you and your family well.

Our final New Year's celebration in Hong Kong was an absolute hoot, and prompted me to get back in touch.

We were once again at the Country Club dancing the night away, when the DJ shouted, 'Does anyone remember 15 years ago, when we had the fabulous legends Showaddywaddy live here at HKCC?' to which Pam and I screamed at the top of our voices Yeah!!! He followed up by playing five or six of your big hit songs, one after the other, and we were truly in our element, as was everyone at the club.

The night stirred up such good memories of meeting you all those years ago, and made me smile when I thought of the numerous postcards we exchanged – which I still have hidden away in a folder – from all over the globe.

I'm retired from the force now at the grand old age of 57, and with my baby Melissa, who is 20 now, off travelling in Europe with her boyfriend, we figured it may be time to realise some of our own ambitions and take a 'gap' year – six months actually – ourselves.

What I'd dearly love to do, if it's OK with you, is to start the cards rolling again. I know you're still travelling the world, and besides it would be great fun.

We leave HK on January 29th for Toronto in Canada, then travel all over to Montreal, Quebec, Calgary and Vancouver etc. After this we cross the US border and head due south through the Grand Canyon into California, through Mexico, Central America and eventually reach South America. We'll do the River Amazon, Machu Picchu, Iguazu Falls on the way down to Ushuaia in Southern Argentina where we catch a cruise ship to Antarctica. It's truly the trip of a lifetime, and we honestly can't wait! Come the end of our adventure we will return to Pam's native Norfolk, which as you well know I grew to love too. We plan to renovate a chocolate-box cottage we own in Wroxham, right next to the Broads. That will be a true labour of love!

Should you have any shows in the diary anywhere nearby from July onwards, it would be wonderful for us both to see you perform again, and maybe we could begin to catch up on the last 15 years or so.

If you can let me know as soon as possible, and on the postcards I'd be most grateful.

I very much look forward to hearing from you.

Wishing you a very happy new year

Your Friends

Pam & Bill

In truth I hardly knew the guy, yet I was so elated to hear from him. One of life's little oddities is how sometimes you seem to identify and connect with certain people. This had very much been the case with Bill.

I replied within a couple of days and explained that, coincidentally, we would be playing four dates in Norfolk during early August, so not only would we be reunited, they'd even have a choice of venue. Embarrassing though it may have been that they'd get to see the band in the less salubrious setting of one of these parks, they were after all down-to-earth people, and the opportunity was too good to miss and so I figured what the heck!

Two more letters followed on top of an echoing call from Hong Kong, and everything was arranged for them to see the band in Hopton-on-Sea on Friday August 5th, after which I'd spend the night at their idyllic cottage by the Norfolk Broads.

Tragically, I was never to see Bill Williams again.

Out of the blue Bill's sister Gwen contacted me a week or so before we hit the holiday park trail, stressing she was concerned that Pam and Bill hadn't been in touch with any family members for more than six weeks. Their daughter Melissa had mentioned the postcards and tracked down my number, and desperately clutching at straws she asked if I'd received any mementos in recent weeks, and if so what countries had they been sent from.

I dug out the cards and got straight back to her, saying I'd received just five. The first had been from the Niagara Falls, followed by others from Flagstaff, Arizona (close to the Grand Canyon), Acapulco in Mexico (signed by Great Train Robber Buster Edwards), Chichen Itza also in Mexico (one of the seven wonders of the world) and the final one from Panama City which read: 'What a dump, kind regards Robert Mugabe.'

Gwen was most grateful and promised to keep me up to speed as to any ongoing developments.

On August 5th we arrived in Hopton-on-Sea at, dare I say it, one of the more upmarket camps. Once we were settled into our pleasant, recently decorated chalets (there was still the lightly gaseous fragrance of emulsion), I made my way over to see the ents manager to double check that suitable arrangements had been made for Bill and Pam to see the show.

I'd elaborated a little when I'd called a couple of weeks ahead, and had mentioned that the Chief of the Norfolk Constabulary wished to attend the show, which they'd fawningly swallowed hook, line and sinker, and had gone out of their way to reserve a table for my esteemed guests in a prime position.

The table remained empty all night; but it wasn't until two years later when I visited Pam in their charming waterside cottage on the outskirts of Wroxham that I belatedly found out why.

Pamela and Bill Williams spent sixty-six days in a Columbian mountain range, I hasten to add not by choice.

They were kidnapped on June 7th 2005 along with four other tourists (two Dutch and two American) as they slept in wooden huts en route to the Lost City of La Ciudad Perdida in the heart of the tropical jungle of the Sierra Nevada. Their captors had been a rag-tag bunch of left-wing guerrillas, some of whom were only sixteen or seventeen years of age; however, the AK47 rifles they carried belied their youth, and made them all the more unpredictable and terrifying.

The desolate hijacked group were forced to march for mile after mile into deep jungle terrain, having no clue as to what fate awaited them; initially the only communication they had was through American tourist Lena, who propitiously spoke fluent Spanish. The guerrillas knew only a handful of English words, the most frequently used being 'money' and 'dollars', but it appeared that someone had tipped them off that Bill was a VIP and was consequently worth his weight in gold.

After the first few brutal days the captors became a little more relaxed as Bill's magnetism began to take hold, and even dubbed him 'El Presidente' as they took a shine to the man. Over and over through Lena, and eventually in pidgin Spanish that he'd picked up himself, he used his powers of persuasion in attempting to convince the rabble he was of no importance at all, and was simply a retired policeman; but his efforts seemed to fall on deaf ears.

The party were moved on, trekking some days for a backbreaking twenty hours or more, surviving on sugar-cane, Kraft cheese slices and yucca plants, and sleeping huddled together under sweaty plastic tarpaulins. Physically and mentally exhausted they finally took refuge in a small wooden house where they were held for twenty-five days, only for the level of interrogation to be stepped up. Day after day the hapless captives were given the third degree for details and names of wealthy friends or acquaintances who could meet the kidnappers' excessive ransom demands; but incredibly even after the occasional beating the group stood unflinchingly firm, eventually wearing down the exasperated custodians who at last believed Bill to be a case of mistaken identity.

Using his charismatic personality he even befriended the mob's surly leader Paulo, and they were often heard laughing and joking together in broken English (much to the chagrin of the prickly minions), though the humour soon wore thin as alarmingly the stress of being in captivity was finally beginning to take its toll with Bill's health deteriorating rapidly.

As Pam continued their dumbfounding story, I saw that this woman could see evil in no one, and had come to believe they'd been fairly treated. True to say there had been the odd occasion when the guerrillas became aggressive and jabbed them with their rifle butts, demanding money and threatening worse violence should their wishes not be met. However, tales their friends had heard of excessive cruelty and rape were completely unfounded.

On August 9th Bill suffered a serious stroke. Pam pleaded with the captors to get him to the nearest hospital; and mercifully Paulo, now riddled with guilt, wanted no blood on his hands and acted immediately. Two days later, after being dragged on a shabbily constructed stretcher and transported on a rickety bus ride, Bill lay receiving treatment in Santa Marta Hospital.

Pam's prayers had been answered, and Bill miraculously survived the stroke, which ironically had been the unfortunate tourist's saving grace. The couple flew back to London from Bogota on August 19th 2005.

After all the suffering they'd been through, quite what prompted Bill to send what was to be his last ever postcard, I'll never know. It came from the Bogota Plaza Summit Hotel, and poignantly in one word read: 'FREEDOM! Love Bill and Pam.'

My visit to their picturesque Norfolk retreat was a sad one. Bill had been plagued with illness from the moment the couple arrived back in England, and suffered another massive stroke in 2006. This one he heartbreakingly didn't survive.

Pam had aged alarmingly, and the once lucid bright eyes had become heavy and forlorn, as she pensively recounted the trip of a lifetime that had turned into a horrible nightmare.

She returned to Hong Kong to be with her friends in 2008.

17

HOUND DOG MAN
(FABIAN)

Saturday August 6th 2005

Danny was looking forward to today's short trip inland to Belton, as the camp was situated close to his beloved Norfolk Broads, to which he enjoyed escaping for a few days from time to time to be in his element fishing from a hired boat while his family enjoyed the untainted air, and to add to the attraction make regular pub stops along the way. The prospect of an unexpected bonus visit thrilled him to bits.

I in turn was looking forward to the opening day of the Championship football season, where my team Leicester City would be beginning their 2005/06 campaign with a twelve-forty-five p.m. kick-off in what was to be the season's curtain-raiser. A tricky away game at Sheffield United, which in recent years had not been a happy hunting ground, was far from the ideal start, but I figured if there's no cause for optimism on the opening day, then there never will be!

With fourteen camps behind us, many of which had been dispiriting, it was a pleasant surprise to arrive in the unusually leafy surroundings of the Belton park. Even the weather had taken a turn for the better; and, as we pulled up outside the venue, to our surprise we found Steve laughing along with his new best buddy, the gregarious and extremely generous entertainments manager. The super-efficient head honcho had furnished the boys with able-bodied assistants, sandwiches, and cooling pints of lager, and I hadn't seen Steve so relaxed and happy in his work in a long time.

Trevor was the only member of the party not delighting in the high temperatures, as the humidity played havoc with the creation on top of his head, where occasionally the preparation he used would liquefy in the heat and cause black streaks to run down his face, which we cruelly referred to as 'meltdown'! To spare himself or indeed ourselves any embarrassment, he'd somehow managed to find a powerful electric fan, and had parked himself by the open window of his caravan, with the sun on his face, enjoying the protection gusting from the overworked whirring blower.

Dan had persuaded Rod to join him on his Broadland excursion, while I'd borrowed a radio from the amiable controller to keep up to speed on the latest footie score. Stef's perpetually pale body was stretched out on a bedsheet borrowed from his caravan, attempting to catch some rays, as Romeo sat inside busy reading the bulky Saturday broadsheets. Steve, after his earlier exertions (and lunchtime tipple), had now fallen asleep in the truck.

Looking around there was a far and away more laid-back ambience to this place, which doubtless emanated from the friendly management team through the onsite staff, who pleasingly couldn't seem to do enough for us.

During the half-time break I switched off the radio in disgust, as Leicester were two down already! There were noises coming from the venue which suggested that some kind of matinée show was taking place, so I inquisitively popped my head through the stage door to check out what was going on.

There were twenty kids, give or take a couple, mostly seated cross-legged on the dance floor in front of the stage, while their mums sat in a row behind them, chatting quietly together or doing a spot of knitting. On stage was what I presumed to be a magician, performing tricks with a top hat, cards, brightly coloured props and balloons. However, the most entertaining part of his show was his patch-eyed mongrel dog who lifted up his (I'm assuming it wasn't a bitch) head and grunted *wuff-wuff* every time a trick was successfully completed. This memory has long remained with me, and frequently rears its head to silently amuse my warped sense of humour and cause me to snigger, much to the puzzlement of those in my company at the time.

In spite of the comical connotations, ten minutes of the calamitous conjuror and his slobbering canine friend was more than enough, so I quietly slid away back to the latest sports bulletin on my borrowed radio, snickering to myself as I walked across the grass.

The smile was soon wiped from my face forty-five minutes later when the result of the game came through: we'd been stuffed four-one, which felt way below the belt. I agonised over what went wrong and mused, 'Perhaps this place isn't that great after all!'

I was in the midst of taking forty winks when the smell of culinary delights came wafting on the breeze from Jeff and Trevor's caravan, and just like nosey neighbours do I went outside to investigate.

Not content with the regular morning fry-up, there were sausages, bacon and small round croquette potatoes on the go, attended by the band's in-house gastronome Jeff, who offered: 'Want some?'

Breathing in the aroma made it difficult to resist, so I gratefully replied, 'Mmm, wouldn't mind!'

'Okay, just nip to the shop and get a big can of beans, and there'll be plenty for the three of us,' said the budding celebrity chef.

Knowing full well that – as opposed to fresh fruit – the mini-mart would hold ample stocks of the fifty-seven varieties, and licking my lips, I jogged across and purchased a couple of large tins and, hey presto! ten minutes later we were sampling the nearest we'd come to home-cooked food in two weeks on the road. This was more like it and quickly removed the bitter taste of defeat as we sat outside with plates on our laps, happily devouring the lot!

Dan and Rod arrived back looking windswept and red in the face. 'Bloody hell, what a scorcher it's been!' Dan exclaimed, and continued: 'We rented a boat out for an hour, but couldn't do any fishing as some gyppos had slung a load of crap in the river; what's been going on around here?'

'Not much, we've all been chilling in the sun. City lost!' I told him.

'I didn't even know they were playing,' he countered.

'How did Derby get on?' anxiously asked Rod (who always looked for the Rams' result, as he'd lived in Derbyshire for a number of years).

'Lost nine-one,' I said.

'Bloody hell – you've gotta be joking,' said Rod in disbelief.

Grinning like a Cheshire cat I admitted: 'Indeed I am – I don't know any other results yet, only that we got hammered at Sheffield United!'

At the sound-check it was soon realised that Jeff could have forgone his cookhouse duties, as plates of sandwiches, slices of pizza and cakes were lavished upon us for our post warm-up refreshment by four smiling yellow-coated young ladies. The air of gloom that had been prevalent a couple of days before in the drizzliest part of England had well and truly lifted, as the revitalised happy clan optimistically looked forward to a well-organised show later that night.

The lightening of our disposition was further enhanced at the end of the rehearsal, after Trevor returned his guitar to the dressing room and strode back to the food table without realising he'd stepped into a small pile of dog-doings at the side of the stage, causing hilarity all round as he despondently sat and removed his trainer before scraping off the offending excrement with Steve's loaned Swiss Army Knife. Needless to say a competent flock of yellow coats were soon on hand with mops and buckets to spotlessly clean up the mutt's smelly heap, and as we looked on admiring their diligence Jeff added: 'What was coming out of that amp sounded like a pile of shit Oaksie!'

It was an unusual gig as the room had been laid out in theatre style, with row after row of bolted-together plastic seats, which seemed strangely out of sorts in this type of venue; but after a couple of songs it was soon apparent that the sun-baked revellers were in full party mode and itching to shake a leg. Our new pal the ents manager (also called Steve) was quick to grasp that the concert format was far from ideal, and the staff hurriedly remodelled the seating arrangements, much to the chagrin of the sedentary few, to allow ample space for the party animals to get up and boogie.

The show was going like clockwork, with the buoyant atmosphere inherent during the day being extended to the balmy night-time, and it was refreshing for once to witness six or seven hundred revellers genuinely enjoying their family holidays.

Halfway through the set we broke into our big hit *Three Steps to Heaven* with the crowd linking hands and swaying from side to side, aided and abetted by my good self. During the song's spoken passage midway through, I knelt towards the brow of the stage and took the hand of a rosily cheeked lady stood right at the very front, gently placing a peck onto the offered paw but finding myself dragged roughly into a passionate embrace as a full-blooded snog was planted upon my quivering lips.

Slightly alarmed I turned back towards the stage to escape her clutches and hoist myself back up; and what did I see but the magician's canine accomplice, shuffling across the stage as though he were wiping his backside, in search of his master who was observing the night's action from the wings. Bum notes abounded as the band briefly lost control and cracked up helplessly, astounded by what was indeed a 'first' in our long careers.

In the midst of the hilarity I quickly improvised and ranted into the mic: 'Who Let the Dogs Out?' to which the crowd instantly responded with barking noises, something akin to the answer-backs on the original Baha Men recording.

It was a while before anyone was able to regain their composure and complete the show without further incident, but the receptive punters had lapped it up and we'd rounded off a good day in fine style.

♬

With Rod in the driving seat the tickled troupe hit the road home heading in the direction of Norwich, and barely five minutes into the journey the fun started. Dan kicked it all off by saying, 'Why didn't we play *Puppy Love* tonight?' and in no time everyone was in on the act.

'We could've done *Bird Dog*,' said Romeo, followed by an endless stream of canine titles brought to mind over the next ten minutes that frivolously had the gang in convulsions. The following is an abridged selection of the witticisms banded about that night:

1) *Hound Dog* (Elvis)
2) *Black Dog* (Led Zeppelin)
3) *I Love My Dog* (Cat Stevens)
4) *The Bitch is Back* (Elton John)
5) *Me and You and a Dog Named Boo* (Lobo)
6) *The Boxer* (Simon and Garfunkel)
7) *Walkin' the Dog* (Rufus Thomas)
8) *Lonely Pup* (Adam Faith)
9) *Old Shep* (Elvis)
10) *A Four-Legged Friend* (Roy Rogers)
11) *Good 'Collie' Miss Molly* (Little Richard)

and of course the one that nobody wanted to embarrass themselves with, but trust Trevor: *How Much is That Doggie in the Window*, which met with derisive groans.

He felt he was on a roll now and followed it up with, 'How about the theme tunes from *Rin Tin Tin* and *Skippy*?' and it was starting to get silly, until Romeo curtly nipped things in the bud, admonishing Trevor by carping:

'Skippy's a fucking kangaroo, you knobhead!'

As the tomfoolery finally died a death, we saw to our alarm that the bus was being stalked by a police vehicle, and had no idea as to how long they'd been tailing us. The boys in blue promptly flashed the car's blue light and signalled for us to pull in.

Rod who was at the wheel thought it best to get out and chat directly with them, and with the window down we heard the PC enquire: 'Your vehicle was rocking around a little there sir, have you been drinking?'

'Not touched a drop, we were just having a laugh and joke,' Rod replied.

The second patrolman butted in: 'You're not a band, are you?'

'How did you guess?' Rod asked.

'I could just tell,' he said, pausing and chuckling to himself before continuing, 'because in my experience all bands are completely mad!'

At the time it would have been difficult to disagree with him!

Since then the unique episode often crops up in conversation, with a couple of other silly dog titles added to the list such as *All the Young Dudes* by 'Mutt the Hoople' and *Whip It Good* (whippet) by Devo, fully justifying the long-suffering cop's barbed comment.

18

REMINISCING
(BUDDY HOLLY)

Monday 8th August 2005

I suppose you could call me a lucky kind of guy, as my Mum was the first person really dear to me that I'd ever lost in a life that had now spanned fifty-three years. The family's immediate concern, however, was my Dad, and how he'd react to losing his lifelong wedded partner of sixty-one years.

He was ensconced (happily I might add) in a small private nursing home not far from the semi-detached house they shared for fifty years, after suffering two heavy strokes in recent times; but, as an old RAF man, in true military style he'd grittily soldiered on and taken everything that was thrown at him as simply part of life's tangled web.

Always a gregarious man with a mischievous sense of humour, those around him soon warmed to his affability and easygoing nature. Indeed he was popular with all the other homebound inmates and the nurses, but didn't go too much on the Monday-morning 'Knit & Natter', so today's funeral paradoxically provided him with an excuse to miss the social calendar's riveting weekly instalment.

Arrangements had been made for the hearse and cars to assemble outside at the nursing home, before continuing on to the church service; and by the time we arrived Dad had been smartly decked out in his best black suit and tie by the on-duty carers, who genuinely tried to make things as painless as possible for the old feller.

He greeted everyone with a warm smile and a hug, and we made the necessary arrangements as to who would go in which car and a few other formalities, before wistfully departing for the church.

It is a sad and remiss testament to the modern age how en-masse family get-togethers are so often restricted to weddings and funerals. Long-lost relatives, some that we hadn't seen in decades, together with their adult children that the family hadn't laid eyes on since they were knee-high, stood congregated outside the church, all offering kind words and their condolences; and in spite of the occasion being a sombre affair, it was heart-warming to reunite with our kinsfolk and friends giving up their time to celebrate the life of a special woman.

The service was a little bit of a blur. I delivered my lengthy eulogy confidently enough, other than a couple of emotional cracks, but held it together by constantly keeping an eye on Dad, just to be sure things were under control. My sister Pat was very tearful, but ably supported by her partner and two sons toughed it out and by and by came through the ordeal unscathed.

Family members and close friends then moved on to the crematorium some ten miles away for a short committal, close to where the post funeral gathering had been organised.

In the middle of circulating amongst aunts, uncles, nieces, nephews and even some old family friends who'd travelled from New Zealand, I bumped into my cousin John, who I hadn't seen in many a year. Always one for a laugh and joke, he bought me half a lager and we proceeded to chat about old times, and stories about Mum's awful smoking habit (she'd smoked thirty strong untipped Park Drive cigarettes a day) when we were both youngsters. He cracked a couple of hackneyed gags, but pleasingly still retained his youthful sense of fun.

Suddenly out of the blue he asked, 'Are you still gallivanting around the world with the "Waddies" Dave?'

'Not exactly the world, John; we're travelling the length and breadth of Britain doing a string of holiday camps for the next couple of months,' I answered.

'Oh yeah, which ones: Butlins, Pontins?' he queried.

'It's actually a large chain of caravan parks, but the money's okay in spite of the venues being a little basic,' I said.

As we continued chewing the fat I happened to mention the name of the holiday company we were working for, to see his expression furrow into a huge frown as he exhaled and rued: 'Bloody hell Davy, that's a bit of a comedown ain't it?'

'Ah, they're not that bad,' I said going on the defensive.

'They bloody well are, mate: we stayed at one in Helston in Cornwall about three years ago, and it was "hell" all right, worst holiday we've ever had. The place was a dump; we had to leave the cooker on to get warm. Thank God we only went for a week, it felt more like a prison stretch,' he said disparagingly.

'Thanks a bundle, John, we're doing that one in a couple of weeks I think,' I tutted.

'Well, rather you than me mate!' he exclaimed.

'Oh well, at least you've given me something to look forward to,' I joked.

'I'd better get you another lager, it sounds as if you're gonna need it,' he kindly offered.

Dad had coped admirably with the day, and had even enjoyed seeing his relatives and the other well-wishers, but he was clearly tired, and as the throng began to disperse we made our excuses, leaving a handful of stragglers behind, and headed for home.

Understandably emotionally and physically drained he closed his eyes in the car; and, when we reached the nursing home, we figured the best option would be to leave him in the hands of the carers to help get him ready for bed and that he'd be out like a light as soon as his head hit the pillow.

'Where are you going now?' he asked inquisitively.

'Oh, we're just off to Jim's (my brother's) place for a nightcap,' I informed him.

'Can't I come?' he asked, beseechingly.

'I thought you were knackered!' I said in semi-disbelief.

'I could still give you a run for your money,' he claimed.

'You old bugger, I don't know where you get your energy from; of course you can come!' I chortled turning on my heels.

Dad's bones creaked like an old floorboard as we helped him back into the car, and once he was settled my wife Cathy and daughter Holly piled in alongside as we formed a three-car cavalcade to join forces for a *tête-à-tête* on the terrace of my brother's place barely a mile away.

The small gathering sat peacefully studying the starry sky, pondering if there may be a new addition tonight; and, under the light effects of the afternoon's alcohol, reminisced the night away, as if almost in a dream.

My reverie was instantly interrupted when something suddenly dawned on me, and I abruptly disturbed the serene temper by exclaiming, 'Bloody hell, I've got to go all the way down to Dorset in the morning to another one of those hell-holes!'

'I thought you said you enjoyed your work,' Jim said questioningly.

'Mmh, not so much these days,' I replied pensively, without wishing to dampen the surrealistic air any further, as myself and the girls said our goodbyes and quietly sloped away.

19

IT'S ONLY MAKE BELIEVE
(CONWAY TWITTY)

Tuesday 9th August 2005

The M1 motorway is not the most pleasant of roads to travel at the best of times, particularly on a weekday around lunchtime when an incessant stream of white vans, cars, and above all else articulated trucks bearing foreign plates – and equally alien driving habits – fills the congested carriageways.

The chocker mini-bus proceeded past the Newport Pagnell stop-off with the intention of pulling into the next rest area at Toddington for the obligatory 'sweetie stop' and to refuel, when from the rear seat Jeff panted, 'Thank God for that, my guts are giving me hell, I'm seriously in need of a dump,' as he spotted the road sign showing *Services 7 miles*.

'Shouldn't be long now,' I reassured him from the driver's seat; but in typical fashion, three or four miles further along the main drag, hazard lights began flashing and a garish sign indicated *Congestion – slow down*. Sure enough within a couple of minutes the traffic had ground to a complete standstill.

I looked around at Jeff to see him fidgeting uncomfortably as he whimpered, 'I hope this bloody car-park starts moving soon or I'm going to have an accident!'

'Have you brought a change of trousers, or even a bucket?' Trev cracked.

'Piss off Oaksie, is that supposed to be funny? I had a kebab last night and haven't felt right since,' he responded.

'Never mind spare trousers, it sounds as if you need incontinence pants!' Danny suggested.

'I'll bloody need something in a minute; how far is it now to Toddington?' Jeff pleaded in desperation.

'About two more miles,' I answered.

'Can't you just overtake on the hard shoulder or I'm gonna be in big trouble?' Jeff begged.

'Just clench your buttocks and hold on; I'll give it a go when we're a little bit closer,' I said.

The casualty breathed a huge despairing sigh, and I noticed that his eyes had begun to water as inch by inch we crawled frustratingly forward, covering barely five hundred metres in the next five minutes, but still nowhere near his salvation.

'Dave, I'm in agony, for fuck's sake!' he bawled desperately.

Heeding his call I quickly manoeuvred from the middle lane into a gap, only to jump on the brakes as an AA van attending a mechanical failure was stopped at the roadside blocking the majority of the escape route. Eventually I swerved and pulled out to make a mercy dash for the services as the queuing motorists tooted and shouted abuse, which met with an aggressive two-fingered salute as this was clearly an emergency of sorts.

As finally we glided through on the inside of the gridlock, Jeff sullenly informed everyone that the panic was over, and we were too late. The poor guy could have saved his breath: the putrid stench emanating from the rear seat was overwhelming, as hands flapped everywhere in front of the guys' noses. That was until Rod suddenly raised his voice: 'Bugger, there's a copper,' as we idled by on the port side of the jam-sandwich, to which the police vehicle immediately responded by thrusting out behind us with the blue light flaring into action.

'Bollocks!' I yelled, as I jolted to a halt, to see the PC in the rear-view mirror walking purposefully towards the bus. I wound the window down, and the officer leaned inside placing his elbows on the door frame.

'In a hurry are we sir?' he sarcastically enquired, but before I had the chance to make my excuses he stepped back a pace and screwed up his face in horror, saying, 'What the hell is that disgusting smell?'

'My mate in the back has just had an accident, that's why I was in a rush to make it to the services,' I explained.

'Good heavens above,' he said pulling a nauseated face and wafting his hands around; and then kindly, 'Go on, get the hell out of here!' I thanked him, and toed the accelerator, heading the final half a mile to our sanctuary.

Romeo was beside himself, almost crying with laughter, before he spluttered out: 'Did you see that pig's face?' This prompted further jocularity, and a stream of quips to which we all fell about in stitches, with only Jeff excluded, who was hanging his head in shame and disbelief.

Cleaned up and refreshed with fizzy drinks and chocolate bars, we returned in trepidation to the bus to find Danny fumigating the interior with an air-freshening spray, as he prepared to take the wheel. 'Better now Jeff?' he asked.

Without realising, the disinfected bass-man replied: 'Yeah, not bad ta, but what a crap start to the day,' which following a short silence soon met with a predictably jocose reaction to the Freudian faux pas.

The remainder of the journey down to Hamworthy was tedious in the extreme, with the usual southbound weekday freight and business travellers interspersed with mobile homes and drab-looking caravans, especially as we approached the ultra-touristy Bournemouth area.

'Have you never heard of Hamworthy Boilers?' a guy in my local pub had asked during the previous Sunday lunchtime session, in which he was regularly involved.

'Is that a house of ill repute?' I'd joked in reply, as the pub's resident polymath nosily interjected: 'I think you'll find that Hamworthy Boilers are based in Surrey, not Dorset!'

None the wiser, there was a gig to be done as we advanced towards the suburb of Poole with some apprehension as the place appeared to be deserted. The temperature had dropped a full ten degrees, and the rain once again was unyielding, completing an acute aura of bleakness all around.

Had the weather been more inspiring this could actually have been an attractive spot, as I looked across the panoramic views down to Poole Harbour and the nearby millionaire's row at Sandbanks. This, however, was clearly a day to be indoors, and explained fully why the denizens had gone into hiding.

Upon reaching the encampment we were provided with clean but soulless apartments in a cheaply decorated modern wing, where paint had speckled onto the windows. The accommodation was well-equipped, with TVs, kettles and welcome packs, and on the plus side it was a welcome relief not to have been allocated the more usual dismal, poky caravans, particularly in light of the miserable meteorological conditions.

Dan and Rod were comfortably reclined with their feet up watching afternoon TV, and I had a good novel on the go, so wandered off in search of a hideaway to indulge myself in a bit of historical fantasy, without any disturbance.

To my surprise I found a small computer room that doubled as a library, though there were far more comics strewn around than anything of literary importance. A couple of green-felted card-tables were positioned against the far wall, one of which I plonked myself down at, observing there was just one other person in the den, who made eye contact with a friendly nod and smile. The man looked busy, with spreadsheets, writing pads, invoices and a calculator all laid out in front of him, and not wishing to distract him from his business I returned the acknowledgement with a similar gesture.

Turning away, I had just settled in my chair and removed my bookmark at the next chapter when he summarily exclaimed: 'This is unbelievable!'

I looked over inquisitively and conversed, 'I'm sorry, I'm not quite with you!'

The guy stood up and ruefully said, 'Silly me, please accept my apologies; I was thinking out loud. The name's Peter,' (I didn't quite catch the Polish sounding surname) 'I can see you came in here for some peace and quiet!'

'Not a problem,' I said, adding: 'Are you having some difficulties?' as I rose and offered my hand with a reciprocated introduction. He began to explain:

'My mobile-phone business went belly up eleven months ago, and after holidaying abroad for the last twenty years, we decided to follow New Labour's tourist drive and go away in good old Great Britain, mainly with the intention of saving a few quid; but I was just looking through the bills and it really doesn't add up.' Without realising I was part of his evening's value-for-money cabaret, he posed: 'Which model van are you staying in?'

'I'm only here for the day on business, and they've put me up in an apartment,' I coyly informed him.

'Well, lucky you! I've been here with my family for nine days now and can't say I'm enjoying it one bit. The weather's been blowing a gale, we're all bored out of our minds, and it's costing a bloody fortune,' he beefed.

He seemed a reasonable enough guy but was obviously not best pleased, so in an effort to placate him I enquired: 'Where did you go to last year?'

'We flew down to Albufeira on the Algarve, and had a lovely holiday with endless sunshine, and it cost a darn sight less than what we've paid for this dump; so never again, bloody tourist drive or not – it's just a soddin' rip-off,' he complained dejectedly. On a roll he continued: 'Two-and-a-half bloody grand this has cost me, and we've had to eat out most nights because the food's all garbage on the camp.'

'Tell me about it; it's not exactly geared up to a healthy diet is it?' I concurred, going along with him.

'What is it with this country, everything's such a bloody rip-off?' he asserted, before calming himself and saying, 'You didn't come in here to listen to me whingeing; I'm sorry to burden you with my problems mate, I just thought this would be an enjoyable thing to do, but it's a hard lesson learnt. Do you fancy a pint next door? Let me buy you one.'

I thanked him, but turned down the kind offer and said, 'Maybe I'll see you later for one, I've got some work to catch up on right now,' and shook his hand before bidding him goodbye.

Walking across towards the Show-Bar I could scarcely believe what I'd heard. Two-and-a-half thousand pounds for a fortnight in a dingy caravan? Admittedly I'd been to worse places, especially on this tour, but this was something else and it was hard to conceal my amazement.

I grabbed a cup of tea with powdered milk at the side of the stage from the yellow-coats' brewing kit, but only drank half of the foul-tasting swill, whilst observing the movements of the crew boys, who'd clearly be busy setting up for a while yet, so it was back to the apartment to chill out for an hour.

The weather had brightened up a little, but it was surprisingly cold for August; so I was shocked to find Danny with his shirt off as I entered the kitchenette, and greeted him with, 'You un-freckly bastard, what's going on? It's bloody freezing out there.'

'I've come out in a rash, look,' he said, scratching the top of his shoulder.

Sure enough there were red blotches all over his arms, as I unhelpfully diagnosed: 'I think you must be allergic to something!'

'Yep, you're right, it must be caravan parks,' he jested.

'Where's Rod, has he gone to get you some lotion or something to ease it?' I asked.

'No, the lazy git's flat out having a kip; all those phone calls have taken it out of him!'

'I'll go and see if they've got a medicine cabinet at reception if you like,' I offered.

'Good idea, in fact I'll come with you,' Dan said, pulling on his shirt.

As we walked he told me: 'At first I thought it might be scabies or bed-bugs from some of these rat-infested caravans, but I had something similar a few years ago in a hotel that came from the detergent they wash the bedsheets with!'

At reception we were sourly greeted by a large swarthy-looking chap who looked as if he doubled as a hit man in his spare time. 'My friend's come out in a nasty rash; have you got any ointment back there that may help?' I asked.

'Come out has he?' he answered, chortling at his own pathetic excuse for wit, but then followed up with: 'This is a 'oliday centre, not an 'ospital!'

He'd taken no time at all to get right up my nose, and I retorted sarcastically, 'I can see that you're trying very 'ard to be 'elpful, so perhaps you could point us in the direction of someone who may be better equipped to assist, as I'm sure this is not the first complaint of this nature you've ever come across!'

'Are you being funny?' he queried, wearing a pained frown.

'No my friend, you're clearly the comedian around here, and there's nothing funny about an irritating twa… rash!' I retorted – stopping myself, but really wishing I'd said twat!

A lady who'd overheard the exchange appeared from the adjoining office, hoping to bail out her unmannerly lackey, and sweetly offered: 'There's a chemist in Hamworthy that usually stays open 'til late; here, let me show you where it is on the map,' which she retrieved from a plastic holder.

Back at the apartment we woke Rod, who had the bus keys. 'What time is it?' he yawned.

'Just before five p.m. Sound-check's at six; we're just nipping out because Dan's finally come out and urgently needs some cream!' I joked.

Rod looked at me with a bemused expression, questioning whether he'd heard me right, and just said, 'What I'm not with,' as he turned over for a little more shut-eye.

The over-helpful Asian lady in the pharmacy blinded us with science in an extraordinarily affected accent, and after eventually recommending a new-fangled gel that would relieve the inflammation admonished, 'If the symptoms persist you must see a doctor, as it may need an antibiotic to clear the infection,' to which we both expressed our gratitude and rushed back to camp for the early evening run-through.

Upon entering the Show-Bar the park manager fervently informed us that tonight's performance was for an exclusive 'owners only' function to be held in their own custom-built clubhouse, accessed by a private drive on the far side of the camp, which was also a ten-minute walk.

The more upmarket building was well-constructed with attractive exposed timbers, but not ideally equipped to put on a six-piece rock-and-roll band, so yet again we were faced with a 'suck it and see' situation as Steve stood, cap in hand, scratching his head in puzzlement. A decision was made to change in our apartments and drive down to the doors at the rear of the stage area, as the allocated rooms to the side were poky in the extreme.

Later on as we changed I noticed Dan had a large pair of scissors, and was attempting to cut off the sleeves of his shirt to allow some air to his dermatological problem. He laddishly joked: 'I hope this rash doesn't spread to my bollocks, or I'll have to go on with mi' knob out,' to which I quickly retorted:

'Don't worry about that, nobody would notice anyway!'

'The Grand Owners Ball' as it was ostentatiously billed was like being caught in a time warp, and akin to a re-run of a 1970s episode of *Dallas* with buckets and spades! The ladies had donned their glamorous evening dresses, and there was a glittering display of bling on show, with the men in unfashionable lounge suits and outmoded blazers, but unfazed they all appeared to be living the dream, and seemed to be in high spirits.

Pre-warned of volume restrictions we wisely decided to tone things down for our performance and adopt a very un-rock-and-roll approach, seeing that the occasion was far more suited to an out-and-out cabaret style.

The proud owners dined in highfalutin' style (chicken and chips it looked like to me), chinking glasses together at every opportunity, but it was soon apparent that getting them onto their feet to party was another matter. There was nothing for it but to turn on the charm Las Vegas style, and shiftily heap praise upon them. The ploy worked to a degree, as a few couples sloped out onto the floor, but hardly exerted themselves with the stiff ambience taking precedence and preventing them from letting themselves go. That said the performance was politely received, and we certainly hadn't shamed ourselves.

An invitation was extended for the band (after we'd changed and applied a little antiperspirant) to hobnob with the glitterati for a ceremonial flute of 'champers' which we cordially accepted, not wishing to rub anyone up the wrong way. Freshened up we arrived back at the clubhouse in our civvies some fifteen minutes later, where a group of contemptuous, spruced-up people were gathered in the foyer looking down their noses at the unwelcome posse of scruffs attired in jeans and T-shirts, as if we belonged in the gutter.

A heavily sequined lady affectedly laughed and affirmed, 'Oh, it's the band,' when to our relief the man accompanying her interjected in a more pleasant tone, 'Please come in lads and help yourselves to the buffet; great show by the way!'

He arrogantly clicked his fingers, summoning a tarty waitress in a short black mini-skirt and laddered tights to offer us cheap champagne; but most of the guys opted for a beer, and when the initial novelty of our presence had worn off, we were happily left to our own devices.

Jeff and Trevor piled cold cuts onto their plates, while the remainder of us just picked and nibbled, before parking our backsides for a post-gig natter, and to take in the unreal milieu.

People-watching had long been one of the band's favourite pastimes on our travels, and here was an irresistible opportunity to comprehend the air of self-importance that bewitched many of these mere mortals, some of whom gassed so boorishly that it was impossible not to nosily eavesdrop on snippets of their conversations, one of which oddly bugged me. 'My husband and I have a six-berth Prestige with personalised decking, and now we're looking to purchase a further De-Luxe model in Watchet down in Somerset,' pronounced an overtly pompous lady.

Had this been part of a well-planned business venture I would happily have taken my hat off to them, but this self-centred nonsense was purely about one-upmanship and status, the effect of which was over-glorified and even disturbing.

I pictured the guy I'd met earlier, whose business had taken a tumble, and how palpable his disappointment had been; he most certainly wouldn't be investing his hard-earned cash into one of these unremarkable temporary refuges. Perhaps I was still grieving a little and being over-critical, but in reality the whole charade came over as spurious and pathetic and had gotten the better of me.

Thoroughly bewildered I bid the boys goodnight and walked the half-mile to where our apartments were located. It was a cold, breezy night, but my blood was boiling. I tapped into the web on my phone and saw that my football team had triumphed four-two in the first home-game of the season; but in a strop the glad tidings made little difference, and on the way I vandalised an already damaged litter bin with my right foot, without stopping to retrieve the mess I'd made.

20

I CAN HEAR MUSIC
(THE BEACH BOYS)

Wednesday 10th August 2005

In 1978 the band were riding on the crest of a wave in the midst of a string of Top Five hits, and were playing sellout theatre shows wherever we went. One such concert was at the Queensway Hall in Dunstable on a late springtime evening, when our latest single *I Wonder Why* was perched at the dizzy heights of Number Two in the charts, and the place was littered with hordes of screaming fourteen-year-old-girls.

Laura was also fourteen at the time, and being a huge fan of the band had bought tickets to the show, which she would attend with her Mum.

Tragically, the day before, she'd been involved in a fatal motor accident, which had taken the life of her brother and left her in a coma in the intensive care ward at St Albans Hospital.

Beside themselves with grief and worry, her parents kept a constant bedside vigil, to the point of exhaustion, only to see that Laura simply wasn't responding to any tests at all, until a cassette tape of the band's songs was played to her through a set of headphones.

The medical staff immediately saw a faint glimmer of hope, and continuously piped the music through to the teenager, as one of the nurses pointed out that the band were performing only a matter of miles away, and took it upon herself to contact the theatre.

The caring helper outlined the devastating circumstances of the collision, and was put directly through to Tony, the band's tour manager, who in turn relayed the heart-rending tale to us all, soon after which arrangements were made for us to visit Laura at the hospital on our way north after the show.

Tears welled in my eyes as we sat at the bedside listening to her parent's heart-breaking story, as monitoring devices beeped and lit up. Understandably they were inconsolable, but showed immense courage, clinging onto each other's hands and bravely attempting to smile through the sadness.

A young African doctor explained in detail how Laura's respiratory system was being continually scanned on a VDU via an electrocardiograph that measured her breathing patterns and heart rate, but a senior nurse had already indicated in confidence that there was little hope, other than the music therapy that had been known to trigger an amazing response in certain cases, particularly the happy-go-lucky, upbeat, rhythmical genre that Showaddywaddy were renowned for, so they most certainly hadn't given up hope yet.

The cassette was stopped after thirty minutes to allow the medical staff time to investigate the effects; and only minutes later, to gasps of astonishment, the wide-eyed doctor reported that her response had been nothing short of remarkable. Her father walked over to me with the faintest gleam of hope in his over-burdened eyes, and asked: 'Would you hold her hand?'

Physically moved and a little nervous, how could I possibly refuse, and so I whispered 'Of course' as I pulled up a chair beside the bed and sat gently caressing her petite hand.

'I'm Dave, the lead singer of your favourite band,' I choked out, followed by a few softly spoken words of encouragement; after which there was absolutely no doubt in my mind that she could subconsciously hear me, as her fragile hand twitched and she blinked before moving her head the tiniest amount in recognition.

Stirred by the experience, I looked around at everyone as my jaw dropped, enlightened and full of optimism, until one of the band – I can't remember who – put a hand on my shoulder and intimated that it was time for us to leave. Contact numbers were exchanged so we could be kept informed as to Laura's progress, followed by further words of support, as we quietly said our goodbyes and slipped away from the ward into the night.

A handful of days later I received an update through our office, saying that Laura was still on a life-support machine but that she was putting up one hell of a fight, and hopes were high.

Two more weeks had elapsed when further information was passed on saying that incredibly she'd battled through the worst, and although she remained paralysed would undoubtedly survive the accident. The wonderful news came as a heck of a fillip, but was the last we heard from the family for a very long time.

Ten years later the band were playing a series of dates at the incongruously named Caesar's Palace in Luton, and were relaxing drinking tea in the dressing room when the manager of the club came in to ask if we would see a couple of guests backstage, who as he put it 'owed us an enormous debt of gratitude'. Slightly puzzled we nodded our assent, and shortly afterwards found ourselves re-introduced to Laura's inspirational parents.

With the preliminaries out of the way, they explained that their now twenty-four-year-old daughter was very much alive and well, and although permanently in a wheelchair remained in good spirits, and still loved her music. When our *Very Best Of* album had been released in 1987, she had insisted on adding it to her collection and was said to have been elated to have all our big hits on CD for the first time.

Laura, however, suffered from a semi-comatose condition that occasionally would kick in and affect her for days at a time. Her doctors and specialists had kept a close watch on this for many years, and though much research had been carried out on the subject, essentially there was nothing they could do but wait. They further explained that these fugue states are incredibly difficult to monitor, as parts of the brain simply switch off, and experts are convinced that the condition is psychological.

Having already been to hell and back her parents had learnt to live with these difficulties and had stayed hearteningly positive, particularly as the semi-comas were nowhere near as frequent in recent times as they had been only months before. The family were now making plans to uproot and move to the south west coast, with Devon or Dorset being their favoured locations as her father was closing in on retirement and, being a man of the sea, loved to therapeutically while away the hours on his boat.

We once again wished them well as they left the dressing room, and talked of our huge admiration for their strength of spirit, remaining steadfastly undaunted by the avalanche of misfortune that life had seen fit to throw at them.

♬

Weymouth is a beckoning coastal town, with an inherent nautical feel about it, largely due to the fact it boasts a sizeable marina with shops and restaurants aplenty lined up along the jetties, where boats and yachts of all distinctions putter in and out of the harbour at all hours of the day.

During the previous spring we'd been in the resort as part of a nationwide package tour to play a concert at the town's Pavilion Theatre, when on the afternoon of the show we were surprised to find two silver-haired middle-aged people patiently waiting by the stage door for us to arrive, who once again turned out to be Laura's parents. With only a hint of recognition there, it was difficult to put a finger on who they actually were, as sixteen years had elapsed since we'd last seen the couple; but as her father walked across to us and reintroduced himself, it soon became apparent. As he quipped: 'Three times in twenty-six years – I bet you think we're a right pain in the backside!'

He explained how they had moved to a place ten miles or so from Weymouth called Abbotsbury back in 1994, and how they loved the quality of life down in Dorset, adding that the sea air suited them far better than that of clammy, landlocked Bedfordshire.

The obvious question had to be asked: 'How's Laura?'

He smiled and proudly enunciated, 'She's an amazing girl that one, we're so lucky! Would you believe we had a huge party for her fortieth birthday last month, and she even managed to get up and dance. We were hoping to bring her along to see you tonight but sadly she's had a couple of bad days, so we'll have to do it some other time.'

'You can still make the show, we can easily fix up some tickets,' Rod suggested.

Though clearly upset that Laura couldn't be there they both did their best to disguise it, as her long-suffering Mum declared, 'We would've loved to have come, but we really must get back home; we'll look out on your website for when you're down this way again.'

Grabbing a piece of paper I wrote down my mobile number and the office email address and said, 'If anything changes, or there are any other shows you'd like to come along to, just pick up the phone and let me know, and you can come along as our special guests.'

Mum became tearful at this, as Laura's Dad sighed and said touchingly, 'We think the world of you boys, you know.'

Little moments such as that make you realise how music can cross borders in a way that no other art form can, as I thought back to their daughter lying in a hospital bed with a pair of headphones carefully placed over her bandaged head. The man's sincerity was deeply moving, and there was nothing left to say as we once more bid farewell to this special couple whose lives we'd affected with a short gesture of goodwill all of twenty-six years ago.

A couple of days before we set off for the Dorset coast, an email had been sent to our office, which had been forwarded on to me. It came from a lady who lived not far from Weymouth, who mentioned she'd found out that the band were scheduled to perform at a holiday park in the Preston district of the town, before going on to say that she'd been a huge fan of the band since the tender age of thirteen, but due to problems with ill-health had never been able to see us play live. She was now, as she humorously put it, 'an old biddy' in her early forties, and it remained her greatest ambition to someday meet her all-time heroes.

She had contacted a representative at the holiday camp to explain all this, only to be told that the event was exclusively for people staying at the centre, and they would in this instance be unable to help as unfortunately the show would not be open to the general public.

She further stressed in the email that she really didn't like to ask, but was there a possibility we could intervene and have any influence in helping make her dream a reality.

At the foot of the page it read: 'Your Friend Laura. PS My Mum and Dad send their warmest regards!'

I was gobsmacked; this was someone I didn't actually know, but at the same time a person who had occupied my thoughts so many times over the previous twenty-seven years. I immediately emailed her back, and promised I'd do anything within my powers to help arrange for them to see the show, and how much we'd look forward to meeting her.

Seconds later I was onto the camp and spoke to a lady named Tracey, who sounded like a starlet from the cast of *EastEnders*, and laying it on thick explained the whole story, to hear her sigh as if she were captivated by a tearjerker of a movie. But patronisingly all she could say was, 'Aah, if it was left to me luvvie they'd have front-row seats; but leave it with me and I'll have a word with the manager Mr Noakes after he's finished in his meeting.'

Annoyingly, the call wasn't returned until the following morning, when via a receptionist, a self-important sounding man whom I assumed to be Mr Noakes (though he failed to introduce himself) contemptuously informed me: 'I'm afraid we've had to put a veto on your request for guests, as the centre is fully subscribed.'

I pleaded, 'Oh, come on – these are exceptional circumstances: this lady has been in and out of a coma for the last twenty-seven years!'

'I'm sorry but rules are rules. Health and safety will come down heavily on us if the restrictions are breached, so regrettably my hands are tied and there's nothing I can do!' he imperiously snapped.

'Can't you relax the rules and show just an iota of humanity for one night only?' I implored him.

'Company policy is very clear; if I allow just one member of the general public on site, I could be for the high jump,' he argued.

Not helping matters at all I began to lose my rag, and could contain myself no longer: 'Company pissing policy is it? Well, in two days from now when I get there I'm gonna kick your arse so hard you'll go higher than a pole-vaulter, and see how that fits in with your bloody rules and regulations!'

Not surprisingly the phone clicked off, and I sat there staring into the silent handset, totally disbelieving.

Worst of all, I now had to relay the bad news to Laura and her family; but the only form of contact I knew of was from the email address she'd originally sent, which I felt would be horribly impersonal, so I composed a message that read simply 'Can you please call' and left the number.

An hour later my phone chirped into life, and it was Laura's father. 'I just had a text from the girls asking me to call you – it's great to talk to you again. They're out shopping; is everything okay?'

As we spoke I had a gut feeling that he'd sensed the nervousness in my voice, so I cut to the chase and told him of the problems I'd had with the camp manager, and his overblown refusal to bend the house rules.

We chatted, putting the world to rights like grumpy old men, discussing political correctness, bureaucratic red-tape nonsense and the like; and I laughed out loud when he joked: 'The only problem with common sense is that it's not very common!'

However, as the conversation drew to a close we did manage to come up with a temporary solution that would at least soften the blow, and arranged to meet up for a bite to eat when we arrived in Weymouth on the tenth of August.

'All's not lost; you'll be down here again sometime,' Laura's father had said as I'd apologised for failing to keep the promise I'd made the previous year; but what I hadn't realised until the very end of our confab was that the band were scheduled to play at another camp close to Weymouth some eight days later, so indeed we would be back down this way, far sooner than anyone thought. The minute this dawned on me I was straight on the blower.

A helpful Scot took the call, and without delay put me through to a lady named Jacqui, who was unforeseeably delighted to hear from me. 'Our bookings went through the roof when we did our mailout advertising that you guys would be coming to the park!' she told me enthusiastically.

A little taken aback by this – but pleasantly so – I condescendingly replied, 'We've always had a soft spot for Weymouth, so it'll be great to be in that neck of the woods again.'

I briefly and courteously outlined to her the story of Laura and her forbearing parents, and said that I'd be eternally grateful if a day pass could be granted for three special guests, emphasising how much it would mean to them to see the band live on stage.

She quickly curtailed my waffling by interrupting and saying, 'There's really nothing to worry about – I'll ensure that evening passes are left at reception for when they arrive. There are two tables that are situated directly by the disabled access ramp, so I'll reserve one especially for your guests.'

She then added: 'I also think it's a lovely gesture: it's wonderful when artists take the time to actually show they care about their fans!'

I was almost speechless – in stark contrast to the manager of the neighbouring camp, this woman was a decent human being – but I managed to squeeze out: 'I really can't thank you enough, and I look forward to meeting you on the eighteenth.'

I came off the phone and had metamorphosed into a different person: Mr Angry had disappeared, and Jacqui's colleague a few miles up the road had become an insignificance I'd have to grin and bear. I decided to keep the good news as a surprise for when we met the family for lunch later that week.

♫

The curmudgeonly mid-life crisis may have abated by the time we arrived in Weymouth for the first show, but I was nevertheless determined not to risk any kind of confrontation with the niggardly manager who'd made my hackles rise only days before. We grabbed the keys to three caravans and dropped off our stuff – along with Trevor who had been irritable all the way down, and Romeo who was feeling under the weather with a streaming cold – and headed straight back out in search of a pub on the harbourside called The Old Rooms Inn, which had been highly recommended for its delicious fresh-crab sandwiches.

Walking into the marina I spotted Laura's Dad right away, as he was sitting talking with another guy at an outside table. As we made our way through a mass of sunburnt bodies he greeted us warmly and introduced us to Wiktor (pronounced Victor) from Poland, before nipping off to grab a waiter to take the lunch order.

Wiktor's pidgin English was pieced together and difficult to fathom out, but the gist of his words appeared to centre on his son Sebastian, who was it seemed a medic working somewhere in the south of England. As he communicated I looked towards the waterfront, breathing in the sea air, and couldn't help noticing a couple laughing and enjoying the afternoon sunshine. The lady, who was in a wheelchair, radiated happiness, and as I smiled taking in the balmy scene, it became apparent that this was the girl whose hand I'd held some twenty-seven years before on a St Albans hospital ward; and what was more this unbelievably brave woman, who'd fought like a tiger for more than a quarter of a century, was in love.

Her father returned and snapped me out of my reverie. 'I'm pleased to say we have something to celebrate,' he announced, looking over his shoulder and catching Laura's eye. 'Darling, our special guests have arrived,' he gesticulated waving her over.

She sped up the concrete ramp under her own steam with her man in tow, as we all rose and pecked her cheek in familiar fashion, as if it were only recently that our paths had last crossed. Beaming beneath the sunlit sky she proudly introduced us to her fiancé Sebastian, who we were informed was a male nurse at Weymouth's main hospital, the Westhaven. Incredibly the couple had become engaged just three days before, and not wishing to be left out the lucky man's father climbed precariously onto his chair and raised his glass before clumsily pronouncing, 'To Laura and Sebastian, *nazdrowie!*'

Cries of 'cheers' and variations on the Polish equivalent rang out as glasses clinked and compliments came raining down amidst the joyous mayhem. Sebastian – in perfect English – explained that an authentic Slavonic toast should be conducted with vodka, but was swiftly overruled as it was felt to be a little too early in the day.

His robust father Wiktor had clearly taken a shine to me, as he retook his seat and powerfully hurled his arm around my shoulders and said, 'You and me, we make proper party wiz my son on zis night!'

'I'm sorry, my friend, I've got a show to do and we'll have to be making tracks soon,' I laughed.

'In zat case I vill come and bring my accordion,' the burly man offered.

'I don't think so, Wiktor; we're going out for dinner tonight,' interjected Laura's Dad, coming to the rescue.

In all honesty the world couldn't have been a much better place that day, and though during the preceding weeks there had been innumerable moments of abject misery, it was uplifting to witness how a family had rebuilt their lives from the depths of despair.

Laura's father openly explained: 'She still suffers the odd lapse from time to time, but Seb is a brick and is so wonderful with her; we feel blessed that he came into our lives.'

'What are you doing next Thursday night?' I quietly asked.

'Nothing that I know of – why?' he answered inquisitively.

I explained in hushed tones that everything was fixed for them to see the band perform on the outskirts of Weymouth the following week, and that I'd get a pass fixed for Seb too; to which he warmly clenched my hand with both of his, and simply said, 'I honestly don't know what to say – thank you so much!'

We'd shared a relaxing couple of hours with the happy soon-to-be family, but the hour had arrived for us to get back on parade; and after hugs, kisses and warm handshakes it was time to experience the stark precision of Mr Noakes' military operation.

I'd been half expecting Steve to call during our break in town, to inform me of the nightmare he was having with the overzealous park manager, so it was a welcome relief to find the gear successfully set up when we arrived back at base camp.

The fun, however, started the moment the band struck up to run through a couple of tunes, when two men – one shaped like a Toby Jug in a white open-necked shirt and black trousers, the other in a royal blue blazer with white strides, his blond quiff kind of resembling a Mr Whippy ice-cream – proceeded to position themselves in different corners of the Show Lounge, and switched on the little black plastic boxes they were carrying.

Right away we realised these gadgets were decibel level meters, which are often used by council employees to monitor the volume of the sound being pushed out into a public place. The small portly man just had to be Mr Noakes, who'd been my nemesis with all his health-

and-safety tosh a couple of days prior, which he'd antagonistically used as an excuse for the non-admittance of our worthy guests.

The little man arrogantly strode to the front of the stage as we finished our warm-up, and looked up to say: 'You're peaking at ninety-five dBs – the environmental recommendations for this hall are restricted to a maximum level of eight-five decibels; put simply, the volume will have to come down.'

My dislike for this man had been simmering for seventy-two hours now and all at once boiled over, as I answered firmly, 'Will it, now? Firstly, don't talk down your nose to me; and secondly, the health and safety guidelines for obesity state that you are putting your well-being at risk if you are in excess of one stone above your recommended body weight, and it looks to me as if you're three stone or more above yours, so you're not so much of a stickler when it comes to that one are you?'

'What?' he spluttered out, but somehow clammed up.

I smelt blood, and went back on the offensive. 'What's more, if you don't take your clipboard, your poncy friend and your fat face out of here, I'll soak that little black box in grease and slide it where the sun don't shine!'

Mercifully he didn't utter another word and was gone in a flash.

Steve defiantly pushed the PA system right to the limit that night, but the well-oiled vacationers' eardrums didn't in any way appear to be adversely affected.

We'd had our pound of flesh, and perhaps more importantly had notched up the tour's seventeenth show.

21

STUCK IN THE MIDDLE WITH YOU
(STEALERS WHEEL)

Thursday 11th August 2005

The nation was in the grip of cricket fever, and even some of the band who'd been ambivalent towards the sport in the past seemed on this occasion to be showing an interest.

Freddie Flintoff and co. had been thrashed in the opening Ashes test match by Australia, but had countered strongly to defeat Ricky Ponting's side at Edgbaston in an epic second encounter. Today saw the opening day of the third test which was at Old Trafford in Manchester, and hopes were high. This was the strongest England team we'd had in many a year, and having always loved my cricket – I'd even played for my local village sides on and off for years – all I asked was that there would be a working TV set at the next camp in the suburbs of Hastings, so we could catch some of the action.

The road from Weymouth to Hastings is a long haul, and it seemed that more vintage cars traversed this old southern coastal route than in the rest of the country put together. We passed Morris Minor 1000s (Moggies as we knew them), Ford Anglias, an ancient NSU Sprint, a Jensen Interceptor (never the most economical of cars doing nine miles to the gallon), and a beautiful gleaming old E Type Jaguar.

The major problem we were faced with was that on a single-carriageway road many of these vehicles were slow-moving in the extreme, and after the first hour's crawl we'd barely covered thirty miles out of the hundred and forty to our destination, which was rather unkindly referred to as 'God's waiting room'. However, the first over of the cricket was soon to be bowled, so we could find redemption as the radio's *Test Match Special* broadcast crackled onto the airwaves.

The boredom factor's rev-counter had gone well into the red as we continued idling along behind a lagging procession of holiday-bound traffic. Trevor and Jeff in the back seat were doing a grouchy impression of the Muppet characters Statler and Waldorf without realising, as Rod had nodded off with his nostrils making a light fluttering sound. Romeo was reading the *Times* and Danny and I in the front were busy complaining at the lack of progress.

England had won the toss and opted to bat, and the innings had begun without too many problems from the supposedly lethal Aussie attack, although much to my annoyance the ball-by-ball commentary couldn't be located in this part of the world, and we were left with no choice but to rely on updates from Five Live.

The mood lightened as, in the queue of traffic heading in the opposite direction, we spotted a mobile catering caravan bearing the logo 'The Hound of the Basket Meals', which triggered off a stream of not dissimilar plays on words, as Rod stirred and asked what the rumpus was all about before joining in the fun.

The next twenty minutes or more were spent chortling over some of the crazy shop names that we'd observed in our travels over the years, the highlights of which were:

Ryan Hair – hairdressing salon
Abrakebabra – Turkish kebab house
I. M. Smellie – solicitors
T. Watts – skip hire
Cycloanalysts – bicycle shop
Belvoir Hair (pronounced Beaver) – hairdressers
Thai Me Up – restaurant

House of the Rising Bun – bakery
Florist Gump – flower shop
Piston Broke – car spares
Penis From Heaven – German sex shop

Pride of place, however, was reserved for:

Spruce Springclean – carpet cleaners, and
Master Bait and Tackle – fishing gear

The amusement soon wore thin as the heavy traffic persisted unceasingly; but England were going well in the test match, so things could have been a lot worse.

We pulled in to refuel and the irritable troop alighted, clinging to their stiff backs, ready to stretch the legs and purchase some unhealthy garage snacks. The seemingly interminable journey had already taken almost three hours, and we were still the wrong side of Brighton with another sixty odd miles to go, leaving us rueing that we hadn't set off earlier; but these tedious travelling days were inevitable once in a while, particularly during the warmer summer months, close to the coast.

As we climbed back on board England had just lost their second wicket, with blond lady-killer Shane Warne entering the record books by claiming his six hundredth test scalp. The boys, however, didn't seem at all impressed, and just wanted to get to Hastings – and, the excitement of the cricket apart, so did I! At long last we arrived at the camp at five-thirty p.m., and I was forced to finally tear myself away from the dramas of the test match with just an hour to go before close of play.

It was back to the grindstone as we were handed keys to three jerry-built chalets that contained a rancid, fusty smell and were in serious need of fumigation. Sticking from the top of the TV was a rusting metal coat-hanger that doubled as an aerial, but attempts to tune into the Ashes test were futile.

A thumping knock came at the door and Rod shouted, 'Come in!' The youthful-featured Stef graced us with his presence, not at all looking his usual effervescent self.

'What's up, is everything okay?' I asked.

'Yeah, I think so, the gig's a decent size but the stage is a bit tight. Can I have a quiet word when you've got a mo Dave?' he coyly asked.

A little mystified, I answered, 'Of course you can,' thinking maybe there was a problem with Steve (which was a regular occurrence with crew members).

'I'm just over there in number twenty-four,' he said pointing through the window.

'Okay, give me a couple of minutes to unpack my stuff and I'll nip across,' I replied.

Chomping on a Mars Bar I trudged over to his chalet, taking my time through a set of deep tyre-tracks that had become entrenched in the muddy grass, and knocked before entering the dilapidated hut.

'Bloody hell, this is worse than ours!' I exclaimed.

'The bed's damp, but the telly works and at least it's spacious,' he said making unnecessary excuses.

'What's up then?' I queried.

'I've got a little personal problem,' he shyly divulged.

'Go on then, spit it out: what is it?' I unsympathetically urged.

He pulled down his shorts to reveal his pale, limp penis, and apprehensively muttered: 'I think I might have a dose – that slapper from Great Yarmouth had a funny smell about her!'

I could only smile and quipped: 'I told you your knob would drop off before the end of this tour!'

'How do I know if it's the pox?' he earnestly asked.

'Try squeezing up and if there's anything untoward going on there should be some discharge,' advised the supposed voice of experience.

Allowing him a little modesty he nipped to the loo and returned to tell me that fortunately all was clear, but that his fatigued todger was bright red and slightly swollen.

'There's half the problem: that bloody thing's permanently swollen. Just try and keep it in your pants for a while; you've probably picked up a rash, but see it as a warning,' I brusquely advised.

I sat and chatted to him in a kind of fatherly tone, pointing out that there would be no shame in attending a clinic for a check-up, and that young promiscuous lads would always run the risk of contracting something, especially when out on the road.

The good humour continued as I recounted a tale of one ex band-member who visited the special clinic so often that they gave him a loyalty card, and quoted an old adage that: 'VD in the music business is as common as lumbago in the building trade!'

Laughing our hats off, the little heart-to-heart seemed to have done the trick and my young pal was much more relaxed now, as I chirped up: 'Oh well, there's no alarm bells ringing; you'd better get dressed 'cause it's time to go and make some noise,' referring to the imminent sound-check.

The spartan venue was bleakly uninspiring, and yet again reeked of heavy disinfectant; and it seemed that every time an instrument struck up a strange reverberating effect slapped back from the rear wall. Steve mumbled to himself, clearly not overly impressed, but in a way had become resigned to his fate in recent days. The shallow stage looked out over an area of filthy red linoleum tiles that doubled as a dance floor and surely would have excited any environmental health people had they taken the time to pay the camp a well-overdue visit, but happily the staff on hand were accommodating with no sign of sinister-looking monitoring gadgets anywhere in sight.

The Channel 4 news was blaring from the snowy TV as we arrived back at the chalets, and I was soon on cloud nine when I heard that England had ended the day on three hundred and forty-one for five, and had given the Aussie attack a bit of a pasting, in the process maintaining the sporting nation's spirits at an all-time high.

Content with the tidings I reclined on my bed hoping for a short power-nap, but bewilderingly my buttocks almost hit the floor as the mattress bowed like a hammock, bringing into question just how old this bed and its frame were!

I then noticed a large sheet of plyboard poking out from behind the wardrobe, which I crouched down to retrieve from its dusty hideaway, quickly catching on that many previous inhabitants of this room had met with a similar problem. Lifting up the rank mattress and bedclothes from the wire frame, I shoved the board firmly underneath into position, and what d'ya know it fitted like a glove. Briefly standing back to admire my work, I dragged the threadbare sheets and blankets back onto the bed and lay down; it was far from perfect, but would simply have to do, and at least I wouldn't wake up with a stiff back.

Hands behind my head on the crumpled pillow I reflected to myself, 'And some people dream of an opulent rock-and-roll lifestyle,' before dropping off for twenty minutes, with visions of Harmison, Hoggard and our talisman Freddie skittling out the old Antipodean enemy at Old Trafford the following day.

A group of excited youngsters outside awoke me, but refreshed from the siesta I did the right thing and put the kettle on. I was wondering where Rod had got to when I heard what sounded like farmyard noises filtering through the adjoining room's wafer-thin partitions, the suid rattle of which almost shook the chalet's dubious foundations.

Realising that my immediate neighbours were indulging in an animalistic afternoon romp, I took solace by looking out of the window, only to spot Trevor surreptitiously creeping back towards his chalet with a clinking brown paper bag. Guessing the contents of the package, this was not what I'd hoped to see and, shaking my head, I figured it may be time for a friendly word in his ear, as everyone was desperate for him to stay on the straight and narrow. That however, would have to wait for now as my immediate concern was the job in hand later that night.

An unprecedented and amusing incident occurred on stage during the band's performance that night during the segment of our show where, for more years than I care to remember, we'd paid homage to the great Elvis Presley by playing a rendition of his classic song *Jailhouse Rock*.

After the first three verses and an instrumental passage, it had long been the norm to invite a few of the more exhibitionist audience members to join us up on the stage to boogie and have a little fun. The daredevil party animals were encouraged to kick their legs in the air, demonstrate their jiving skills and for the most part make complete asses of themselves, with their final act being to form a line and take turns to run across the stage and wrap their sometimes strapping legs around my ever-suffering midriff.

Over the years this part of the show had resulted in some outrageous consequences, with people soiling themselves, exposing their naughty bits with no undergarments, overexcited females simulating the sexual act as they enveloped me, others who fell flat on their faces, and many of them giving my poor old back a pounding due to the excessive baggage they were carrying.

Perhaps it should be included on my CV that a whole host of partying celebrities have also bestraddled my persecuted torso during many a private function; if you'll forgive me a little name-dropping, the who's who includes Sir Ian Botham, Kerry Katona, snooker guru Barry Hearn (he's even bigger than the mighty Botham), a host of Premier-league footballers and other sporting stars, and on one occasion to my delight the entire cast of Hot Gossip girls (whom you may well remember from the *Kenny Everett Show* et al) to name but a few.

The merrymakers in Hastings were arguably not quite as celebrated as any of the big guns mentioned, but they were equally enthusiastic; and it was good also to see a large proportion of kids making up the crowd, who – with little encouragement from their parents – frantically jumped up and down attempting somersaults, as if they were as inebriated as their seniors. The small stage began to bow as their exuberance overflowed, and video handy-cams flickered into life as eager relatives attempted to catch the antics of their loved ones on camera.

A hulking middle-aged woman, who grossly reeked of urine, launched herself at me punching the air as her legs wrapped themselves around my tortured girth, screaming incoherently as she fervently leapt into the polluted air mercifully to the opposite side of the stage; but taking it in good part it seemed she'd enjoyed her five minutes of fame, and perhaps more so the physical contact.

Two small kids to stage right began imitating the jump routine and looked as if they were having a ball, as I grabbed each of them by the hand and walked towards the microphone.

'Isn't it fabulous to see young kids enjoying a bit of old-time rock and roll?' I proclaimed to the audience, whereupon I heard a squeaky voice to my lower left side that was quick to reprimand me:

'I'm not a young kid!'

Looking down to my left, to my amazement I saw that the person grasping my left mitt was a midget. His Lilliputian face looked innocently up at me, and for once in my life I was rendered wholly speechless.

The guys in the band began wickedly creasing up at my embarrassment, as almost lost for words I squeezed out, 'I'm really sorry,' to the elfin fellow; to which he deferentially replied, 'No problem, it often happens,' as he rolled his miniature body into a cartwheel across the stage to the crowd's applause, which instantly diffused the situation, and helped dig me out of the gaping hole I'd gotten into.

At the end of the show there followed in the dressing room a stream of gags and yet more crazy song titles (I'll spare you the list) about little people, but on reflection I refused to rise to the bait, as it was easy to see the funny side in the midst of my humiliation.

We'd arranged to meet in a small bar situated well away from the entertainment complex, and as I walked in Jeff asked: 'Are you having a pint, or perhaps you'd prefer a "short" tonight?' at which everyone cracked up including myself. The next hour somewhat predictably got a little out of hand, but it was refreshing to see the guys letting off steam, even though much of the hilarity – as well as a good few rounds – came at my own expense.

I'd turned in at just after one a.m. and was out like a light, until an hour later a loud knocking came on the chalet door, which a bleary-eyed Rod stumbled over to answer as I placed a towel around my naked midriff and peeped through a crack in the curtains. Stood outside was a large track-suited female who coarsely grunted, 'Where's the lead singer?' to which Rod laconically replied, 'In bed I think!'

'Well, does he want some company, 'cos me and him have got some unfinished business to take care of,' implied the drunken woman.

'I don't think he'd be capable,' Rod told her, adding deceitfully, 'He's in agony with his back!'

Stock still and trembling by the bedroom door I whispered to myself, 'God bless him, that's what mates are for,' as her voice boomed in response: 'And I suppose that's my fucking fault for jumping on him!'

Rod sleepily tittered, 'Maybe it is, but I've got to look after him as we've got another show tomorrow, so goodnight,' and then closed the door in her face before noisily sliding the bolt across to prevent any further intrusion.

I tottered out of the bedroom and asked, 'Who the bloody hell was that at this time?'

'It was that big muscular woman who you said stank of piss, the one with the tattoos who jumped on you. I think she'd have half killed you if she'd got hold of you,' he quipped.

'Thanks, I guess I owe you one. If you're up in time for breakfast give me a knock,' I yawned, hugely relieved.

22

TEARS OF A CLOWN
(THE MIRACLES)

Friday 12th August 2005

Connie was lonely, and had been on the bill with us previously in Berwick and Caister, when Jeff had enjoyed her company so much he'd befriended her – suffice it to say with no ulterior motive.

The discontented throng were sitting together having a life-saving cup of tea after another dreadful three-hour trek along the A27 in the westward direction to Pagham, near Chichester, where the next port of call was located.

Further north, in Manchester, England had finally been bowled out for a more than healthy total of four hundred and four, and had the Aussies on the ropes at a hundred and twenty-nine for five, so all the way over I'd been driving the guys bonkers with permutations about the impending follow-on and other geeky cricket stuff.

Jeff's new bosom buddy went under the sobriquet of 'Connie Comedienne', with no prizes for guessing her theme tune, where she'd take to the stage with her own rekindled version of the old Culture Club song *Karma Chameleon*, which would fade out into her routine after the lyric: 'She comes and goes, she comes and goes!' Boasting a chequered career, she was fifty-seven years of age and had trodden the boards for almost forty years, including two years as one of the legendary Tiller Girls in London's West End.

What had long become our pet subject once again reared its ugly head when Connie unexpectedly blurted out: 'These bloody camps are doing my head in!'

'You and me both,' agreed Jeff, while the rest of us nodded and mumbled in accord.

'I much prefer doing my blue adult stuff,' she chimed in, before adding: 'I'm bloody awful at these kids' shows; it scares me half to death thinking I'm going to drop the odd F-word in – I have to be permanently on my guard. Plus the travelling is so tiring,' she sighed, stopping for breath. 'But I suppose it was similar with you guys; I couldn't just turn away a couple of months' work,' she continued, going on to explain that the tour may also offer her the chance of some male company, as she'd been alone since husband George had passed away in his sleep two-and-a-half years before.

'Anyway, I can't sit around tittle-tattling all day; I'd better go and get me frock on for the matinée,' she brooded.

'Do you want us to come and give you some moral support?' offered Jeff.

'You must be joking – I don't want you lot there, I'll go straight into blue mode if I hear a bunch of fellers laughin' at me gags,' she shot back in her endearing Brummie accent, as she rose and sauntered away towards the complex.

Her likeable character and sharp-wittedness had proved fascinating, and in need of a laugh or two we gave her ample time to change before running the gauntlet and stealthily creeping through the stage-door, and hiding behind the tall drapes waiting to take to take a look at her act.

Within minutes the strains of her introductory music filled the room, and out she trooped looking like a cross between *Coronation Street*'s Bet Lynch and Joanna Lumley, carrying a goodie bag from which she threw out sweets to the young audience, which we figured to be a smart idea to get the kids on her side from the word go.

She then launched into her routine, beginning with a number of knock-knock jokes, which the excited sprogs lapped up:

'Knock knock!'

'Who's there?' shouted the kids.

'Annie.'

'Annie who?'

'Annie one you like! Knock knock!'

'Who's there?' was the cry.

'Alli.'

'Alli who?'

'Alligator!'

She then roared 'Arrrrgh!' wildly into the mic, scaring some of the little ones half to death, but totally in control showed what a good pro she was, with the kids soon eating from the palm of her hand:

'What do you get if you cross a teacher with a vampire?' she bellowed.

'We don't know, what do you get…?'

'Lots of blood tests,' she yelled to the appreciative young crowd.

Connie rattled off gag after gag continuously for thirty minutes, and left the stage to high-pitched cheers, announcing she'd be back later with her Mums-and-Dads' routine.

Jeff and I decided to come clean and pay a visit to her dressing room, but creeping along the narrow passageway at the rear of the stage could hear a sniffling sound, and after knocking and entering saw small rivulets of tears on her cheeks that showed she'd been crying.

'What's up, Connie?' Jeff asked.

'Oh, it's just my eyes are sore from taking off my make-up,' was her excuse.

Black mascara tracks had streaked down from beneath her eyes and I noticed her wipe away another tear with a tissue as I enquired: 'Are you sure you're okay?'

She took a seat and said, 'I'd be bloody depressed if you lads weren't around, that's for sure. I've done eighteen of these camps and you're the first human beings that have given me the time of day. Why is everyone so damned unfriendly in these places?'

I answered, 'Because they have to spend months on end in them; I'd be miserable as sin if I had to do the same!'

'I never looked at it like that. But some of them are just downright cruel,' she rued, before going on: 'Do you know what that snidey compere just said when I came off?'

'No, what?' we asked in unison.

'He said the last time he'd heard those jokes he was about the same age as the kids in the audience! No one in these dives has ever got a good word to say,' she groaned.

'You just went down a storm with those kids; what more do they want, blood?' I said raising my voice, as Jeff chipped in:

'Don't worry about that orange-faced twat – he's so far up himself he's irretrievable!'

By this time I'd forgotten all about the cricket. She began opening up to us, lamenting, 'I've not had the easiest of lives but I've always been a grafter, and all I've ever wanted to do is to make people happy,' after which she proceeded to tell us all about her complicated background, beginning: 'My life story would be twice the size of *War and Peace* you know!'

Connie was born in the West Midlands town of Tipton, the second of two girls. Her father had been employed as a sheet-metal worker, but was fired from the job at the age of forty-seven when he was found on the factory floor unfit to work after an excessive lunchtime drinking session.

The same night after drowning his sorrows he'd come home from the pub shouting and swearing and had laid into the girls' mother, leaving her face badly bruised, but not content with the assault had marched up the stairs and entered Connie's bedroom with one thing on his mind – to have his evil way with his own daughter. She'd defended herself stoutly with a wooden bedside lamp, which she'd smashed into his face, managing to break the bullying ogre's nose, after which he stormed out of the house cursing at the top of his voice that he was going to kill her.

Connie's sister Kim had acted quickly and was about to call the police when their distraught mother intervened and persuaded her not to, thinking the man would soon see the error of his ways and come crawling back apologetically; but the damage was done and the once close-knit family were in turmoil, so much so that Connie packed her bags and left home at the age of seventeen, in search of a new life in the nation's capital.

As so often happens when youngsters leave home, she fell in with a bad crowd, and shortly after her eighteenth birthday began a stage career as a striptease artist, performing nightly in three seedy Soho clubs; but as the novelty and excitement of the big city began to wear thin she walked out of the job, feeling degraded as nightly she studied her audience's salacious expressions.

The very next day, after answering an ad in the post office close to her digs, she found herself waitressing in a busy little East End café, where she met a young musician called Sean who worked an afternoon shift at the café to subsidise his paltry earnings from night-time gigs.

Connie soon became popular with the regular clientele as she sang her way around the tables, which Sean's educated ears soon picked up on, thinking the girl had no little talent and a sweet singing voice. Within no time at all they'd moved in together as flatmates and practised every day for hours, soon learning a string of tunes and deciding to cash in and tout around for some gigs, which weren't long in coming.

Musically there was a good chemistry between the twosome, and inside a few months they had built up a sizeable following around the East End pubs and clubs they were playing, on top of which they began making a fair crust, even attracting the attention of talent scouts from a couple of record labels who kept regular tabs on them, which all added to the excitement.

Connie's life was on the up with everything panning out like a dream, when out of the blue she received a cry for help from her distressed mother telling her that sister Kim had been arrested and taken into custody by the police.

Jeff and I had been hanging on every word for well over an hour, completely engrossed, when the sound of Romeo pounding on his drums thundered from the nearby stage, causing her to pause mid-sentence and signalling that the time was nigh for the early evening sound-check.

'Oh lord, I must've been boring you pair witless; your rehearsal's come to the rescue,' she said self-deprecatingly.

Looking over towards Jeff and back to her, I asked: 'Why was Kim arrested?'

'Ah, maybe I'll tell you later. I've known some gluttons for punishment in my time, but you pair take the biscuit,' she muttered, collecting her things and disappearing from the room.

'Where the hell have you been?' asked Rod as we appeared from the wings. 'I thought you'd want the cricket on in the caravan and tuned the telly in especially,' he added.

'Bloody hell, what's the score?' I enquired with bated breath.

'A hundred and ninety for seven, with about half an hour's play to go,' he let on.

'Connie's been telling us her life story; she's a fascinating woman,' I said.

'You what? I used to think cricket was boring, but it's got to be more exciting than that,' he claimed; but it mattered little what he thought as we'd been captivated by her story, and were eager to hear more when the run-through was over – and besides it was close to stumps-up at Old Trafford and there was little else to occupy ourselves with for the next three hours.

'She just needs a bit of company, that's all,' Jeff said as forty-five minutes later we wandered through the maze of mobile holiday homes looking for Connie's overnight boudoir.

'Come on in, boys,' she said welcoming us into her caravan, which was decked out like a palace compared to the ones that had been allocated to the band.

'How come you get such special treatment?' Jeff asked.

'Bloody right, ours are like pigsties compared to this,' I added.

'Ah, well, I know people in high places,' she jested, adding: 'But I can assure you they haven't all been as pleasant as this! Would you care for a cup of coffee?' she offered, leaning over towards a shiny new-fangled Italian percolator that was bubbling away in the kitchenette.

The pair of us sat contentedly, feet up on the pouffe, socialising in Connie's lap of luxury as she apologised for boring us senseless earlier on with her self-indulgent tale, blaming it all on the excessive amount of time she'd spent alone in recent months.

Jeff had been right – all she craved was a little company – but that apart we were still anxious for her to pick up where she'd left off earlier and continue the absorbing ripping yarn, and he could wait no longer: 'You didn't finish telling us why your sister was arrested!'

Connie giggled and, replenishing her coffee cup, asked, 'Are you pair for real? You sad buggers! You really do want to hear some more?'

Her father had returned to the house in Tipton some six months later, pleading with her Mum to take him back, and stressing how meaningless and pathetic his life was without her. This time she'd refused flatly to have any more to do with him; and, as she saw the first signs of anger in his crazed eyes, escaped into the adjoining kitchen, urging him to 'Get out!' But the brute was having none of it as he forced his way through the latched door, only to find Kim waiting with a face like thunder. At first he froze when he saw her, calling her a 'shit-stirring little bitch', and moving threateningly towards her with a clenched fist.

Determined to defend her mother at all costs, Kim had been ready for him with a long sharp carving knife concealed behind her back, which she wielded, cutting the man's hand as his attempted blow flew towards her head.

Yelping violently he grabbed at her neck in retaliation; but the blade slashed wildly across the side of his face, covering the man's neck and clothes in blood as, utterly defeated, he stumbled out onto the street, crying for help from the startled passers-by.

The police were soon alerted and on the scene, after neighbours had spotted the claret-spattered miscreant; and an ambulance had also been called, as Kim was led away by the boys in blue for questioning regarding the violent act of self-defence.

Later the same night it transpired that the wrong-doing scumbag wished to press charges against his own flesh and blood who had only sought to protect her Mum, and after being subjected to a lengthy grilling the unfortunate Kim was detained in a holding cell, where she was to spend two days and nights before finally being released.

The recalcitrant father refused to cooperate and drop the charges, and in an act of retaliation Kim informed a female officer of the attempted rape of her sister the year before. Her outspoken confession opened up a real can of worms: the police had unsuccessfully been investigating a case for the past eighteen months involving two similar offences, and after putting two and two together smelt blood, treating the allegations with the utmost seriousness. Upon his discharge from hospital Connie's wayward father was apprehended and taken into custody, pending interrogation.

The CID boys were intent on speaking to Connie as part of the ongoing investigation, and knowing that her Mum and sister were desperately in need of her support, she decided it was time to return home.

The two unfortunate female victims from the unsolved cases were tracked down and requested to attend an identification parade, scheduled whilst the man was still under lock and key. Connie meanwhile was persuaded to undergo a rigorous medical examination, after which forensic studies revealed some old scar tissue, with the evidence proving beyond doubt that the police had their man.

At the ID parade the first girl – who was still traumatised from the assault – picked out a poor guy who'd been on the street selling *The Big Issue* barely thirty minutes earlier; however, the second injured party instantly recognised Connie's father as the perpetrator of the vile crime.

The case dragged on for months, with Connie itching to return to London, only to find to her disappointment that Sean had joined a band, which immediately put a large dent into her singing ambitions and prompted her to answer an advert in a theatrical magazine looking for attractive, long-legged girls. To her surprise within days she was invited to attend an audition.

Only weeks later, incredibly she found herself on the stage of the London Palladium learning the ropes to become a Tiller Girl. It was hard, physical work, but relishing the challenge she took to it like a duck to water, whilst also enjoying the camaraderie of her fellow dancing hopefuls.

During her second year at the famous theatre she began seeing a wily old entertainment-agent named George who, although twenty years her senior, captured her heart as she fell head over heels for him. George was enraptured by Connie's personality and sharp-witted sense of humour, and before long had other plans mapped out for his vivacious young partner; but as their romance blossomed in its embryonic stages Connie was summoned to a Birmingham court to stand as a witness for the prosecution and corroborate the serious allegations made against her immoral father.

In a moving testimony – along with a dreadful outpouring of grief from the second of the defiled girls – the evidence presented proved sufficient to keep the man behind bars for a two-year sentence, which might well have been far less lenient had the first unfortunate girl's recollections of the incident been more convincing.

Saddened by the ordeal, but to some degree relieved, it was time for the family to move on with their lives. Things soon took a turn for the better as Kim was accepted into medical college, and purely by accident the girls' Mum met an old family friend named Sid, and within weeks they were engaged to be married as soon as her divorce was finalised.

Connie, as a result of George's know-how and persistence, had been offered a residency at London's high-profile nightspot 'The Talk of the Town'; and, hugely excited at the prospect, the two of them spent weeks honing an elaborate cabaret act, which included her doing comic routines for the very first time.

Her experience of 'The Talk' was nothing short of invaluable, but the venue's popularity had begun to decline with George well aware there was bigger money to be made on the burgeoning Northern club circuit. Within a couple of months the diary was full and the Brummie lass was all set to wow the north-country public with her unique brand of music and comedy.

Travelling together far and wide as the chain of nightclubs expanded in a southerly direction, Connie was making a fabulous living, and even performed on TV's *Seaside Special*, but without ever quite making a breakthrough to the big time.

Like a ghost from the past, whilst on stage at a Birmingham cabaret-spot she observed the familiar features of her father seated at a table close to the front, with the new woman ('floozy' as Connie described her) in his life in tow.

Composing herself, but obviously shaken by the apparition, she stayed cool under pressure and managed to see out her act, after which she fled to the relative safety of the dressing room, before shortly afterwards a knock came at the door, which was answered by George.

The disgraced man stepped into the room alone, and said embarrassedly, 'Hello sweetheart!'

Connie immediately perceived a much changed man, but still in shock remarked: 'You've got some nerve; how was your time in Bedford prison?'

'I'm hoping that's all behind me now; I'm a changed person these days. The inmates don't take kindly to rapists on the inside, you know,' he said repentantly.

George interrupted: 'I'm sure they don't. What do you want with Connie? Don't you think she's been through enough?'

'What can I say? I've had more good hidings than a punch bag, and I know what I did back then was unforgiveable; but I've learnt my lesson and I'm trying desperately to make up for all those lost years. I was a complete bastard but I can't turn back time. Please say you'll have lunch with me tomorrow; there's so much I want to say to you... Please!'

Disbelievingly Connie felt a small twinge of sympathy for the tortured man who'd clearly done his time; and reluctantly agreed to meet up, on the sole condition that George would be close at hand at all times.

Her father's attempts at any form of reconciliation proved futile, as the wounds remained deep-rooted and tender. There was no doubting the man had changed; but to remove the picture from her mind of the lustful, evil person who had been the central character of many a nightmare was something she found impossible to do. And yet here was the same loose cannon back to haunt her again; but with too much water under the bridge it was too late for any form of *rapprochement*.

Finishing off her lunch, Connie left the restaurant without any physical contact whatsoever, still feeling betrayed and heartbroken by what had happened all those years before; but this time she genuinely believed it would be the very last time she'd see her father.

She stopped, looking at her watch, and panicked. 'Blow me, is that the time? I'd better get myself garbed up for the show.'

Jeff and I had been enraptured listening to her story, but couldn't help feeling that there was something more that she really needed to get off her chest, and sure enough as we stood to make for the door she dropped the missing bombshell.

'He contacted me only three weeks ago, saying he's desperate to see me, and blubbered like an old fool when I told him Mum died of cancer last year. He's living in Bournemouth now, and I honestly don't know what to do; I haven't seen that man in thirty-two years but the thought of doing so is upsetting me like you wouldn't believe!'

She picked up her things and we escorted her across to the Show-Bar, which pleasingly was packed to the rafters. Jeff went off back to his caravan for a nap, while I made my way to the dressing room and sat strumming a few melancholy chords on the acoustic guitar, inspired by her story.

Fifteen minutes later the disingenuous emcee distortedly bellowed something inaudible into his microphone, which was soon followed by the musical introduction, 'Connie, Connie, Connie, Connie, Connie Comedienne, she comes and goes, she comes and goes,' and it was time to head back to the caravan to get showered and ready.

♫

The whole entourage was present at breakfast the next morning, including Connie who was in fine fettle, especially on the gag front; although there wasn't too much to laugh about after the previous night's unspectacular gig, where the band struggled tiresomely on a two-tier stage and never quite broke into second gear. Still, it was history now, and by no means could it have been termed a disaster.

Trevor was busy giving Jeff some stick about 'his new bird', which after overhearing Connie nipped straight in the bud with a cruel wisecrack about the boot polish on his head; we cringed with amusement, and wickedly nicknamed him 'Cherry Blossom' for the rest of the day.

With a greasy start to the day the gang quickly dispersed, and as we ascended the stone steps Connie murmured: 'Thanks so much for listening yesterday; I needed someone to tell my troubles to but you must've been bored out of your minds!'

'Not at all. What do you intend doing – are you going to see your Dad again?' I posed in hushed tones.

'It's tearing me apart; I just don't know Dave. I only wish George was here – he'd have known the right thing to do.'

'How did your father find you?' I asked.

'That's a good question: he phoned around just about every entertainment agency in the country trying to track me down. He's a tenacious old bugger all right,' she replied with gritted teeth.

'I really don't envy you this one, Connie. How old is he now?' I asked.

'Oh, he's got to be eighty-six or eighty-seven,' she guessed.

'Wow, he's an old-timer now,' I declared.

'I know he is; maybe he won't be around for much longer,' she hinted pensively.

'There's an old saying I remember from my schooldays which goes, "There is no revenge so complete as forgiveness",' I quoted.

Breathing a long sigh she began sniffling, but with typical resolve came back with: 'You soppy sod, why don't you bugger off with your mates and I'll see you in Watchet: that'll be me last one so I'll be more than ready to let me hair down.' Giving me a peck on the cheek she sashayed off in the direction of her state-of-the-art caravan.

Roaring claps of thunder could be heard in the distance, and ten minutes later the downpour began with the wind swirling around carrying just about everything in its path, as the flimsy caravan walls shuddered like clapperboards.

We switched on the TV in the hope of catching the morning session of the test match, but in true Manchester fashion they weren't to be outdone in the precipitation stakes, and play had been suspended indefinitely, with an inspection due at lunchtime.

Staring out at an eyesore of a telecommunications mast situated in the adjoining field, I picked up my cell phone and in turn punched in the guys' mobile numbers, and made the decision to cut and run a little earlier for the trip to Rochester in Kent.

23

BADLANDS
(BRUCE SPRINGSTEEN)

Saturday 13th August 2005

It was a grim day as we traversed through heavy, eddying drizzle, having a stroke of good fortune at one point when the bus briefly aquaplaned for thirty metres or so: fortuitously we were the only vehicle on the M3 carriageway at the time and were able to count our blessings before easing off the throttle to join the dreaded M25 in an easterly direction.

The clock read three-thirty p.m. as we reached the former city of Rochester, believing the trek to be almost over; but little did we know that the Allhallows park was a further fifteen miles away, with the only mapped route being via an isolated single-track road.

Manoeuvring the bus around the final bend of the approach road to the camp gates we were welcomed by a cordon of police vehicles blocking the entrance, with Rod the first to wind down his electric window before shouting over to one of the officers to ask what was happening.

The barrel-chested PC sporting a bright yellow jerkin walked over and said with authority, 'You can't go in there until the medics have given the all-clear!'

'We're supposed to be performing here tonight,' Rod explained.

'I'm sorry, but my hands are tied,' said the bobby, adding: 'There are two suspected cases of bird flu on site and the last thing we need is an outbreak. You'll have to come back later,' he dramatically concluded.

I called Steve on his mobile. 'They won't let us through the gates, and said it's something to do with bird flu,' I unfolded.

'This is the biggest shithole yet,' was all he could muster.

'Have you got the gear in?' I asked.

'Yeah, it's in, but we're nowhere near finished setting up yet,' he replied.

Explaining we could be delayed for quite a while, I asked if he knew anything about the suspected epidemic on the camp.

'They just told us to stay in here and that they'll let us know later what's going on. Apparently some old biddy's collapsed or something. Anyway, wait 'til you see the fucking caravans,' he went on, not exactly raising my expectations.

'I can barely contain myself. At least we don't have to stay the night,' I replied sarcastically before signing off.

The wretched weather swept viciously across the coastline, which meant there was still no play in the cricket, though the rain up north had abated and it was thought there may be an hour or more's action before the close of play.

The only thing of note in the vicinity was a fish-and-chip restaurant about a hundred metres from the camp gates, so we drove along and parked up before dashing inside to ask if we could get a warming cup of tea.

'You can 'ave chipsa an' tea, butta notta only tea,' said the Greek proprietor (his nation's distinctive flag was displayed on the back wall); and Dan being a sucker for fish and chips was straight in to order haddock and fries, 'plussa a bigga potta of da tea please,' he cheekily quipped.

By the time we'd all ordered there were battered sausages, two varieties of fish, chicken and mushroom pies, curry sauce and bread and butter strewn across the tables we'd shoved together, along with the life-saving pot of tea that had finally arrived, as we tucked in and chatted away awaiting the reopening of the stricken park.

'I knew we'd have problems at this place,' I said.

'Why's that?' Romeo asked.

'I saw some reviews online that weren't exactly gratifying: one of them said simply, "Don't go to Allhallows;" another said, "Without a doubt the worst week's holiday I ever had," and loads more,' I pointed out, adding: 'Guess what Steve thinks of it?'

Five voices boisterously shot back in harmony: 'Fucking shithole!'

We all creased up, until the Greek guy chastised us: 'Hey you guys, minda the language and keepa the noisa downa, this ain't a pubba you know!'

As he spoke two ambulances came screeching around the bend towards the park entrance, and looking a trifle concerned Jeff exclaimed, 'Can't we just piss off? It's a bloody killer that bird flu you know!'

Romeo chipped in: 'We're here now, and if it's anything contagious they'll soon have 'em out of there; so let's just get on with it!'

Roughly an hour later we were stood in a packed reception area, where a profusion of concerned holiday-makers were flapping around in a panic, believing they were in grave danger from the suspected epidemic, as flustered members of staff attempted to pacify them.

After sweet-talking a blue-coated Bonnie Langford lookalike, we were eventually given our caravan keys and escaped the mayhem by winding our way through the complexity of wheeled homes in search of sanity and safety.

Unbelievably the caravans, as Steve had implied, had plummeted to a new low, and were degrading and utterly filthy. I recited another of the online complaints I'd read: 'You must be joking, never again,' which summed it up, as it was so bad it was almost laughable.

The caravan itself was at a severe tilt, which felt disorientating, and the curtains and sofa were covered in horrible black mould, with bugs crawling everywhere. The sink was full of dirty cups, plates, and glasses and the overall stench was fetid and foul.

There was though on this occasion a saving grace, in that we'd be hitting the road back to base straight after the show, and not only that we actually had a short break with all the home comforts before setting off again the following Thursday.

The small TV had also seen better days, and in keeping with everything else any attempt to tune it in proved a hopeless task. Cussing to himself Rod reclined onto one of the tiny beds, but in seconds flat sprang bolt upright shouting, 'For fuck's sake!'

'What's up now?' I enquired.

'This bloody bed's covered in pubic hairs; do these people think we're bloody animals?' he bitterly complained.

I couldn't help myself and burst out laughing: it was either that or cry – the place was purgatorial and truly beyond comprehension.

In a vain effort to lighten the proceedings Dan and I started behaving like children, running up and down the slope with arms simulating aeroplanes, careering around the disgusting debris; but the novelty soon wore off, and rather than spend any longer than necessary amongst the squalor the three of us trudged disconsolately over to the venue to see what delights awaited us there.

The Clubhouse as it was inaptly named was predictably on the small side, and frankly we should have packed up and moved on; the crew were being made to suffer yet again, needless to say through no fault of their own, as the incompetent and unhelpful staff simply got in the way.

Steve though was keeping mum and realised that making any waves would've been a waste of breath and that we'd all be content to just see the day out.

A wall-mounted TV seemed to be arousing some interest in the adjacent bar area, where men clad in white could be seen gesticulating and appealing to the stoical umpires, and I could scarcely believe that the test match was finally under way in Manchester; but in true keeping with the day's events I saw to my annoyance that the Aussies had fought back and avoided the follow-on, and spin bowler Shane Warne was closing in on a maiden test century.

Transfixed until close of play I tramped back to the tilted trailer and saw that Rod was sitting alone with his head in his hands. 'Is something wrong?' I asked.

He lifted his head, looking a little red-eyed, and deeply sighed.

'I just had some terrible news: my brother Mike died today. His wife Jane just called to tell me.'

In something of a trance he explained that Mike had been battling with lung cancer for ages now, and that it had finally got the better of him. Realising exactly how he must be feeling, I offered my condolences and allowed him some time alone to reflect and gather himself.

The day had been thoroughly depressing for a number of reasons, but there was just cause for a shred of optimism, as when this gig was out of the way a four-day hiatus lay ahead, with some time to regroup and get our heads together before trekking back down to Weymouth to begin our assault on the south west of England. It was effectively half-term.

♫

The sound board, or mixing console as it is often referred to, is arguably the most important piece of equipment used by any band or theatre production group, and is the epicentre from which the engineer routes and alters the level of audio signals for every on-stage instrument, by skilfully mixing together the drums, guitars, vocals etcetera to provide the desired overall stereophonic effect that is thrown out through the towers of speakers situated to both sides of the stage.

These high-tech desks can also be extremely costly, and to splash out thirty or forty thousand pounds on a well-respected make would not be deemed at all out of the ordinary.

The size of the board is determined by the number of channels it is equipped with, and for a band such as ourselves a thirty-two-channel console would normally suffice – though we'd curiously been carrying an all-singing, all-dancing digital forty-eight-track model for these dates, with a view to updating and finally moving into the twenty-first century.

My mobile chirruped, with Steve's name flickering on the screen, which I assumed to be a call to say they were ready for us to sound-check; but instead my ears soon began taking a battering.

'Those fucking idiots have tried to shift the desk and dropped it,' he ferociously groaned.

'What, have they damaged it?' I queried.

'The idiots said it was blocking the fire exit; one end is all smashed up, and I've lost a load of channels. I've managed to get it running again, but I'm not sure it'll get us through the gig,' he angrily unravelled.

'Can't we just cut down on the channels and wing it for tonight?' I asked.

'I doubt it. The manager's trying to find another board from some other camp to get us out of the shit,' he eloquently informed me.

I blew a gasket. Not only had these people moved an expensive piece of equipment without our permission, they'd also caused a serious amount of damage through their total ineptitude. As if things could have got any worse, this was nothing but an unprofessional shambles, and after putting up with small stages, ignorant staff, crappy caravans and generally appalling facilities for going on five weeks, they'd now seen fit to interfere with the tools of our trade, which had only added insult to injury.

I strutted over to the venue in a foul mood, striding past the mini-mart: and became distracted, thinking I'd spotted an orange through the window next to the counter. Was my quest for some life-giving fresh fruit finally over, here on this depressing day in what was surely the bleakest corner of Kent?

I went inside, eager to see if I was right… and picked up a plastic netted bag containing two solid wooden rackets and a bright orange ball. The pallid assistant looked across and said, 'They're eight pounds ninety-nine.' I explained to her I'd mistaken the ball for an orange, to which she sharply retorted: 'I think you need an optician's, not a supermarket!'

'Nothing super about this store,' I snapped back, and strode out with my dour demeanour intact.

The manager was glued to his mobile phone, with Steve beside him looking on anxiously, exhaling loudly through his fluttering lips as I joined them.

'I've lost ten channels on the board; it'll be a hefty bill to get it fixed,' he said.

The manager interrupted us. 'They have a sound desk at Herne Bay, but you'd need to go and collect it.'

Steve interposed: 'What size is it?'

The perspiring guy delivered the same question into his mouthpiece, and whispered across, 'He's just finding out, won't be a sec,' pausing for breath and then saying, 'Yes, still here,' before relaying the information: 'It's five feet six inches by three feet six.'

Steve gritted his teeth and yelled 'Aaargh!' to the skies before griping, 'I fucking give up – by size I meant how many channels does the sodding thing have, not the fucking dimensions!' Almost at boiling point he stormed off muttering, 'Don't even bother!'

I took the bewildered manager to one side, and let him know my feelings. 'I know he's giving you a hard time, but your staff had no right moving our sound board without asking for permission first. It could be a very costly affair, and I don't see why we should have to fork out for it.'

'I'm really sorry I wasn't around at the time. I'd better inform head office, and hopefully something can be sorted out with them,' he suggested.

In fairness he was a half decent bloke, and was only trying to help. However, if something couldn't be resolved there was no way the gig could possibly take place, and with people already taking their seats in the venue, and the band's scheduled performance just two-and-a-half hours away, the party pooping holiday company would be facing the wrath of a whole load of dissatisfied punters expecting a night of nostalgia and rock and roll.

Steve was crouched over the desk, working diligently with a smoking soldering iron at the ready, as I tiptoed over and asked him again what the chances were; but he disdainfully shrugged his shoulders and said, 'Who knows!'

Feeling a little jaded I went back to the listing trailer and took a quick shower. Though the water was cold, as it hit my skin I found it invigorating and something of a tonic. I dried myself down and, expecting the worst, called Steve for a progress report.

Miraculously he had sixteen workable channels up and running and the show would go ahead after all. The petulant but dexterous sound engineer had again risen to the challenge and saved the day.

The atmosphere in the dressing room was as grim as the park, with the band sitting heads bowed, feeling a little sorry for ourselves. The last run of dates had been beset with problems, and the feeling was that we were in dire need of a good gig to raise everyone's spirits.

Quietly perched in the corner I hatched a sneaky plan to entertain us all on the journey back to base; and fifteen minutes later we took to the stage with mischief glowing in our eyes, and pulled off a satisfactory show, in spite of the venue's limitations and the potentially costly damaged channels on the sound desk.

♫

Trevor had long possessed a penchant for living dangerously, and his reputation as a womaniser preceded him, as he often sought to use the lure of a successful rock-and-roll career and its obvious attractions to entice the odd nubile female into his tangled web.

His carefree nonchalance constantly landed him in hot water when unsuspecting partners got wind of rivals that had emerged onto the scene, thus threatening their position; but Trev in masterly fashion convinced them time after time that it was all just idle gossip.

During this tour he'd boasted of having five young ladies in his life at the same time, and to avoid confusion when they contacted him had set up a handful of individual mobile phone accounts so he would instantly know from the different ringtones and handsets exactly which of his mistresses was calling.

Through a little devilish skulduggery, between us we'd managed to get hold of each different number, and to amuse ourselves with a little wicked buffoonery decided to set him up on the way home. Upon a signal from myself in the front, where I'd raise my right hand to the back of my head, each band member would punch in their own individual digits, with the sole intention of creating mayhem; and just like a bunch of excited schoolkids we could hardly wait!

Half an hour into the journey with the radio switched off, I could feel the eyes to my rear burning into me like hawks, and shuffling in my seat lifted my right hand as planned, and with fingers on mobiles at the ready the mischief began.

Trev was soon in the thick of the action as he answered the first call, followed swiftly by two, three, four and then five simultaneous incoming calls, with a cacophony of ringtones chiming together and a sense of confusion that was utterly priceless, and uproariously gut-busting.

It wasn't until the fourth call – by which time he'd begun having a panic attack – that he actually cottoned on, and yelled, 'Very funny, you bunch of bastards!'

The remainder of the jaunt back was far more high-spirited, apart from Trevor going into a sulk and refusing to mouth a single word, almost as if the world had turned against him; and, well aware that he wasn't in good fettle, it felt as if the joke had almost back-fired. Still we'd had our fun, and the journey flew by, as the butt of the prank grabbed a cushion and ignored everybody totally, before feigning sleep for the remainder of the trip.

24

LAZY SUNDAY
(THE SMALL FACES)

Sunday 14th August 2005

There's nothing quite like a good old-fashioned English Sunday! A couple of lunchtime pints in the quaint local pub, smattered with topical jokes and all the latest lighthearted tittle-tattle, then it's back to the wonderful aroma of the Sunday roast emanating from the kitchen, as we merrily re-enter the house.

My wife Cathy is an excellent cook, and had always gone out of her way to make Sundays that little bit special, being patently aware that on the vast majority of Saturday nights I'd be out on the road plying my trade, returning home knackered more often than not as the next day was dawning.

The band's live performances were always physically demanding and at times could even be attritional, and after several back-to-back gigs along with all the other machinations I would often be hoarse and muscle-weary. However, the perfect antidote to a stressful rock-and-roll lifestyle was a traditional weekly feast in the company of my family and friends with a carefully selected bottle of full-bodied red wine.

It's one of life's extraordinary quirks how often the phone rings as a family is seated and ready to tuck into a sumptuous meal, and annoyingly this day was no different, when on an afternoon that was intended to be restful and over-indulgent the odd vagary reared its ugly head once again.

The call was from the self-esteemed head office of the caravan holiday company, and the man's voice bore a kind of military authority as he explained that a complaint had been received from the Allhallows centre with reference to the alleged mishandling of the artists' sound equipment.

Unable to get a word in edgeways, I was further informed that the conduct of the artists' crew manager had been abusive and unreasonable and that this kind of behaviour would not be tolerated, and should be addressed with immediate effect prior to any further scheduled dates.

The high-and-mighty spokesman then insolently enquired: 'What have you to say in your defence?'

Dumbfounded, I took a deep breath and retorted, 'I'm more interested to know what you have to say in your company's defence,' and equally contemptuously added, 'There is potentially thousands of pounds' worth of damage caused to our sound equipment as a result of the total ineptitude and clumsiness of your employees, and furthermore if you expect my sound engineer to be thrilled to bits then you are very much mistaken!'

An altercation ensued, but this guy's intransigence knew no bounds as he went on: 'It is not our company policy to reimburse visiting artists for damage to their equipment if it is assembled in a manner that contravenes the in-house health and safety regulations; indeed, let me refer you to clause 14A in your signed agreement that states: "All visiting performers' articles and apparatus shall be set commensurate with management regulations, and shall cause no obstruction or encumbrance to public areas in accordance with the health and safety act of 2001."'

The guy's dictatorial manner had really got my goat and I fired back with both barrels: 'And clause common sense states that unauthorised imbeciles do not take it upon themselves to move valuable pieces of equipment, or as you put it apparatus, without the prior consent of its rightful owners!'

The row had now become heated, but it was abundantly clear that no recompense for the staff's ham-fistedness and incompetence would be forthcoming and that the company and I had reached an impasse. It was crystal clear that the cards were forever stacked in favour of this implacable and arrogant organisation, and to top it all they'd even had the audacity to wreck my cherished day of rest. Something would surely have to give, but I wasn't about to go making any rash or hasty decisions on a civilised Sunday afternoon, and tucked back into the delicious roast, as the wine helped numb my senses; but deep down inside I was fuming and just wanted the tour to be over.

Like millions of other males on the sabbath day, I finished my lunch, helped dry the dishes, switched on the TV taking command of the remote and flicked between the football and cricket coverage. Within half an hour I'd soundly nodded off.

♫

Feeling a trifle sensitive the following morning, it was time for me to take the bull by the horns, and picking up the phone I dialled the company number and asked to be put through to someone in senior management.

The long-winded man who'd disturbed my Sunday lunch had taken the day off (I secretly wished I could call him on his day off and exact some revenge for his interruption the day before) and I was connected to a chirpy guy with a London cockney accent.

'What can I do for you, guv?' he asked familiarly.

Over breakfast I'd jotted down a whole page of notes in preparation for this *tête-à-tête*, and cut right to the chase expressing my dissatisfaction with the technical limitations of the various venues, the unhelpfulness of ninety per cent of the staff, the squalid accommodation that had been provided and every other gripe I had to hand, ending the diatribe by explaining that the damage caused to our sound desk by interfering morons had been the final straw, and that the lack of understanding and arrogance shown by his colleague barely twenty-four hours earlier had been totally unacceptable.

I then steeled myself and with a hint of regret said, 'I think it may be best if we cancel the agreement forthwith; we can't go on like this!'

There was silence at the other end of the line and then hurried breathing, as he quietly spoke. 'What, you want to curtail the tour prematurely? I've 'eard there's been a few 'eadaches along the way, but you can't leave everyone in the lurch and just pull out! What about the families who've booked specially to see you? 'Ave an 'eart mate!'

The guy had conducted himself well with a manner that was calm and considerate, not at all like his workmate on the Sunday, who'd talked down to me the whole time. I explained that our contract had not been honoured, and that we were deeply concerned at how the lack of professionalism and facilities were affecting the band's reputation.

He asked for a couple of hours to discuss the matter with his board of directors, and assured me he'd do everything he could to come up with a mutually agreeable solution to help rescue and improve matters.

By five p.m. the decision to cancel had been reversed. My new cockney pal had promised to keep a close watch on the remaining dates, and the company had further agreed to contribute towards the sound-desk repairs upon receipt of an invoice.

The outcome was as good as it was going to get; but what I hadn't realised at the time was that, with thirteen dates to go, I'd been sticking out my neck and playing with fire!

The Aussies were eight wickets down at Old Trafford, so in need of a little cheer I put my feet up for the final few overs of the match, to see to my delight that the ninth scalp was captured soon after; but from then on things didn't go according to plan as Brett Lee, the Oz bowler, had put up a spirited rear-guard, with England just failing to secure the final wicket and claim the victory the nation craved.

As the umpires finally signalled stumps, Cathy brought in a cuppa to where I was slothfully reclined, and sweetly asked: 'Shall we go out for the day tomorrow… perhaps to the seaside?'

'You've got to be kidding,' I said. Thankfully she was!

25

LET'S GET PHYSICAL
(OLIVIA NEWTON-JOHN)

Wednesday 17th August 2005

Plans were in progress for the recording of the band's first full album of new material for almost fifteen years, the early details of which I'd promised a sneak preview of to a long-standing journalist buddy who worked for the local rag, the *Leicester Mercury*. Rising from my pit just before nine a.m., I sluiced my face and brushed my pearly-whites, vainly picking up on a fresh batch of worry lines in the bathroom mirror that had begun blending in with the hollowing bloodhound sacs beneath my jaded eyes.

In little more than two weeks, following a short period set aside to get my house in order, my good lady and I would be jetting off to a Portuguese retreat filled with endless sunshine, to replenish the batteries and finally put to bed a summer that had been eventful in the extreme, mostly for all the wrong reasons. Lethargy was fast setting in, with the countless inactive hours of travelling (not to mention the burden of dealing with all the unnecessary headaches) taking their toll, hastening the need to snap out of an afflicting bout of burgeoning indolence.

Having relocated from neighbouring Northants back into my native Leicestershire only months previously, my regular fitness regime had been restricted to jogging the leafy country lanes nearby, as opposed to a weekly shakedown at the gym. My growing concerns for my well-being were once again highlighted as, tuning into the satellite news, I heard a tongue-tied scientist banging on about a breakthrough in anti-ageing strategies, skincare and even chemotherapy, by means of manipulating a master gene to control dermatological disorders.

'Perhaps I should get my name on the list good and early for when it becomes available,' I half joked to my wife, popping some trainers and gym-clothes into a bag and setting off to spill the beans, before putting myself through hell.

♫

Arriving early at the trendy new city-centre bar, I ordered a cappuccino from a familiar-faced guy I'd bumped into working in various hostelries and establishments in the town over a number of years.

'It's Roly isn't it?' I asked as his name sprang to mind.

'Thank God for that Dave, I thought for a second you were ignoring me,' he postured in camp tones, clunking the dispenser onto the coffee machine.

'No, I never forget a pretty face, how's everything going?' I kidded.

'Good thanks. If I didn't know better I'd have said for a minute you were coming onto me there, you cheeky so and so,' he embellished.

'Sorry, you're out of luck there Roly, and anyway I'm old enough to be your Dad,' I responded, pausing to suck the froth from the cup. 'Listen, you don't happen to know of a good gymnasium around here, do you?' I queried. 'I need to tone up my biceps and six-pack.'

'I know just the place: there's a fantastic new health club and spa over at Meridian Park that only opened recently. I've got a mate who works as a private trainer down there. I could give him a call if you like; and who knows, he may even offer you an introductory freebie,' he helpfully tipped me off.

'That would be cool if you don't mind,' I replied, as a tap came on my shoulder and I span round to find my journalist pal Lee greeting me with a smile and outstretched hand.

As I sipped coffee and divulged the exclusive 'hot off the presses' details to the young hack, Roly called over: 'Hey Dave, sorry to interrupt but I just spoke to Freddie down at the gym and he'd be happy to put you through your paces at 3.30 this afternoon if that's okay?'

'Yeah why not, that's brilliant, thanks a million,' I retorted, pondering just what I was letting myself in for.

♫

My old hometown was looking a little tumbledown and disappointingly shabby as I progressed along the bustling, cosmopolitan Narborough Road and headed out to the modern leisure complex. The prospect of a galvanising hour of calisthenics, together with a sauna and swim, seemed the perfect way to unblock my benumbed grey matter and start the juices flowing again.

My cellphone trilled into life, distracting me from the mounting chaos caused by illegally parked vans of all descriptions and the restless multicultural hubbub of the suburb. Pulling into a service station to fill up, I paused to take the call. Flashing intermittently on the screen I saw it was Jeff, and I replied in the usual laconic fashion with: 'Alright boy, how are you enjoying your little bit of freedom?'

'It's similar to being released from the nick. Hey, you're not gonna believe this, but I just bumped into a guy in the Nag's Head who took his family down to that pisshole near Clacton we played a couple of weeks ago,' he relayed, sounding a trifle tense.

'You mean Saint Osyth? I'm not sure I really want to hear this, that wasn't one of the better camps or performances,' I answered sceptically.

'Don't worry, they actually enjoyed the band, but he couldn't believe we were playing in a dump like that. They checked out the next day and now he says he's going to sue the bastards and has asked if I'll swear an affidavit to confirm that the place wasn't as advertised on the website. What do you reckon?' he inquired.

Quickly mulling over what he'd said I responded: 'You know that old saying "never bite the hand that feeds," well I'd steer well clear if I were you; there's precious little to be gained from stirring up a hornet's nest!'

'Yeah, I figured you might say something along those lines, but he said their attitude stunk and he's determined to take things further, maybe even to the papers,' Jeff informed me.

'Ah well, wish him the best of luck, it's about time those jumped-up cronies had a dose of their own medicine,' I bickered before signing off.

The fact remained there seemed to be no escape from the clutches of the dreaded chain of holiday parks, but undeterred I returned to the car steeled by the satisfaction that the final onslaught was drawing ever nearer, hell-bent on doing a professional job in spite of whatever may be thrown our way, motivated and ready to pump some iron.

♫

A dead ringer for an army drill instructor, Freddie greeted me clad immaculately in a white logoed vest and skintight cycling leggings that enhanced the muscular contours of his toned calves and thighs, sporting a military style haircut and neatly trimmed moustache and appearing the perfect picture of health.

'Roly's given me the full lowdown on you; it seems we have a celebrity in our midst – but don't think for a minute that'll get you off the hook,' he barked, putting the frighteners on.

'This sounds more like *Bad Lads Army* than a visit to the gym,' I jested, desperate to inject a little humour into the proceedings.

An hour later, following a white-knuckle ride that consisted of being strapped into a range of weird contraptions, sit-up apparatus and a host of other newfangled appliances, with me literally on my knees and begging for mercy we toned things down on a selection of free-standing weights, the exercise serving as a cruel reminder that I was no longer in the prime condition of my life.

'Just do a few stretches to warm down and then take the load off relaxing in the sauna, but beware of the plunge pool – it's like ice,' Freddie warned, finally leaving me to my own devices.

To the rear of the locker rooms leading into the sauna lay a green matted area set aside presumably for recuperation and kitted out with a selection of giant plants along with two comfortable reclining couches which looked just the ticket for a power-nap once the grubbiness of the preceding weeks had seeped through my clogged-up pores.

Stuffing my sweaty togs inside a locker and grabbing a towel I mooched into the log cabin, spooning water over the hot coals to build up a head of steam and feeling the searing humidity pinching at my nostrils whilst reclining to breathe in the woody vapour.

Reinvigorated, with my heart palpitating at nineteen to the dozen from a ducking in the benumbing ice-bath, I tiptoed over to the rest area before collapsing in a heap onto the tilted couch, closing my eyes and drifting away into an almost surreal state of relaxation.

Subliminally aware of a presence in the quietude of my repose, I suddenly heard a voice close to my ear asking softly: 'I don't suppose Roly said anything about this?' I opened my eyes to find the shadow of Freddie's well-proportioned penis looming just inches from my face.

Leaping to one side like a bovine from an electric cattle-prod, I panicked: 'Whoa, easy tiger... I think you've got the wrong idea about me pal!'

'It's only a spot of post-workout fun; after all, the session was complimentary. Are you trying to tell me you've never been pierced?' he audaciously asked.

'No I fucking haven't, and what's more I most definitely won't be getting my cherry popped here today!' I snapped disbelievingly, scampering back towards the locker room and changing in seconds flat.

♪

'How was your day?' my wife enquired, joining me at the dinner table for a generous portion of mushroom risotto.

'Not too bad thanks – I did a trial workout at the new gym complex close to the M1; it's full of really hi-tech equipment but I think it's too far out to go on a regular basis,' I replied, being economical with the truth. 'Anyway,' I continued hastily, 'what have you been up to?'

'I had coffee with the girls this morning. Yasmin's lent us a pirate DVD that her husband Richard brought back from a business trip to China; it hasn't even been released yet but apparently it's set to take the movie world by storm. What say we have a quiet night in and watch it – what do you think?' she hinted.

'If it's what it's cracked up to be then why not; what's it about and what's this new blockbuster called?' I queried.

'It's entitled *Brokeback Mountain* and it's about two cowboys stuck out on the prairies for months on end who fall in love and become embroiled in a gay affair,' she elaborated.

'Second thoughts, I think there's an international match on Sky tonight which I'd quite like to see, maybe we can watch it some other time,' I fabricated, topping up the wine glasses and for the first time in weeks bizarrely looking forward to getting back on the road.

♫

Lost in a deep slumber the same night, I mentally recited Rudyard Kipling's classic poem 'If' (which I'd learnt by heart from a framed tapestry that had adorned my bedroom wall for years as a kid) in its entirety, waking in a stupor with the words still swimming around in my head: *If you can keep your head when all about you are losing theirs and blaming it on you...*

Stretching and rubbing at my eyes first thing I mused: 'Perhaps if I'd kept my head in the first place I wouldn't have been such a money-grabbing git and could forget all about today's Dorset trip and flip over for the luxury of a lie-in!'

26

LA CIENEGA JUST SMILED
(RYAN ADAMS)

Thursday 18th August 2005

The approach road suggested an odd location for a holiday camp, and it was first thought we'd taken a wrong turning on the way in as the wagon careered through a large industrial estate; but true to form we were soon confronted with a mass of caravans sprawled before our eyes on a barren hillside that led down to a coarse sandy beach.

Jacqui was super-efficient, helpful, humble, organised and friendly in the extreme, in fact she was just about everything that ninety per cent of the site managers thus far hadn't been.

We'd arrived at the second Weymouth camp in good time after an early start from base; and, with no traumas on the way down, to be greeted with such cordiality was like a breath of fresh air. In no time at all tea, coffee and a home-made Victoria sponge cake (Trevor greedily grabbed three slices before anyone else had a chance) had been laid on by ultra-smiley staff in the spotless lounge, and it was plain for all to see that this place was run with pride.

Jacqui invited me to her office for a brief chat, and explained that she'd received a call from head office pre-warning her that there may be some difficulties upon our arrival, but to ensure that we were properly taken care of; as she made it clear, 'That's the way we do things around here anyway,' adding: 'We have four comfortable Platinum caravans for you and some strapping bodies on hand from three p.m. to assist with the load-in, but should there be even the slightest problem please let me know immediately.'

I was gracious and grateful in assuring her that the majority of the headaches we'd thus far encountered had only partly been of our own making, but by some quirk of fate seemed to keep finding us; but that I had every confidence things would run smoothly in this place.

Our allocated mobile homes were, as Jacqui had put it, 'luxurious and spacious', with plasma TVs mounted in the lounge area and main bedroom, a well-stocked fridge, sheets and pillowcases that were crisp and white – in fact everything was spick and span.

A chilly easterly wind was blowing, so I donned my jacket and walked in the direction of the Show Lounge, spotting the trouser-suited Jacqui chatting to someone on the steps leading inside.

'Oh Dave,' she said personably, 'I'm glad I've seen you, let me show you where your guests will be seated tonight.'

Having temporarily escaped my mind, my memory reignited remembering that Laura and her family would at long last be coming to see a show. Not only this but the consummate manageress had laid on the best table in the house, right by the disabled exit ramp as promised.

'I'll personally put a complimentary bottle of bubbly on the table for when they arrive,' she offered.

'That's wonderful, you're an absolute star Jacqui – thank you,' I sincerely replied.

The venue yet again was far from ideal; but the staff here had a different mindset and were eager to please, repositioning all sorts of stuff to allow the band's set-up a little more space. Satisfied that everything was in hand, it was time to embark on our daily expedition, in the direction of Weymouth harbour.

The swarm of people in the marina area were like bees round a honeypot, and parking was virtually impossible. Dan suggested: 'Shall we give it a miss and go and see Portland Bill instead?'

'Who's he?' I asked, being totally ignored.

'Supposed to be nice down there, and it won't be anywhere near as crowded,' chirped the guitarist.

'I'm sure I read an article about a wartime submarine wreck just off that stretch of coast,' Rod chipped in.

Following the signs in the direction of Wyke Regis we pulled in at the roadside on the route out of town where a group of wet-suited divers appeared to be preparing themselves for an underwater odyssey at the southern end of the harbour; they greeted us enthusiastically as we showed an interest in their maritime quest. Rod was correct: there was indeed an old submerged vessel that lay on the seabed not far from Portland, which was precisely the dive these intrepid shipmates were about to embark upon.

A wild-haired salty seadog, who on this occasion couldn't make the dive due to his arm being in plaster, was keen to give us a brief history of the ill-fated submarine, and began elaborating: 'The M2 was an amazing bit of kit and was the only one of its kind to double as an aircraft carrier; it had been developed between the wars and was capable of launching and retrieving a seaplane, which was used to seek out and identify enemy ships. Once the plane returned to the carrier it was winched back on deck and held in a watertight hangar, before the sub once more plunged beneath the ocean. It tragically sank during an exercise in 1932, when the doors malfunctioned leading to the deaths of sixty men. The plane was salvaged, but the M2 was sealed; but, seen as a bad omen, it was left to rot in Davy Jones' locker.'

These days the submarine has become a magnet for bodacious scuba divers, this group of which were scrambling aboard a small vessel in readiness for their very own deep-sea adventure. 'I bloody wish I could go out with 'em,' the man said, as we bid them all *bon voyage* and drove on.

The Fleet Lagoon is an unusual stretch of water; overlooked by Chesil Beach, it extends across a muddy morass that at low tide looks deceptively sturdy, and ideal for a gallivant close to the silty seaboard.

The expanse was almost deserted and the wind bracing, with only a young guy tossing a stick for his dog to chase across the sticky surface, and further inland two elderly anorak-clad birdwatchers setting up a tripod for an afternoon of ornithological pleasure.

The air was invigorating as each of us inhaled stimulating deep breaths, relieved to be away from the constant odour of recycled burger-fat, whilst observing a slapstick scene as strong gusts of wind sweeping across the foreshore prevented the bird men from erecting a protective tarpaulin.

The youth was still busy teasing his pet by throwing the branch ever closer to the water's edge as the trembling canine returned the stick time after time to its frivolous master, until he launched an enormous fling that catapulted towards the lagoon; but this time the dog was having none of it, despite the prompting of his master: 'Go on boy, fetch it, go and get it,' he urged, but his faithful friend quivered nervously and began barking, as all the lad could do was trudge into the silt and retrieve the object himself.

'Silly sod, he'll get covered in sludge going all that way out,' commented Rod, as we left him to it and, in need of a refreshing cuppa, turned away and plodded along the stodgy ground in the direction of a ramshackle old wooden café that lay at the far end of the beach.

Half an hour later the twitchers had finally erected the troublesome windbreak, and appeared thoroughly exhausted by their efforts. What had been intended as a relaxing afternoon's birdwatching had turned into a monumental task, leaving the pair of them collapsed into their deckchairs snoozing away catching flies.

Further in the distance the dog was now yapping with renewed force, and looking across to see what all the fuss was about we noticed that the beast's provocateur was up to his knees in mud, flapping his arms and shouting something incomprehensible, but unmistakably distressed.

'I'm sinking, I can't move my legs,' we made out with difficulty between the noisy gusts of wind.

'He's in a spot of bother; I swear he said he's sinking,' Dan exclaimed.

'He basically said he's stuck, and can't get out,' I affirmed.

The dog was going berserk, so I trod carefully towards him, a little unsteady on the soft silt underfoot, as he padded his way towards me; and I softly patted him on his watery coat, managing in part to pacify his undisguised fretting.

Dan was now charging across the compacted mud back to where our vehicle was parked, and minutes later returned with a yellow tow-rope that had been stashed in the boot since our earlier complications with the starter motor.

Frighteningly the young guy was slowly becoming immersed in the quicksand, as the three of us removed our shoes and carefully waded through the wet slush in his direction, with Dan taking the lead doing his Ranulph Fiennes impersonation, already ankle-deep in the morass, until I yelled to stop him and took off my waterproof, urging, 'Quick, tie this to your belt!'

He hurriedly tethered it in a double granny knot, and Rod did the same by securing his jacket to my midriff, and in a small chain-like formation we squelched forward, sinking deeper and deeper into the sludge.

Dan was now submerged to his knees and progressing further forward was no longer an option; but with just twenty metres or so between him and the engulfed youth he hurled the tow-rope with all his might, failing to get enough purchase and leaving it frustratingly short, but reeling it back in like a madman he tried again, and this time got within touching distance as the guy scrambled forward and attempted to spreadeagle himself towards the offered olive branch. A combination of natural instincts and determination sufficed to propel the juvenile far enough forward to cling to the end of the rope with his fingernails, but somehow Dan bulldozed his way even closer to him, allowing the youth to frantically get a firm grip on the line.

'Heave!' Dan shouted, as we unyieldingly tugged in true herculean style.

The lad, albeit slowly, inched his way towards us until my weatherproof disconnected from Dan's waist and I toppled backwards into the mud; but I was in no mood to throw in the towel yet and briskly hoisted myself up before lunging at Dan's outstretched hand, as we strained every muscle in our flagging bodies.

The guy was no longer motionless and began slithering on his stomach across the squelchy surface, until his delirious dog splashed excitedly towards him, as crying he knelt and embraced the relieved animal.

Leading the mud-spattered canine by the collar, the teenager slopped laboriously away from the quagmire and became emotional as, hanging his head in shame, he reached his rescuers.

'I don't know how to thank you; I acted like a complete twat,' he snivelled.

'No problem matey, but where shall we send the bill for the laundry?' Dan quipped.

Resembling a quartet of Indian Kushti wrestlers we were covered from head to toe in mud, but seeing the funny side gave the kid a sloppy hug before finally moving well away from the silty sand.

Further back on the beach a small crowd had gathered, including a member of the coastguard who now came over to greet us in complimentary fashion. 'Well done lads, another few minutes and I'd have had to call in the chopper!'

He walked over to the shaken youth, offering him a blanket which he draped around the lad's shoulders, escorting him away for a few private words, closely followed by the loyal golden retriever; I overhead him say, 'Any more stunts like that, you'd be better off with a Saint Bernard!'

Having reached a happy conclusion, we scraped off the excess dirt and began tramping away, when the dozen or so onlookers all at once burst into spontaneous applause, to which we took a bow.

'You know that's the warmest ovation we've had all tour,' I cracked as we reached the bus.

♫

Caked in dry sludge the bespattered heroes arrived back at the camp to be greeted by the agog but ever-dependable Jacqui.

'What on earth happened to you lot?' she enquired.

'We had a small mishap down at Fleet Lagoon,' I replied, explaining briefly what had happened.

'You wouldn't have a laundry here would you? I've only brought one pair of jeans away with me,' asked Dan.

Jacqui immediately came up with an ingenious solution. 'Would you mind posing for a couple of photographs with the children's skin characters in your stage clothes?'

'What, now? We'd need to get cleaned up first!' I said.

'Of course, I'll get two of the girls to launder your dirty things whilst you're in your stage outfits,' she helpfully offered.

'What a great idea! They don't want to see us in our undies then?' enquired a hopeful Dan.

'I think not, you've had enough excitement for one day; we'll see you back here in thirty minutes,' said Jacqui discouragingly.

Romeo posed with Toby the Tiger, Danny with Cheeky the Chimp, Rod was arm in arm with Looby Loo, Jeff sidled up to Sidney the Snake, and I was stood alongside Nellie the shocking-pink Elephant. Trevor, somewhat typically, had thrown a wobbler with Big Ted (a giant teddy bear) who'd attempted a show of affection by ruffling his carefully coiffured thatch with a furry paw.

'Thank you so much for your kind cooperation, I'll make sure the photos are featured in next year's brochure,' Jacqui informed us.

A headless character, with just the top of his bonce visible from within the furry torso, wheeled in a trolley full of goodies which amongst other things contained hamburgers, soft drinks, and pots of tea and coffee.

The voracious party were sitting devouring the greasy snacks with aplomb, when a young lady in a red sequinned mini-skirt arrived with three neatly folded piles of our freshly laundered clothes.

'Jacqui says that the cleaning is on the house,' she said smilingly, before wiggling provocatively away to sharp intakes of breath and leers as we admired her shapely rear.

Walking back to the Platinum caravan, I suddenly thought out loud, 'This has got to be the one!'

Dan, looking puzzled, asked: 'The one what?'

I surmised, 'Look at the people here: hardly any of them are lard-arses, the staff are all bronzed, workmanlike and healthy-looking and the place is spotless – this has to be it!'

'What?' Rod and Dan exclaimed together.

'Let's find the mini-mart – they surely must have fresh fruit here! Jacqui looks the healthy type; I bet she has it for breakfast every morning,' I asserted.

'Bloody hell, it's become an obsession,' claimed Rod.

Just then a lady with two carrier bags full of groceries passed by, whom I asked where the store was located, before the three of us marched off in hot pursuit of my holy grail.

Irritatingly the shop was closed, but reopened at seven p.m.; with an appalling Schwarzenegger impersonation I posed hands on hips and said: 'I'll be back!' With the sound-check looming large and our bellies full we dropped off our things at the caravan, and trudged back to make some noise.

Unsurprisingly the supermarket didn't stock any items of fruit; and though I could quite easily have nipped out to a local greengrocer's to buy some, that would've been cheating. But Rod's comment had been justified, as my quest to find a few pieces of fresh fruit had become a preoccupation, and with only two weeks of the tour remaining it was looking increasingly unlikely.

Trevor's volume at the run-through had left my ears ringing, but leaving the building I noticed a different beeping sound that turned out to be a call from Laura's dad.

'We've arrived a little earlier than planned; are you around?' he asked. Explaining that indeed we were, the little trio did an about turn and went to join them in the Café-Bar for a small caffeine boost.

Sebastian was on night duty, so sadly was unable to make it, and without her man around Laura somehow looked pale and withdrawn; but she was still enthusiastic about seeing the show. Nonetheless she was clearly very tired and appeared discomfited by the noise and clatter of the room.

'If you'll excuse us for a sec I think we'd better get some fresh air,' her mother urged, and then suggested, 'Let's take a walk to the beach before we go and find our table.' Sipping up the dregs we allowed them some space and arranged to see them after the show.

It would have come as no surprise to have heard from Laura's family saying they needed to make an early exit, as it was plain to see that she having a bad day, but pleasingly there they were at the table Jacqui had laid on, wide-eyed as we sprang into action.

During the show I glanced over regularly to where they were seated as I paced around the stage, until at one point I detected pained expressions of concern from her parents.

They stuck things out for around two thirds of the show, when a welcome burst of air entered the room. I spotted a member of staff opening the emergency door by the ramp, as Laura was wheeled out by her father with us performing her favourite song *Three Steps to Heaven*.

Whilst changing later I noticed there was a new text message on my phone, which read: 'Thanks 4 everything the excitement was 2 much sorry we had to leave early fab show see u soon.'

Afflicted by a tinge of sadness that Laura hadn't been well enough to enjoy the show to the full, I called her Dad the following morning, comforted to hear one of our songs (*Dancin' Party*) playing merrily in the background.

'She may not have been at her best last night but she's full of it today, we can't get a minute's peace,' he excitedly told me, before passing the phone to Laura who touchingly said, 'I just want to thank you all for bringing me so much happiness over all these years.'

I swallowed hard. This was one of those truly precious moments that make life's little traumas evaporate into thin air, and whatever problems and unpleasantness we'd suffered throughout this tour, in that split second I'd have done it all over again.

The ever-efficient Jacqui had organised a buffet breakfast for the whole gang in a quiet corner of the canteen, and was full of praise for our efforts the previous night.

'What a shame those delightful people couldn't stay for the whole show,' she said caringly.

Her competence and hospitality had been without equal, and were in no way influenced by my complaints to head office a few days previously. The simple truth lay in her being a consummate professional: this was the way she did things, and what a welcome relief it had proved.

We thanked her in turn, pecking her cheek as we prepared to leave, and she appeared genuinely sad that we were moving on; in fact I swear I saw her eyes well up as the bus finally pulled away.

27

GRAPES OF WRATH
(SPEAR OF DESTINY)

Friday 19th August 2005

Travelling for weeks on end can play havoc with one's general well-being, and together with the inactivity of constantly being sat in a vehicle, the differing hardness of the water, not to mention the effects of regular junk food, the human body can often react in a very negative way.

During the band's fifty-date 2004 UK tour I'd suffered from throat problems, constipation, a twisted ankle, back spasms and gout, along with the added fatigue of the daily grind that is inescapable; but the alarm bells were ringing as this run of albeit less glamorous dates was beginning to have a similar effect.

From *The World English Dictionary*:
> **haemorrhoids** *(non technical name: piles)*
> swollen and twisted veins in the region of the anus and lower rectum, often painful and bleeding

On the journey down from Weymouth I'd begun experiencing some discomfort in my nether regions, which I imagined to be similar to sitting on a bed of hot coals, as I continually fidgeted around in the passenger seat as if suffering a bout of St Vitus's dance.

The malaise horrifyingly intensified as the jaunt ground on, and by the time we began winding our way through the narrow Cornish lanes on the approach to Perranporth I was woebegone and in agony.

The untidy but endearing little camp was situated on the outskirts of the resort, close to one of the sandy beaches for which the small town is renowned. Fearing the worst after the wonderful hospitality afforded us on the previous day, there was an air of expectancy that we were about to come tumbling back down to normality with a resounding bump, so it came as something of a surprise to once again be extended a warm and courteous welcome.

Using the map provided in the envelope that contained our keys, we navigated our way through the confusing grid in search of the night's accommodation, which albeit adequate was a far cry from the Platinum luxury experienced in Jacqui's pristine Dorset centre.

The guys in the band mocked derisively as, in a hackneyed Max Wall routine, I waddled like a chimpanzee, bow-legged up the steps of the caravan with the insides of my thighs causing friction burns as they constantly rubbed together.

There before me was the comforting sight of a bed-settee, where within minutes I lay prostrated from the ordeal, a strategically placed cushion beneath my rear as I dozed off dreaming I was trapped inside an inferno.

As I stirred I saw Dan with his feet up watching TV. He looked over and asked, 'All right squire, d'ya think you could manage a stroll into town?'

'Yes, why not; maybe I should see if there's a doctor's surgery to get my arse looked at?' I suggested hopefully.

Realising the park was situated more than two miles from civilisation, and not wishing to be too ambitious, we drove to a public car park on the edge of town and legged it the rest of the way, only to find that the wonderful NHS could do nothing for me, with no doctor's sitting until the following Monday morning; so after muttering some curmudgeonly un-PC comment I hobbled off in search of a chemist.

There were scores of people ambling along the attractive main street, dotting in and out of bakeries, souvenir shops and amusement arcades, but more importantly in between the row of shops stood a more modern building indicating it was the settlement's pharmacy.

Two female assistants greeted us with a smile and asked if they could help; but understandably I was a little slow in coming forward due to the nature of my disorder, and uneasily began muttering that I had a slightly embarrassing personal problem, only to be interrupted by Dan who laid it on the line: 'What he's trying to say is that he's got a nasty case of the Plymouth Argyles!'

The confused ladies offered blank looks, so he added, 'I mean piles – it's rhyming slang!'

'Oh, my goodness – is it really painful?' asked the senior assistant, adding, 'My husband suffers terribly you know!'

'Let's put it this way, they've never been quite as sore as this,' I admitted to her.

'I may have some prescription-strength ointment hidden under the counter, and applied together with some suppositories hopefully they'll ease matters considerably,' said the voice of experience in a pleasantly maternal manner.

On the way into town I'd called my close friend Richard, whom I knew had suffered with a similar complaint, in the hope that he could provide me with a few pearls of wisdom; helpfully he'd suggested a whole range of products that may do the trick, none of which had been supplied here, or indeed were on the list I'd jotted down. He'd also recommended that I buy a rubber ring to sit on (which I thought must be a wind-up) to allow a little air to the inflamed patch, to which the white-smocked assistant looked puzzled and agreed, 'That may actually be a good idea, but I'm afraid we don't have anything suitable in stock.'

Rod and Danny were having a new lease of life as we began exploring the back lanes of Perranporth in search of a more substantial model than the gaudily flimsy children's rings on offer in the souvenir shops, which wouldn't have lasted five minutes underneath my sylph-like fourteen-stone frame; but as if by magic we stumbled upon a shop that sold fishing tackle, and with Dan keen to take a look inside, to my delight I noticed a sturdy-looking blue-and-orange-coloured life buoy. Although five times the price of the kiddy alternatives on display it would surely do the job, and I hastily laid claim to it, passing over a small wad of cash to the wizened vendor.

I was drawing some odd glances from the passing pedestrians and idling traffic, as I meandered along the street manually attempting to inflate the life-saver with huge exhalations of breath; and, as we reached the minibus, I carefully placed it on the seat before clambering in like an idiot.

Ridiculously I'd pumped far too much air into the rubbery device, making it impossible to position myself without ducking my head, and like a grumpy old man shifted and cursed whilst manoeuvring the thing beneath my buttocks, much to the amusement of my bandmates as the air slowly released with a squeaky light farting sound.

Attempting to adjust the height of the seat alleviated the situation somewhat, but my noodle was still perilously close to the roof of the vehicle: were we to go over any road humps or bumps I'd surely suffer a mild case of brain damage. The only alternative was for me to slide further down in the seat, and though it wasn't the most comfortable of positions it would simply have to do until the soreness subsided.

'Have you finished buggering about now?' Dan enquired.

'Sorry, am I being a pain in the arse?' I replied unintentionally.

'You could say that,' he nodded wistfully, before hitting the accelerator and heading back to the camp.

♫

My medication administered, I chilled out in the caravan for a while, only to be disturbed by an enormous flurry of activity taking place next door.

Prior to hitting the town I'd noticed a battered old khaki-green Skoda juddering in and out of the space adjacent to us on several occasions, delivering a large complement of what from their guttural sounding accents I took to be eastern Europeans (Danny later deduced that they were Ukrainians).

The jalopy had now shipped in between twenty or thirty foreigners who were garrulously talking over one another as the smell of barbecued food began drifting tantalisingly through the open windows.

There had been much media speculation in recent weeks about the growing numbers of asylum seekers being allowed entry into the country, and perhaps the government had enforced some new legislation that temporarily placed those seeking UK residency into empty caravans in the country's seaside resorts; but, whether or not that was the case here, we figured it may not actually be a bad idea.

The din became almost unbearable as glasses and bottles clinked together, and then a CD of wailing gypsy-type music began blaring out through the open door.

From a window we nosily monitored the proceedings, with the distraction temporarily easing my discomfort, and caught playing Peeping Tom from time to time just smiled and waved, before two bare-chested young guys dressed in tracksuit bottoms emerged from the neighbouring caravan.

The taller of the two was clearly called Ivan (pronounced E-van) as a grey-haired old man shouted an announcement and raised his arm aloft, followed soon by the second guy whose tongue-twisting name was indecipherable, with no one quite able to make it out.

Rod excitedly intimated that this could be a bare-knuckle boxing contest, and that it may be a tradition from their country of origin, but whatever it was curiosity had definitely gotten the better of us as we took our ringside seats to witness what was going down.

Well aware of the attention they were arousing elsewhere, our new neighbours upped and moved to an open space to the rear of the caravans, forcing us to trot down to the far window where they were still in view. They formed a human circle, and after a carnal huddle leapt into the air and let battle commence.

There wasn't an ounce of fat on either of the well-toned combatants as they clenched their taut bodies together in a fearsome grip, in a contest where it appeared that the general idea was to grapple the opponent flat onto his back.

The tussle continued until a withered silver-haired referee blew a whistle – presumably to signal the end of the round – as the gruesome twosome snarled at each other, annoyed at the interruption and itching to get the job done.

They persevered in a similar vein for a further ten minutes, but neither fighter could wrestle the other to the ground. The shrill whistle chirruped again to indicate that the contest was over, with both men's hands raised up suggesting that the brawl was a tie.

The merrymaking eastern Europeans appeared well satisfied with the outcome, which from our perspective had disappointingly been something of a non-event; but the spectacle was far from over.

Bottles of clear liquid (which we assumed to be vodka) were handed to each contender, which incredibly after a united countdown they swigged at eagerly until Ivan spat the remnants from his mouth and collapsed in uncontrollable laughter, while his pal's arm was subsequently upheld in triumph.

The test of manhood was relocated to the inside of the caravan as rain began to fall, thus bringing to a premature close our afternoon's entertainment, which had nonetheless been far more enjoyable than the soporific daytime TV.

I looked at my watch and yawped, 'Bloody hell, we're twenty minutes late for sound-check,' before springing up a trifle too eagerly, only to be reined in by my complaining posterior.

♪

The downpour had descended into a light drizzle as we foot-slogged back towards the trailer, where in the distance the boisterous sound of the Ukrainians partying hard could still be heard. The ear-splitting racket grew even louder as we turned into our boulevard where an accordionist was bellowing out rustic republican anthems to which his inebriated comrades danced passionately, arm in arm going around in circles.

Dan put the kettle on and we ripped open some refrigerated sandwiches purchased from the poorly stocked mini-mart, whilst continuing to earwig the exuberant goings-on. These people doubtlessly knew how to push the boat out and were downing huge gulps of the crystalline fluid as if it were water, hugging and jostling each other at the same time in rough tactile fashion.

The bacchanalia seemed destined to go on well into the night, and in a way we were envious as the camaraderie was infectious; but the burning question was what would happen when they all finally collapsed into a large heap later on, with the beaten-up old Skoda's ferryman clearly in no fit state to take the wheel, as he staggered around yawping at the top of his voice and bumping into the uproarious guests.

The entertainment value reached new heights when a well-endowed topless woman emerged from the caravan wearing just a multi-coloured grass skirt, encouraging the red-blooded males to rub their faces between her ample breasts, which was an invitation none of them were about to pass up.

'I wouldn't mind giving that a go myself,' said Dan, almost foaming at the mouth.

'They're just udders, and if they produced milk we wouldn't need cows!' I remarked.

'And she wouldn't crap all over the floor,' jested Rod articulately, having the last word.

The horseplay was brought to an abrupt halt when unsurprisingly after a number of complaints two police vehicles arrived on the scene, closely followed by a quartet of brightly attired members of staff, who looked on nervously as the boys in blue attempted to communicate with the revellers.

The bare-breasted woman was gallingly urged to preserve her modesty, with the semi-naked males also slipping on their shirts as an altercation ensued where the police made it clear that the majority of the party animals had no right to be inside the park.

In the midst of the turbulence rasping voices were raised, as one of the officers was seen to wield a truncheon in the direction of an apoplectic blue-faced Ukrainian who was fast losing the plot, and things seemed to be getting well out of hand when one of the younger carousers took a swing at an unsuspecting flatfoot before being swiftly handcuffed and despatched into the rear seat of the waiting patrol car.

To their credit the lawmen handled the delicate situation with effective aplomb, as the heated scene was eventually quelled and many of the dejected foreign gatecrashers began drifting away.

In the thick of all the excitement there was another show to be done, and forced to miss out on any further developments we picked up our stage gear before wending our way back to the Show Lounge, with myself trailing in the wake of Rod and Dan at a shuffling pace.

A member of staff later told us that the 'gypsy' caravan had been rented just for the day by a couple named Smith, courtesy of a Newquay address, though quite where all the other guests had sprung up from would long remain a mystery; but whatever, the diverting organised chaos was over with the police making just two arrests, and any other stragglers disappearing on foot into the night.

♫

The morning after a tryingly average performance the three of us awoke to the bone-shaking sound of a tow truck, and peeping through the curtains it appeared that the rickety Skoda had been in a prang with its not-so-proud owner doing a bunk. The powers that be had ordered the banger's removal, and the noisy ratchet winched the crate onto the breakdown vehicle in preparation for its valedictory journey to the knacker's yard; but the old jalopy still had the final say when a side panel clattered to the ground causing consternation amongst the swarf-tainted grease-monkeys, much to the amusement of the bleary-eyed onlookers.

Trev didn't show for breakfast as Jeff croakily informed us that he'd been complaining of toothache all night and needed a little more shut-eye, but there was a touch of anxiety in the conversation as we pigged out on the morning fry-up, hoping that he hadn't begun anaesthetizing the pain during his room-mate's absence.

The back-to-back gigs, uncomfortable sleeping conditions, junk food, incessant travelling, and lack of optimism had, two thirds of the way through the tour, taken their toll, with Romeo suffering a nasty head-cold, Jeff struggling with laryngitis, Rod complaining of severe back pain, Trev's jaw swollen as a result of his dental problem, and my rectal discomfort, albeit on the mend but still literally a pain in the butt.

Embarking the bus resembled an outing from an old people's home, as the walking wounded awkwardly ascended to be greeted by Danny, who now that his rash had cleared was the only hale and hearty member.

Poking fun he announced: 'Ladies and gentlemen, let me introduce to you the world's greatest crock-and-roll band,' the tone of which was not best received as, to the sound of coughing and spluttering, we chugged away, heading further south west to the Cornish cargo port of Hayle.

28

HOTEL HAPPINESS
(BROOK BENTON)

Saturday 20th August 2005

Many people perceive the rock-and-roll lifestyle to be a glamorous existence, full of five-star hotels, luxurious tour buses, limousines, Ferraris, Porsches, rock chicks a-plenty on the arm, being lionized wherever you go, and all the other much publicised accoutrements. However, when it actually comes down to it here in the twenty-first century this manner of living is more likely reserved for vastly overpaid Premier-league footballers – as opposed to honest-Joe musicians – of whom many behave like spoilt brats whilst appearing sadly out of touch with the real world and its moral standards.

Happily the music industry is not really like that at all, though admittedly one does come across the odd egotistical prima-donna; these more often than not fall into the category of ungifted solo artists, who spend far too much time alone believing their own hype and publicity. All the same, in the main the vast majority of troubadours tend towards being a laid-back, wickedly humoured multi-cultural breed, who mostly offer few airs and graces.

There have been, and always will be, exceptions to the rule (as we'd found to our cost years previously, but that's another story), but in reality being part of a band fosters keeping a tight rein on any pig-headedness or egocentricity that may afflict an individual, as in general the unaffected majority are likely to come down hard on the offending braggart by bringing them down a peg or two to ensure they toe the line.

Like any successful band we'd all tasted the high life, sampling luxury cars, posh restaurants, swanky clubs and the like; but, with strong family backgrounds, remaining well-grounded never appeared to be a major issue.

Over the course of thirty-two-plus years we'd lived the five-star fairy tale (once even staying in a ridiculously opulent seven-star hotel in Dubai), but the nature of our chosen industry had a habit of biting us all on the backside by also leading us to many utterly disgusting establishments.

On a tour of Ireland some years prior, we'd checked into an old country-house hotel close to the town of Clonmel in South Tipperary, where upon signing the register at reception we were each handed our room keys, together with a small pile of linen.

'And what might this be?' I'd enquired, only to be semi-admonished by the female clerk who answered: 'What do they look like? It's a pair of curtains – we had some pinched once…'

With a stunned expression I just said, 'Well, I suppose you can't be too careful,' thinking on my way to the room how much easier it would be to simply stuff the neatly folded pile inside my luggage.

Incredibly all the way along the corridor doors were ajar, as I witnessed new residents perched on chairs assembling their curtains into the track, realising that a few minutes later I'd be performing a similar task in my own room.

On the opposite side of the hall I heard a sudden crashing sound, and leapt down to check out what had taken place, to find a dumbfounded Ray (who was our lead guitarist at the time) stood by his toilet which had completely disintegrated as he'd allowed the seat to fall. Within seconds the same ubiquitous woman was back on the scene to inspect the shattered mess, and hilariously exclaimed, 'Begorrah, you must've shit a brick,' before scampering away to promptly find Ray another room as if the bizarre incident was an everyday occurrence.

On the same afternoon an England World Cup qualifying international was taking place, and through the thinly partitioned walls I could hear that the coverage had begun on the TV in the room next door. Keen to see the game I noted that an aerial cable was dangling from beneath where I'd hung the curtains, but that there was no set of my own, and marched back to reception to see if they could supply one.

'Here's the key to room number six: take the telly out of there, and wheel it round to your own room,' she suggested.

Quietly letting myself in I was taken aback to see clothes hanging on the rails, and suitcases full of stuff scattered across the floor, so made a quick U-turn back to the reception desk.

'Excuse me, but the room you told me to take the TV from seems to be occupied,' I said.

'Ah, don't worry your head about that, just take it – they've gone out for the day, and won't be back until late,' she amazingly explained in her lilting Irish tones.

'Are you sure?' I asked.

'Of course I'm sure, begorrah; anyway there's bugger all on later!' she exclaimed.

Whilst staying in an upmarket Hong Kong hotel that overlooked the famous bustling harbour in the 1990s, I made the front page of the *South China News*, which had the biggest circulation of any daily rag in the colony.

On the night of our arrival in the province, the band had been extended a VIP invitation to a notorious bar in the busy Wan Chai district of the city called Joe Bananas, which specialised in exotically named cocktails, one such concoction being tagged a 'Blow Job'. A special technique was required to consume the risqué-sounding drink, where the glass would be placed in the centre of the table, and the imbiber would place both arms behind his or her back and lean forward encircling both lips around the rim, with the idea being to swallow the potent contents all in one go.

It was a sickly sweet potion and also very strong in alcohol, but was in no way unpleasant on the taste buds, and being a novelty each of us gave it a go. Foolishly it was my good self who became rather partial to the compound and the effects it was having on me, and subsequently I downed one over the eight and was somewhat worse for wear by the end of the session, when we thanked our hosts for their superb hospitality and staggered into the waiting cars to be returned to the hotel.

The following morning I received a call urging me to get my backside down to the lobby area for a radio interview that I'd forgotten had been organised, and for which I was late due to the effects of the previous night's liquor. I threw on some clothes and hurried into the lift, pressing the button for the lower ground floor where the recording was taking place, and entered the foyer area to see a couple of heavy-eyed band mates chatting with the loquacious radio DJ, who greeted me warmly saying: 'Good morning lead-singer Dave, and how are you on this fine day?'

Half-jokingly I replied: 'How would you be if you'd had eight blow-jobs last night?'

The look of horror on his face said it all, and after a pregnant pause he announced: 'You're listening to Radio HK, live here from the Harbour View hotel, with our special guests all the way from the UK, Showaddywaddy!'

I gasped and whispered, 'Are we live on air?' followed by a sincere apology, pointing out that I'd referred to eight quirkily named cocktails that I'd taken on board the night before, to which the DJ laughed nervously and smartly changed the subject.

Later in the day I was informed that the European community in Hong Kong were renowned for their over-the-top piety and prudishness, and sure enough the next morning there was the news headline in black and white: 'Rock singer's outrageous outburst, live on the airwaves.' Fortunately the commotion soon died a death, and with slapped wrists only a blind eye was turned to my so-called outlandish rock-and-roll behaviour.

The job of hotel night-porter is an odd vocation, and attracts a nocturnal breed of hireling, similar in many ways to recording studio engineers in that they rarely see any daylight at all, and generally carry wan, almost ghostly complexions.

One such night-man was employed at a notorious Sheffield hotel known many years ago as Hallam Towers, where the band stayed on a number of occasions whilst touring during the seventies and eighties.

His slicked-back hair and cadaverous features made him look a lot like an *Addams Family* character, on top of which he was rake thin, with a uniform that looked some forty years out of date; but on the plus side he was helpful, attentive and happy in his work.

The hour was roughly three a.m., and the emaciated steward had been back and forth serving several rounds of drinks as our convivial bunch relaxed post-gig in the hotel lobby. The marked up prices suggested he would be in his employer's good books the next day. However, as we tried to catch his eye yet again, alarmingly he'd gone into hiding, presumably in the hope that we'd had our fill and that he could get some well-earned rest; but on a roll Jeff rose and went off to search him out.

'Lurch was having a crafty gasper in a little side-room by reception. I startled him and saw him put it out in his pocket; he's on his way over now,' he told us as he returned.

Sure enough the skeletal man soon crept eerily over to our empty-glass-strewn table, and began jotting down the order; but as he scribbled there was a distinct smell of something combusting close by.

Rod suddenly detected that the old boy's jacket was smoking from the right-hand pocket, as almost disbelievingly the porter was alerted to the danger, but not before the garment had burst into flames.

Like a rocket he removed it from his person and began stamping upon the burning cloth, which was now smouldering on the floor, causing a well-oiled group of businessmen behind to retch and cough; but once the smoke and flames were extinguished he coolly picked up the jacket and slipped it back on, chuckling to himself in the process. 'Now then gentlemen, what was it you were wanting?' he asked, completely unperturbed with our undivided attention.

'A fire extinguisher and a bucket of water,' answered Jeff, as Romeo erupted into a bout of raucous laughter, soon to be followed by the whole caboodle.

Hotels, of course, couldn't possibly function without courteous and efficient staff to greet weary travellers as they check in at the main desk, but once again in our experience this is not always necessarily the case, even in more upmarket premises.

On a trip out to the Middle East in the mid-eighties, the entourage had been put up in a luxury resort, situated right next to a private man-made beach on the outskirts of the city of Abu Dhabi.

Each room was done out in Spanish hacienda style and equipped with queen-size beds and bamboo furniture, all in a beautiful setting that felt more as if we'd just arrived on holiday.

Ninety per cent of the in-house staff was Asian immigrants, who were super-efficient and catered to our every whim, but also possessed a great sense of humour which I was soon to be on the end of.

After relaxing on a sun-bed by the ornately shaped pool, and taking the odd dip to douse the heat on my body, I returned to the room to freshen up and prepare for our show in the hotel gardens later that night. As I pulled the lever to the shower I heard a gurgling noise but there were no jets of water flowing out. A call was put in to reception who explained that there was a boiler problem, but that the problem would be fixed within the hour; so chilling out for on the bed for a while I indulged in a spot of light reading.

Trying the wall taps again some twenty minutes later, this time there was a weakly pressurised trickle of cold water, which I thought it best to risk and somehow managed to wash albeit with some difficulty, but revitalised by the coolness of the water and drying myself down I was good and ready to take on the world.

The show had been a wonderful success, after which we were spoilt silly by our hosts, with expensive champagne flowing on tap and compliments raining down as we mingled with the mainly ex-pat crowd (though the prime tables had all been occupied by a sea of towel-headed nationals garbed in virginal white), many of whom were adamant they'd never return to the UK; but all in all things had gone sensationally well, and we too were in our element living it large in the lap of luxury.

The following morning I heard a rat-tat-tat at my hacienda door, but before I had time to move a muscle a pass key clicked in the door as the staff allowed themselves in to afford me the rare luxury of breakfast in bed. There were muffins, toast, preserves, bacon, eggs, sausages and would you believe (I'd forgotten what it looked like as I reminisced) a platter of fresh fruit, along with plentiful fresh ground Arabic coffee, which was poured from ornate polished brass pots.

One of the waiters flicked the light switch, but nothing happened, so he quickly drew the enormous drapes that were banishing the bright sunlight before courteously leaving me to my feast.

I tiptoed to the bathroom to do my business, again doing so in darkness as the small room was also without power, but enjoying the high life I returned to the sumptuous-looking spread and tucked in.

My appetite sated, I picked up the TV remote to try and find the international news, but it seemed nothing was functioning at all, with the electricity as dead as a dodo. Certain in the knowledge that such a classy hotel would surely be on the case I decided to take a stroll in the already scorching sunlight in an effort to recharge my throbbing brain after the previous night's excesses, also figuring that the perfect antidote would be a refreshing dip in the beckoning sea. Having wandered down to the water's edge I slipped off my sandals and began paddling in.

'Sahib, please don't go swim there, it very big danger,' said a concerned-sounding voice over the light breeze.

I looked behind me to see a local man who resembled one of Ali Baba's forty thieves. 'Pardon me – did you say it isn't safe?' I asked.

'Very bad, Sahib: sea snakes, can make very big pain for you, sometimes can paralyse,' he warned, shaking his head from side to side.

Without another word I was out of there like a shot, and patted him on the back, thanking him for his wise words, as he continued along the beach making horrible phlegmatic noises.

It seemed there was no one else around yet, so I strolled back to my room to indulge in a little more reading and, recumbent in a comfortable cane armchair, switched on the standard lamp; but still there was still no power, and it was fast becoming an inconvenience.

I strutted over to reception to find two cheerful Indian guys, who both bid me 'namaste' with their hands held together in praying mode.

'Good morning,' I replied. 'Can you please tell me what is going on in this hotel? Yesterday there was no water, and today no electricity!'

He audaciously shot back: 'And tomorrow no telephones,' before bursting into spontaneous laughter – rendering my complaint as fatuous, but at the same time cleverly taking any heat out of the crazy situation and causing me to laugh along with them.

'The maintenance engineers are making progress sir, so don't worry – you will have power very soon,' he confirmed, as I walked away shaking my head in admiration at the unique handling of my gripe.

♫

'The centre is completely chock-a-block so you're all booked in at the Union in Penzance, which is only seven miles away,' said the receptionist as we arrived at the camp in Hayle.

'What's the Union?' I enquired.

She looked perplexed, and just stated, 'It's a hotel right in the centre of town,' before jotting down the address and booking reference, leaving me dumbfounded at the prospect of sleeping in a clean bed, perhaps with an en-suite bathroom and the added bonus of some privacy.

Thirty minutes later a phantasmagorical vision unfolded before my eyes, as on a picturesque street of a pleasant Cornish town stood a lovely old whitewashed Georgian building. However, on the back of our highly unsatisfactory sleeping arrangements over the past seven weeks, there surely had to be a catch!

Key cards to single rooms were handed out by the friendly manager, who then asked: 'Will you chaps be requiring a late bar when you arrive back tonight? I'm sure by that time you'll have a good thirst on!'

Completely disorientated I croaked out, 'Wow, that would be spot on, thanks!'

'No problem, I'll make sure it's all sorted for you: in fact I'll probably put myself on bar duty,' he kindly offered.

Upstairs the quaint rooms were tastefully decked out with Chinese rugs over aged creaking floorboards with beautiful antique furnishings, and everything was absolutely spotless and pleasing to the eye.

Back down in the lobby the gregarious proprietor insisted on giving us a history lesson, followed by a short guided tour of the hotel that led us into a deserted dining room.

'This was once the famous Assembly Rooms, where the first formal announcement of the death of Lord Horatio Nelson was made from that balcony in 1805,' he narrated pointing upwards.

The man was something of a geek, but was justifiably proud of the unique historic surroundings in his place of work, and continued: 'In 1755 the town withstood an eight-foot-high tsunami, almost as powerful as the one in Asia last year, but they knew how to build towns in those days!'

Full of pride and enthusiasm he explained how good the quality of life was down here in Cornwall, and grabbing a tourist map from a rack pointed us in the direction of several 'not to be missed' attractions, thus allowing us to prise ourselves away and take a good old mosey along the sea front towards Newlyn harbour.

Dan in particular was fascinated by the smelly netted lobster containers that were lined up alongside an array of rusting vessels, where the crustaceans were offered for sale on blackboards suspended from the harbour walls, which caused the three of us to lick our peckish lips.

Closer to the centre of town we noticed another blackboard, displaying daily specials scrawled in chalk, above which was a large arrow pointing down a secluded alley to a tiny, trendy-looking restaurant, with a small courtyard.

'I like the look of this place: are you ready for a bite?' I asked my fellow adventurers, who immediately made all the right noises.

The small eatery was ideal for a light lunch, and was run by young, eager-to-impress student-like staff donned in black pinafores, who without ado took our order and served up homebaked bread with little bowls of appetising nibbles as we perched ourselves outside in a pleasant sun-trap and waited for our main courses, which were not long in arriving.

Rod was given a display of my ambidextrous skill of removing a sardine spine complete with head, which he curiously showed an interest in, but continued to pick at the oily little fish on his plate with a knife and fork.

Enjoying the moment, I was brought crashing down to earth as my mobile vibrated in my pocket, and answered the call from Steve with some trepidation.

'There won't be time for a sound-check as there's a kids' show on until six p.m. I'll do a line check,* but you lot may as well stay put where you are,' he pleasingly informed me.

I thanked him for keeping us posted and raised his spirits considerably when I told him how pleasant the hotel was. 'That's a bloody turn up for the books ain't it?' he commented.

'Indeed it is; I may even buy you a pint later,' I offered, leaving him to press on.

The lunch was excellent, and in a totally relaxed frame of mind after chilling out in the sunny weather, we patted our stomachs and took a leisurely stroll back in the direction of the hotel, zigzagging in and out of tiny alleys and winding backstreets, where the imagination was fired by thoughts of smugglers making hasty getaways from the Peelers seeking them out in the local taverns in days of yore.

All our yesterdays apart, time was getting on and we had a job to do, in what had now become more familiar surroundings barely seven miles up the road; and feeling almost inconvenienced it was back to our historic lodgings to freshen up and make ourselves presentable in readiness for the evening's big event.

While I was showering my mobile vibrated against the chair that my clothes were draped upon, and drying myself off I saw I had a missed call from Jeff. I clicked the green phone icon to hear him answer 'Yeah,' as I barked, 'Alright ba?'

'Oaksie's bloody well pissed,' he imparted, adding: 'He's been wandering around all day with that discoloured bottle of Coke, and now he's fast asleep in his room, and won't answer his phone!'

'Shit! Why don't you go and bang on his door until he wakes up?' I suggested.

'Because he's barricaded himself inside his room! I borrowed a pass key from one of the chambermaids, but the bloody door won't budge an inch!'

---

* See Chapter 9.

Jeff gave me the room number, and I arranged to meet him there five minutes later.

Upon turning the pass key the latch clicked but wouldn't budge, as it seemed there were several articles of furniture stacked up against the aperture, prohibiting anyone from entry, even in an emergency. Taking a run at it I shoulder-charged the opening; a couple of seconds later the sound of something toppling came from within the room, and with a further shove the obstruction finally gave way, allowing me in.

As I entered the room the startled Trevor sat up in his bed with a face as black as coal, as if he'd just swept a chimney, and yawning and stretching said, 'What the hell's going on, what do you want?'

Jeff, just outside the doorway, had begun making whimpering noises which I soon realised were disguised, helpless laughter. Controlling myself and somehow holding it together I managed to force out: 'We're leaving in forty-five minutes!'

'Oh, I'd better make a move then,' he answered, as he struggled to free his torso from the tightly bound blackened sheets. With a feeling of acute embarrassment for him I shut the door, realising his hair treatment had run from the top of his head and covered his face as he'd slept, leaving him looking like an old-time coal-miner at the end of a shift.

Jeff was sitting on the floor chuckling away uncontrollably as he catechized: 'Why on earth does he put that crap on his head?'

I exhaled and replied, 'Each to their own; I think it's called mid-life crisis, but all I know is I'd rather be bald as a coot than wake up looking like that every day!'

The show that night was undisciplined, with the cocktail of over-exposure to the sun, excessive alcohol and general slothfulness failing to provide the ingredients necessary to make for a good performance, and as a result the dressing room was spookily silent as we changed.

The bus was loaded up to the gunnels as per usual as we absconded from yet another resort, looking forward to drowning our sorrows courtesy of the organised lock-in at the hotel.

Dan brought a brief halt to the despondency by saying, 'Hey Dave, you know when I went for a little stroll just before the gig, I popped into the shop to buy a can of Coke and I swear I saw some fresh fruit in there!'

'Oh yeah, pull the other one you bloody wind-up merchant,' I cried out in the gloomy silence, not believing a word of it.

'Well, there was definitely something red and shiny in there,' he muttered.

'Maybe it was Trev's head beneath the camouflage,' I cruelly joked, starting Jeff off again in the back, as Rod hit the accelerator to muted laughs of disbelief.

29

STAGE FRIGHT
(THE BAND)

Sunday 21st August 2005

The mini-session at the hotel had gone on until around three a.m. and was positively what the doctor ordered after such a disappointing gig, in a terribly restricted venue.

It was clear and in a way understandable that the band was a little jaded, and that the parks weren't exactly inspiring us to great things; but efficaciously a few pints of Cornish real ale, amongst a few other wee tipples, had saved the day and lifted the spirits tenfold.

With a late breakfast under our ever-expanding belts, we had a fair old trek ahead of us, and had arranged to meet in the hotel lobby ahead of the journey back north to Exmouth in Devon, with the sojourn into historic Cornwall at an end and the feeling it would doubtless be a while before we resided in such a comfortable and picturesque dwelling-place again.

Rod and I were first down and met at reception to settle our extras signed for during the previous night's bender, only to see that the girl behind the desk clearly had a clerical problem as, fraught with concern, she shuffled through a pile of paperwork in a desperate search for a mislaid document of some importance. Leaning over and whispering with the phone to one side, she said, 'Sorry, be with you in a minute; one of last night's residents has done a runner – I'm on to the police station right now.'

'Okay, we're in no rush,' I revealed.

Stood biding our time it was difficult not to earwig the ensuing conversation. 'Well, he was quite tall, with blond curly hair,' the girl explained, as the distant voice sounded in her earpiece. 'Signature?' she asked stupefied a moment later, before adding, 'I'll see if he signed for anything; can you hold please?' She stretched across the desk to retrieve another folder. 'Goodness, there are a lot of bills here; he's really taken us to the cleaners,' she panicked, donning a pair of glasses, and continuing: 'His handwriting is actually quite difficult to read; ah, this one's a little clearer – it says "E. Presley",' she said earnestly.

Stunned, we put our hands to our mouths to conceal our reaction, and could imagine just what the officer at the other end of the line was thinking.

'Okay, I'll wait to hear from you,' she affirmed politely, putting down the phone and turning towards us. 'Now then, gentlemen, thank you for your patience; what can I do for you?'

'Can I pay the extras for room thirty-six, please?' asked Rod.

'What was the name?' she enquired, understandably still slightly flustered.

'M. Mouse,' Rod quipped.

She began scrolling through the register, and started to say, 'I'm afraid we don't have anyone of that…' before finally cottoning on and looking up with a bashful grin, scornfully waving an index finger.

♫

The hotel receptionist's embarrassment complete (after a string of crazy *nom de plumes* once the boys had been let in on the act), we wound our way through the busy winding lanes of Penzance seeking out the signs for the A30 road up to neighbouring Devon, and most likely the less salubrious surroundings of the next camp on the agenda.

The disappointment of the previous night's gig was very much the topic of the day, and an air of gloom was still prevalent, along with a yearning to step out on stage before an adoring public in a well-equipped theatre.

'What do you reckon is the worst gig we've ever done?' Jeff contemplated, breaking the silence from the rear seat. Thinking caps were firmly placed on heads, but in all honesty there had only been something approaching a dozen of what could be termed 'bad gigs' in thirty-two years, which looked pretty good on the CV.

'That fucking Motorcycle Museum gig near Birmingham is by far the worst I can remember,' harked Romeo.

The show in question had indeed been a pretty awful experience, and even now stuck in everyone's throats as we recalled the event. It had been a corporate function held at the end of a three-day seminar, with delegates present from all over the world, and in particular Japan (where the band were little known).

The venue was an absolute shocker, and in no way conducive to a rock-and-roll concert, boasting nightmarish acoustics in a cavernous, hangar-like setting where, as the day staff meticulously laid out the tables, the sound of crockery and cutlery echoed endlessly throughout the commodious backdrop. To make matters worse there would be no sound-check, as the conference was still taking place in the open expanse, so in a potentially disquieting environment it was very much 'suck it and see' when it came to the quality of the band's performance.

During the instrumental opening number, the barely audible music reverberated from wall to wall, creating an alarming delayed racket which from an audiometric perspective was virtually impossible to control; but to add insult to injury none of the international attendees appeared the least bit interested in any case.

The conceited organiser pleaded demonstratively with us to reduce the volume level, which made very little difference as the clattering room could only be termed a rock-and-roll band's nemesis, with every single note plucked or sung repeating itself several times before tailing off into what would best be described as an unworkable environment.

The evening might well have been a total disaster, with the saving grace being that the majority of the male delegates were far more interested in which PA or female representative may be on their arm accompanying them to their hotel room later on in the night.

Thirty minutes into the band's set the organiser stood in front of the stage, before running his index finger from left to right across his throat, thus indicating that we should curtail our performance at the end of the song. Ironically it proved a merciful gesture, despite the fact that the near catastrophic experience had largely been no fault of our own.

My personal memoir was a night that still gets my back up, and was another show we should never have been subjected to in a large 'fun pub'-type venue situated in the centre of a Catholic estate in Northern Ireland's capital, Belfast.

From the very moment we took to the stage it seemed there was a whiff of hostility in the air, with four menacing barrel-chested security men positioned in each corner, each of whom wore stern faces and intimidating expressions.

A Saturday night out in Belfast is in general terms a boozy affair, and the sociable buzz of the city centre on a summer's evening seems a million miles away from the troubles that blighted the province for so many years. That conviviality, however, was sadly absent from this neglected ghetto as we mounted the stage before a grim-faced crowd, clearly the worse for wear.

A couple of songs into the set and we'd got off to a flyer, until a woman of maybe thirty together with an unshaven, lank-haired man in a leather jacket gave the minders the slip and leapt onto the stage, with the woman grabbing aggressively at one of the mics. Meanwhile her grubby-looking associate attempted to wrestle my own contraption from my grip, to find I was having none of it, as apart from the device being a much coveted and expensive tool of my trade,

I really didn't relish the idea of the unkempt man spouting his dog breath into it.

The man growled an incoherent insult in my direction as his female accomplice blared what were presumably Republican slogans into the microphone in Erse or some other esoteric Celtic language, which auspiciously seemed to fall on deaf ears as the pair were manhandled from the platform by the hateful-looking guards; but the effect had been chilling and unsettling, as I nervously looked to the audience and uttered: 'Quite what all that has to do with a band like us is beyond me – c'mon let's rock!'

The woman's comments had frustratingly doused the crowd's enthusiasm; and though the band had been on fine form, our efforts were fatuous and received with no little indifference, as we managed to see the gig through without any further dramas to huge relief all round.

Rod mentioned a cringeworthy gig we'd played way back in the seventies at a large nightspot in the centre of Derby, during a period when bands and artists were beginning to experiment with sound technology to enhance their live performances.

With a new single out at the time – our vocal interpretation of the Buddy Holly song *Heartbeat* – we decided to jump on the bandwagon, as whilst recording the single in the studio we'd experimented by layering together multiple tracks of vocal harmonies one on top of the other to produce a big fat (almost pre-Queen) wall of sound. In the process some of the band members became a little nervous as to how we'd reproduce the song with the same grandeur in a 'live' situation.

What was most puzzling was that between us we undoubtedly had the vocal ability to pull it off, but with the temptation there to bring things bang up to date and dabble with modern techniques the stage was set to create something utterly ground-breaking.

A reel-to-reel copy was prepared of the multi-tracked vocals, together with an audible click-track (similar to a metronome, to allow the drummer to remain in perfect time with the recording), which after working well in rehearsal was figured to be good and ready for a live airing.

The club was jam-packed with more than fifteen hundred people, and the band was storming the place, when I announced midway through the set: 'This is our brand new single *Heartbeat*,' and bang on cue the backing track started, with the band joining in vocally, mouthing 'ba dap ba dada, ba dap ba dada' in perfect synch with the taped recording, the effect of which to my ears sounded hissy and slightly synthetic.

All of a sudden the accompanying vocal track went dead in our onstage sound monitors, and for some strange reason a couple of the band simultaneously stopped singing too. Within seconds the whole performance had ground to a humiliating halt, as I quickly improvised, uttering some feeble excuse into the mic along the lines of, 'Sorry, but we have technical problems; we'll be back as soon as it's sorted!'

We trooped from the stage like Muppets in single file; but catastrophically, as we were roughly halfway, the taped voices embarrassingly fired up again, blaring out through the front-of-house system. To make matters worse the sound engineer again stopped the tape deck, leaving us stranded to the left of the stage, with a high-pitched whirring, rewinding tape noise clearly audible to the jeering crowd.

This was a rare point in time when the red-faced band wished the stage would open up and swallow us whole, such was the ignominy of the moment; but also a juncture when a band's front man bears a heavy burden, and it was meaningless to lie to the baying, paying customers. So, standing centre stage, hands on hips, I stated candidly: 'I guess that's what happens when you mess with modern technology and don't know what you're doing!'

Following an initial chorus of cynical boos and put-downs we somehow survived the night, although the post-performance dressing-room exchanges were – to put it mildly – furious, with the vast majority of the culpability laying with the ineffectual sound-man.

'The gig that I really hated was that cricketer's benefit function in Birmingham a few years ago,' voiced Dan.

The day had begun well as we arrived at the beautiful Botanical Gardens in Edgbaston for a show that was especially in aid of the talented Warwickshire cricketer Nick Knight (now a Sky TV pundit), who'd persuaded me to ask the band to do a special performance at the final dinner event of his year-long benefit fund-raising campaign.

An area in one of the humid glasshouses had been provided for the band to use for relaxation and for changing prior to the show, where we found ourselves hemmed in by a leafy mass of shrubs, flowers and triffid-like trees in an extraordinarily exotic setting.

We'd been urged to mingle and socialise with some of Nick's team-mates and their WAGS for the early evening pre-prandial drinks, and the ambience had been one of peacefulness and sophistication, with many of the girls flaunting expensive designer-labelled ball-gowns together with Jimmy Choo shoes, while others paraded sexy, brightly coloured cocktail dresses, as the boys more predictably sported Hugo Boss and Armani suits a-plenty.

As often happens at events such as these there was an auction, which we listened to with interest, huddled in a side room abutting the stage, fifteen minutes or so before we were about to burst into life.

A week in a luxury apartment at the fashionable Marbella resort of Puerto Banus, a cricket bat signed by the current England and Australia players, a pair of boxing gloves donated by a world champion from one of the many dubious divisions, and lots of other items that fetched outrageous sums from well-off businessmen trying to impress their friends, all added up to boost Nick's pre-retirement fund.

The odd box-stage was far from ideal and seemed to cramp our style a little, but we were warmly received by the charitable audience, and within minutes the place was rocking with people rushing onto the floor to shake a leg and creating a spontaneous party atmosphere worthy of the occasion.

In keeping with a peculiar British trait the lion's share of the guys jigged politely with their partners for a couple of songs, but then made their excuses before drifting off barwards to socialise with their pals, leaving the floor full of solitary females making shapes around their handbags; and within minutes on the male-dominated side of the room the fun started – big time! Tables were turned onto their sides, chairs became airborne, glasses shattered on the floor and fists began flying in all directions in what resembled out-and-out war.

The bloody battle continued for a full fifteen minutes, with many of those involved blood-spattered and nursing cuts and shiners. Inevitably the original source of the carnage had been a woman, but the scene had been more reminiscent of a wild-west saloon brawl, with the violent aggression displayed proving pretty unnerving. The performance was in ruins, but calmly we soldiered on through to the final song, and to muted but polite applause scampered out of there as fast as our legs would carry us.

I felt deeply sorry for Nick, as being a sensitive kind of guy he would no doubt have been bitterly disappointed by the disgraceful behaviour of some of his colleagues; nevertheless he had been amply compensated by the consolation of making a few quid to soften the blow(s)!

The slow-moving holiday traffic had prompted a couple of hours of conversation concerning gigs that had stuck in the memory for all the wrong reasons, as we hoped and prayed not to be on the receiving end of anything similar at this particular centre.

♫

The Exmouth park was the biggest so far, with a thousand or more caravans clinging to a rocky hillside that sloped down to an expansive sandy coastline. Arriving earlier than scheduled we found that our trailers were not yet serviced and wouldn't be ready for another hour, so to fill in the gap we strolled slowly over to take a look at the evening's venue.

The crew had not long arrived and the rear doors were still swung back whilst the gear was wheeled in up a ramp by a whole host of helpers, who courteously stepped aside to allow us through.

For a split second I thought I was hallucinating as I reached the top and walked out onto the empty stage to find that the place resembled a top-notch Las Vegas cabaret lounge.

The band's body language changed in an instant. This was undoubtedly a far classier venue, and it was plain to see that all concerned were champing at the bit at the prospect of putting on a proper performance, with no unnecessary encumbrances.

One of the stage hands wearing trousers and an open-necked shirt thrust a hand in my direction, as I noticed that even the crew had a spring in their steps. 'Hi, I'm Bob, the general manager; welcome to Exmouth. I've organised your refreshments for five p.m. in here if that's okay, and everything should be set and ready for your technical check by five-thirty.'

It was immediately apparent that he was methodical and full of professionalism, but also that he was *au fait* working alongside bands with large equipment rigs, which was just the fillip we needed, especially after recollecting old tales of woe all the way across the moors into Devon.

True to fashion the set-up proceeded unhindered and smoothly for a change, with the rehearsal lasting for well over an hour without the need for any petty interference or harsh words.

The show quite simply was the best of the entire tour, and the non-restrictive nature of the venue enabled us all to come out of our shells. After performing with renewed confidence, for the first time in weeks we could justifiably hold our heads high, like a professional rock-and-roll band should. We'd absolutely ripped the place apart, and played two genuine encores (as opposed to the usual false-tab routine); and with our pride restored it felt good to be alive again, which extended itself to the long journey home which was far more good-humoured than the majority of trips in recent weeks. With just nine more camps to visit, it seemed the worst was now behind us and surely at long last we'd broken the tour's back.

♪

The following Monday morning after a minimal amount of sleep I had a lot of catching up to do in my managerial capacity, and was on the phone bright and early to an agent friend who'd left a message for me to call him.

'Be careful,' he'd said. 'That company have a history of pulling dates on higher-paid artists once their camps are fully booked, so don't give them any excuse to do so,' he'd wisely added.

Sure enough a call came in that afternoon from a snooty woman who announced herself as 'head of customer services', who immediately went on the offensive, presumptuously tearing into me saying that one of the caravans we'd used for changing in Exmouth had been virtually stripped bare, and that the crockery, kettle, cutlery, cushions, bed-linen and stereo system had all gone missing. It was painfully clear that her accusatory finger was holding ourselves responsible.

'There are only the mattresses and the wall-mounted TV left,' she prodded.

'I can assure you one hundred per cent that no member of our party would have touched a thing,' I reasoned, trying hard to placate her, and adding: 'I'm not jumping to conclusions, but there were a number of suspicious-looking people lurking around nearby; and as you may know we didn't stay the night.'

By now she'd calmed a little and said remorsefully, 'I'm afraid we do seem to be attracting a more undesirable crowd this season, and consequently more and more things are going missing!'

I quickly recalled a white-vested man with an excess of metallic rings attached to his face, who'd parked up an old red van and had been caught peering through the window of one of our designated trailers as we'd returned to change after the show, perhaps believing it had recently been vacated, which I explained to the fretful lady.

'That could be very helpful; we may have the vehicle on CCTV,' she said in a far more endearing tone, and continued: 'I apologise if I got on my high horse when I first called; I'm sorry to have bothered you but thank you for your help.'

Arguably I should have left it at that, but instead I replied: 'I suppose in our desperation to get away we could've left the van unlocked, so I can only apologise if that was the case; but rest assured there are no kleptomaniacs in our party.'

For a moment the agent's words from earlier in the day came back to haunt me, and I thought that after the first really good performance in weeks we'd actually given them an excuse to prematurely pull the remaining dates.

I logged on to my computer and replied to a few emails, listening in the background to my wife complaining that my stage jackets smelled disgusting and were in serious need of a dry clean; and within half an hour we hopped into the car and took the offending 'high' items to the local laundry service to ensure they'd be ready for the penultimate leg of the tour, which began the following day.

30

REDEMPTION SONG
(BOB MARLEY & THE WAILERS)

Tuesday 23rd August 2005

Leicestershire was looking green and pleasant in the glistening sunshine, where the first scattering of autumnal leaves lay at the roadside as we made a late morning getaway bound for the small market town of Watchet in Somerset, situated midway between Bridgwater and Minehead on the marshy coastline by the Bristol Channel.

'Connie will be on with us tonight,' said Jeff expectantly.

Trevor misogynistically butted in: 'She's a right old slapper – she looks like a drag queen!'

Aggressively springing to her defence, Jeff asserted: 'What the fuck do you know? She's a good sort is Connie!'

I muttered my agreement from the front seat, while Trev cruelly insinuated: 'She's almost sixty!'

Instantly Jeff retorted, 'So are you and you still bloody think you look like James Bond!'

This tickled everyone on board, with the exception of Trevor, and happily the subject of Connie was quickly dropped.

♫

I'd visited the same littoral on a couple of occasions before and enjoyed the freedom of the encompassing wilderness, where even on a cloudy, blustery day there was a refreshing ruggedness about the area that would make any intrepid fresh-air freak want to don their waterproofs and get out and explore; so for a little exercise, and with our stomachs rumbling, we trekked the two miles towards the town in an effort to seek out some healthier fare than was on offer at the park.

Following my excruciating experience in Perranporth I'd become determined to make every effort to be kinder to my constitution, with no wish to literally inflame matters further, and untroubled for a few days now felt at the peak of fitness as the invigorating breeze caressed my skin and cleared my head.

Halfway along the hardened sand our resident ornithologist Rod spotted what he thought was a marsh harrier, and following his lead we crept inland to take a closer look at the creature. Dan with his camera at the ready questioned: 'Are the Harrier war-planes named after these birds, and anyway what's so special about them?'

'I just have a thing about birds of prey, and you won't see one of these every day,' answered Bill Oddie.

The nature watch was interrupted by an incoming call on my mobile, which was from the girl in the office who said: 'There's a letter that's arrived marked "Private and Confidential"; would you like me to open it?'

In the briefest of moments conspiracy theories began flying around in my head, prompted by questions such as: 'What've we done wrong now?' or 'Has something else gone missing?'

'Yes, it's probably best to open it: maybe they've fired us or something,' I quipped unknowingly; but after a brief pause she came back on chuckling:

'You're not going to believe this – it's a cheque for £415.20 for repairs to the sound desk.'

Absolutely gobsmacked I gasped and said, 'Bloody hell, I didn't expect to get that without a fight,' before thanking her, with a mental picture of my cockney pal from nine days before beseeching his directors: 'Come on, 'ave an 'eart!'

Danny and Rod were being lectured as to the different species of marsh harrier likely to be spotted in this neck of the woods by a bespectacled man clad from head to toe in khaki-green waterproofs, who explained that this one was a western marsh harrier, *circus aeruginosus*, which is the most common variety seen on European shores.

The guy was on a roll now, and although his ramblings were of some interest, I was pleased my phone had rung when it had, as he garrulously digressed with poor old Dan and Rod having difficulty escaping the excessive barrage of information. In a bid to intervene I punched Rod's number into my mobile, to hear him chirp fervently: 'Route One!'

'Never mind Route One, I can see that twitcher's boring the shit out of you – this is your chance to make an excuse and run for it!' I encouraged.

'You're not kidding; he's a major league geek, and is coming out with all sorts of stuff, most of which I don't have a clue about. See you in a sec!'

Calling over to Dan he proclaimed, 'Come on, we've got to go – we're urgently needed back at the camp!'

Danny's bobbing head soon appeared above the top of the sandbank, and upon reaching us he elaborated, 'What an interesting bloke' – to which the three of us cackled and began attempting some crazy bird impressions, before moving well away from the dunes and setting off along the coastal path into town.

We arrived in the small neighbourhood just ahead of the rain, and hurried into a hotel café on the empty main street, with the weather feeling more like March than August and a dark threatening sky looming large overhead.

'It's a bit black over Bill's back yard,' hinted Dan (this is an old East Midlands colloquialism for when a downpour is imminent).

A lady seated reading a newspaper at the next table interjected, 'According to this forecast we are supposed to be getting eighty-degree temperatures by the weekend!'

'Ooh, I'll have to get some sun cream to protect me white bits,' Dan cheekily quipped in reply.

While we scoffed noisily away there followed a heavy shower for ten minutes or more, and as it subsided we thought it best to make our way back to camp to check out the night's plush accommodation, and also to see if the inimitable Connie had arrived.

My name was scrawled on a white notice-board to the side of reception, almost illegibly in thick black ink, reading, 'Please contact a representative upon arrival,' so in haste I reported to the desk and was informed that one of my colleagues had explained I'd be willing to conduct a live interview for the local station Radio Minehead, sometime during the afternoon.

'Exactly which colleague would that have been?' I enquired, pondering who had passed the buck.

In a polite tone she answered: 'The tanned chap with the dyed hair.'

'Ah, I'm with you,' I said chuckling to myself, knowing instantly to whom she was referring; and, although I didn't mind at all, questioned as to why he couldn't have done the interview himself in my absence.

An old man sporting a Pringle golfing cap and carrying a crooked stick was complaining as an assistant clarified that there was no record of a Mrs Stewart, whom he insisted was definitely staying at the centre. 'I've driven more than a hundred miles to see her,' he protested before plonking himself down looking thoroughly exasperated and even a little sad.

Two teenage youths wearing US basketball vests came rushing out from the bar area; and for a moment I thought it was Ivan and his Ukrainian mate, who'd grappled together for our amusement just a few days before in Cornwall. I soon realised I was mistaken as I picked up on their broad Geordie accents. Some kind of affray appeared to be kicking off amongst a posse of lads outside, but a couple of interested onlookers chewing hot dogs assured me: 'Don't worry, it's just a bunch of young lads having a bit of fun!'

'If that's their idea of fun they can bloody well keep it,' I muttered under my breath, as one guy emerged from the melee with a ripped shirt and a suspected broken nose. Decidedly unimpressed I moved on in search of Sunset Boulevard, which was the idyllic-sounding avenue on which our caravan was located.

Laughter was streaming out of the trailer next door; peeping through the glass I spotted Connie entertaining Jeff and Trevor, and stuck my head in to say hello, noticing she was done up like a dog's dinner.

'Got my early spot in forty minutes, luvvy,' she almost sang in her dulcet Brummie tones, adding: 'It's lovely to see you all again; I've missed you lads, and now it's me last night on this bloody circuit so let's all make sure we have a little celebratory tipple later on!'

Rising from her seat, she bid us a fond 'turrah' before flitting along the path to her own caravan, as we looked on in envy wishing it could also be the band's grand finale.

I headed straight back to the reception area, where my impending interview with Radio Minehead was imminent, to see a slanging match taking place between an irate vacationer, who was leaving prematurely and wanted the cost of his holiday refunding in full, and an intransigent woman sporting a name badge that identified her in gold lettering as the 'Assistant Duty Manager'. Informed that the radio DJ was running ten minutes late, I hung around to do a spot of earwigging and tuned in with interest to the disgruntled customer's ranting gripe.

'I can't stay in this hell-hole for another minute, let alone another night! The TV remote is all sellotaped up and ain't working, everything stinks of dirty wet dogs, there's graffiti on the caravan walls and what's more it's miserable and bloody freezing,' yelled the enraged guy, making sure that all and sundry could listen in.

Condescendingly the uniformed woman replied, 'I doubt very much that your accommodation is as deplorable as you are suggesting, and I regret to inform you it is not our company policy to offer refunds unless there is concrete proof that your complaint is of a more serious nature; the caravans are exactly as advertised in the brochure!'

Her bumptious retort was like a red rag to a bull, and it was a blessing that the reception desk formed a barrier between her and the apoplectic customer, or I swear he would have grabbed the toffee-nosed female and attempted to throttle her.

Before long I'd lost interest, as I'd been listening to this stuff for seven weeks now, and mentally had begun winding down the clock to the final date that was incredibly just ten days away. I again laid eyes on the melancholy-looking old fellow who had now nodded off in the quietest corner of the foyer, hoping above hope that I'd steer well clear of places like this in my own dotage.

A number of cussing residents had rushed inside to take shelter from the latest of a string of ill-timed showers, and I paid heed to how the whole complex was devoid of any happiness whatsoever, until amazingly I saw a smiling face trundling in my direction with a digital recorder under his arm. His outstretched hand greeted me.

'Dave, so pleased to meet you, sorry I'm a little late; there's a handy little office just along the corridor where we can get some privacy and record the piece, so shall we crack on?'

Nodding my assent and relieved to be diverted away from the ever-increasing dissent, I followed in his wake ready to turn on the charm.

♬

My radio buddy gone, I traipsed back to the venue and stumbled across Jeff who was stood by the stage door having a crafty ciggy.

'There's something not quite right about her today; she's definitely got things on her mind,' he counselled, referring to his new best pal Connie.

'What makes you say that?' I probed.

'We were swapping addresses a little while ago, and she suddenly broke down and burst into tears. When the tour's over I'm gonna go down to see her at her place in Essex: a friend in need and all that,' he unfolded.

This seemed like a great idea, as Jeff had also been spending a lot of time alone since an upsetting divorce the year before.

'Whereabouts in Essex does she live?' I asked as if I was well-acquainted with the county.

'She said it's a small town not far from Stansted Airport,' he said, retrieving a little black book from his pocket, flicking through to the page marked 'S' and putting his finger on 'Stewart, Connie, Thaxted, Essex'.

It rapidly dawned on me that the lugubrious-looking old man asleep in the foyer had been searching for a Mrs Stewart – but it couldn't be, could it? Was this the man she hadn't seen in thirty-two or more years: the same fiend that had tried to force himself upon her when she was just seventeen years of age?

'Did she mention anything about her Dad?' I queried.

'Oh yeah, she told me she'd spoken to him, but didn't want to burden me with any more family problems,' he answered.

'I think he might be here at this camp,' I revealed.

'How would you know that?' he asked with a questioning frown.

I described how the down-in-the-mouth senior citizen in reception had been looking for a Mrs Stewart, only to be told that the register had no record of such a person.

'That explains it: she's been twitchy all day. We'd better tell her he's here,' Jeff said with a renewed sense of urgency.

Speak of the devil, almost instantly she appeared from the stage door. Jeff nodded over to me with raised eyebrows, gesturing towards Connie and intimating I should spill the beans. Taking a deep breath I delicately mouthed, 'Are you expecting any guests today?'

At this she froze dead in her tracks and, reading my expression, said: 'You're not telling me he's here are you? The stupid old git was supposed to come to Poole last night, but he got the dates mixed up. All I wanted was to get it over and done with before he curls his toes up,' she babbled cynically.

'There's a distraught old man in reception who was asking for a Mrs Stewart,' I told her.

'He's not bloody right in the head you know; why the hell didn't he tell them I'm performing here? I'm just not ready for this,' she bemoaned, working herself into a right tizzy.

'If you're not ready now, you never will be!' Jeff said purposefully, helping me out; and the least I could do now was offer to go and find the man.

Connie anxiously begged, 'Would you? Is there somewhere we can go and talk – I don't want him knowing where my caravan is!'

'Calm down and leave it with me, I'll get it sorted,' I offered, turning on my heels and jogging back towards reception.

The girl I'd spoken to earlier on was still at the desk, but the area was now deserted and there was no sign of the old stager. 'Excuse me, but have you seen the elderly guy with the walking stick?' I asked.

'Do you mean the chap that was enquiring about his daughter?' she queried.

'Yes, that'd be him. I know this may seem odd but is there any chance I could borrow the office we used for the radio interview for around thirty minutes?' I pleaded.

Helpfully she replied, 'I don't see any reason why not; will you need to use the computer?'

'No thanks, it's just a little bit of family business,' I said.

'Ah, is this some kind of reconciliation? Are you family too?' she posed.

'No, I'm just a friend trying to help out,' I assured her.

'Please just help yourself when you're ready; the room's not locked, and I'll make sure no one disturbs you.'

Complimenting her on her understanding, I went into the bar area to try and find Connie's father. He was slumped in the corner, head bowed, with a newspaper in his lap and a flat half-pint of lager on the go.

'Excuse me, are you looking for Connie?' I asked, slightly startling him.

He peered up at me suspiciously and grilled: 'Connie Stewart?'

'Yes, you're here to see her, aren't you?' I asked him cagily.

'I suppose she doesn't want to see me,' he answered despairingly.

I excused myself for a second and rang Jeff. 'Can you get her over to reception right away; there's a little office where they can both talk in total privacy.'

'Okay, she's just powdering her nose – I'll have her down there in a few minutes,' he confirmed.

With a sense of urgency I led the old chap out of the bar to the business side of reception, and ushered him into the small den. He almost impolitely implied, 'You must be her new husband,' as he squeezed his portly frame into the chair behind the office desk.

Assuring him I was nothing of the sort, and that I was simply a friend, I told him to stay put for a while as I headed back into the lobby to see if there was any sign of them.

'What on earth am I going to say to him? Please say you'll come in and stand guard,' she begged us, only yards away from the door.

With a reassuring hand on her shoulder, I said: 'I honestly don't think he's here to hurt you; in fact I doubt he'd be capable. He's just a bitter and twisted old man looking for some forgiveness. What say we come in with you, and once you feel okay we'll leave you to talk in private – can you handle that?' I suggested.

Becoming a little sentimental, which I saw as a positive sign, and welling up she said: 'I remember what you said about forgiveness the last time I saw you.'

'Well, don't you forget it. Come on – let's do it!' I urged, as we strode towards the door.

We had barely moved two paces when a piercing alarm sounded, and the camp's sprinkler system spurted into life, erratically squirting jets of water in every direction. We ducked out of the way in a hidden cranny, as the foyer area becoming saturated in next to no time.

A tall black guy garbed in yellow overalls suddenly crashed onto the scene and sprinted into a small chamber next to the toilets, and within seconds the gushing jets had come to a halt. The girl manning the desk had seen it all before, and had clearly been well prepared as she collapsed a brightly coloured umbrella and watched as we lifted ourselves up laughing and cursing; but looking over at Connie it seemed the weight had been lifted from her shoulders, as the worried countenance had vanished into thin air, almost as if the distraction was 'meant to be!'

In trepidation I opened the office door with the utmost care, and could hardly believe my eyes, as only the earnestness of the moment prevented me from bursting my sides. The old man was sitting behind the desk, soaked to the skin. Connie stepped inside and froze, before scornfully saying, 'Look at the state of you: your sordid past has come back to haunt you once and for all!' She then coughed and began laughing uncontrollably along with all of us, and the awkwardness of the reunion had been diffused in seconds flat.

The old boy rose from the chair with some difficulty and clambered to the other side of the desk; and, drenched or not, fell into an impassioned embrace with his trembling daughter, tears streaming down his face. It was an emotional, heart-stopping moment that had Jeff and myself choking, but also signalling that it was time for us to leave, as we snuck from the room unnoticed to allow them both some precious space and privacy.

Forty-five minutes later Connie re-emerged into the lobby, and Jeff caught her glance from the inner bar where we'd been lingering sharing a coffee. She looked exhausted, but also bore a look of inner contentment.

'He's just a sad old man who'll go to his grave wishing he could forever turn back the clock,' she said, far too animated to sit and join us, and continued: 'You know, I can't believe he's seen my sister six or seven times, but the sly cow never said a word to me!'

The old-timer came limping across the foyer still wringing wet, but failed to spot Connie talking with us.

'He's off back to his B&B, as he's completely worn out and very emotional. I'll get to see him before I leave in the morning. It's true what they say – that blood runs thick,' she added, watery-eyed.

Her adults-only show was scarcely an hour away, so we accompanied her back to her trailer to prepare, chatting along the way. She surmised that some bridges had been rebuilt, but that the scars sustained were deep. Even so there was an air of serenity about her that had been missing before, despite her inner turmoil.

♫

Since I'd chucked my toys out of the pram after the Allhallows debacle, things had noticeably taken a turn for the better, with the accommodation both clean and admissible, the staff making every effort to appear organised and accepting of our requirements and the foregoing doom and gloom now consigned to the history books.

That was until I overheard Steve forlornly holding court and complaining about how the band were lowering themselves playing gigs like this particular one and how badly it must be affecting our reputation, in the presence of Rod and Romeo.

Unable to perform the customary sound-check due to the pink elephant and his cuddly pals being put through their paces in an early evening kids' revue, I'd taken it upon myself to visit the venue sometime before, and could empathise with Steve's concerns; but that apart we were now closing in on the homeward straight and could hardly be surprised by whatever else was thrown at us from here on in. Accordingly I felt a sudden urge to castigate him.

'What's the point in continually moaning? It's about being a survivor,' I said out of the blue.

The three heads turned my way totally in sync, looking gone out at me. But I wasn't done yet, and launched into a further diatribe.

'That woman,' I said, referring to Connie, 'has had so much shit to deal with in her life, but whatever's been slung her way she's taken it on the chin, dusted herself down and got on with it! We've only got to put up with another eight days of this, so why can't you just bloody well do the same?'

Completely stunned by the verbal attack, Steve belligerently uttered, 'For fuck's sake,' before sloping off disconsolately; but incredibly not a soul heard him utter a single word of complaint for the remainder of the tour.

In all fairness the gig was not the easiest, and yet again the space limitations hampered the band as we never quite reached top gear; but the audience reaction had been responsive if nothing special, and the boys were in good humour as we removed our sweaty togs in the minuscule dressing-room, in readiness for Connie's post-gig farewell bash.

As we walked back through the empty venue Stefan was once more attracting a great deal of attention from a small posse of pimply teenage girls as the crew packed the gear away. Steve – who was clearly relieved that the gig was over – shouted across to them, 'Wouldn't you rather have a real man?' only to be quickly upstaged by Danny who demonstratively stood in the centre of the room with his arms flexed and yawped, 'If it's a real man you need then look no further!'

Watching her socialise with an invited crowd of in-house entertainers as well as ourselves, it was instantly apparent that a millstone had been removed from Connie's person as she happily chit-chatted and gesticulated, seemingly back to her peerless effervescent self.

The drinking went on until four a.m., with the lady in question the real centre of attraction cracking gag after gag, mixed in with a hint of sadness that most us would probably never see her again; but there was no doubt that the day's events had been inspiring, and if nothing else at least we'd done our little bit to help.

31

LIKE A HURRICANE
(NEIL YOUNG)

Wednesday 24th August 2005

December 13th 1981 is a day that will live long in the memories of the residents of Burnham-on-Sea, close to the M5 motorway on the Somerset coast.

Old press clippings report that on that fateful day the resort was pummelled by a massive storm, caused by a combination of high tides and gale-force winds that resulted in an enormous amount of damage to the town with miraculously no lives lost, although the cost of the ensuing destruction ran into millions.

The gigantic waves had literally rolled tsunami-style over the sea walls and into the town, destroying many homes and businesses in its wake, forcing the local authorities to seek outside advice that led to a complete reconstruction of the community's sea defences to prevent such extreme flooding from reoccurring in the future.

Eddie – our amiable entertainments manager – was a local lad, and recalled lugging sandbags on a bitterly cold night at three in the morning through frightening winds that near on swept him from his feet, chatting away as if the devastation had transpired only yesterday, when it had darned near happened again today!

The travelling minstrels showed up at the small Burnham camp just before lunchtime, feeling a trifle delicate post Connie's swansong. Thus far it had been a breezy but pleasant enough day, so within half an hour of our arrival, and after chucking our bags into four super-duper caravans, the three happy wanderers were more than ready to leg it down towards the sea front.

Twenty minutes further on after a bracing power-walk in the direction of the town centre, we took a break at a wooden stall on the esplanade which served up mugs of builder's tea, accompanied by delicious hot dogs on home-baked rolls, with real English pork sausages, which proved the perfect antidote to the preceding night's shedload of booze.

'There's a storm brewing,' the guy who'd served the fare forecast, rolling his r's in a characteristic West Country accent; but we were having none of it as if anything the sky seemed to be brightening by the minute, and decided to walk off the oily fare by continuing our stroll towards the shops getting further away from the camp with every step.

Considering it was the month of August, and presumably still high season, it seemed there was a dearth of people around and as a result very little open, other than the odd supermarket and the obligatory amusement arcades and redundant ice-cream stalls.

Fifteen or twenty minutes passed, and observing the menacing sky with the wind now gusting in every direction, it was plain for all to see that not only had the hot-dog man been a meteorological wizard, we'd been foolish in failing to heed his kindly warning.

With a sense of urgency we turned back towards the esplanade and saw that the waves had begun crashing in against the sea wall, with the overspill gushing vigorously onto the walkway. We stood fascinatedly witnessing the onslaught in all its powerful glory, before seconds later the heavens opened, and in no time at all the rain had become torrential.

The sprinkling of individuals scattered around were running every which way like headless chickens as the intrepid trio scurried along the prom in a desperate search for shelter, soon hitting upon a scruffy little café where, saturated and chilled to the bone by the hailing blizzard, we took refuge from the capricious elements on what had truly been four seasons in the same day.

Devouring a welcoming bowl of hot broth, we dried off, discussing the pros and cons of climate change, deducing that in fact the good old British summertime wasn't at all different from our family holidays as kids, and chuckling at a recent comment that Trevor had voiced on the subject when he'd surmised, 'All that global warming stuff is a load of bollocks!'

The hurricane ultimately subsided, and the rain let up into a light drizzle, at which point we thought it best to make a break for it and try our luck at getting back to the camp. We were not even halfway, however, and battling into severe winds when the rain began bucketing down again. This time we sought refuge in an old sea-front shelter, almost disbelieving at how wintery the weather had become. Within a few minutes the torrent died down but the black clouds and lightning overhead still spelt danger and our only hope was to make a dash for it. Pretty soon panting breaths and bundling footsteps filled the air as we neared the side road that led up to the camp.

Back in the manager's office the genial Eddie had provided towels that were draped across our shoulders, as Rod lounged in his beige boxer shorts while I sported my less trendy M&S briefs. Steam was gently rising from our wet things suspended on an enamel clothes-horse positioned by a glowing electric fire. Dan (who sensibly had been wearing a waterproof) had come out of the escapade relatively unscathed, with only his socks and trainers needing to dry out.

Eddie recalled yet more stories of the 1981 tempest, one after the other, singing the praises of the hundred or more local volunteers who'd pulled together in an incredible show of 'British Bulldog' spirit almost twenty-four years ago and bursting with pride at the moth-eaten tale. As he jovially remarked: 'Today was like a fart in a colander compared to eighty-one!'

The crew had begun clattering around in the gig next door, with Steve trying hard to bite his lip and not rock the boat, particularly as the venue was far and away the smallest yet (I'd been in people's living rooms that were bigger). That said, there was a kind of feel-good honesty and homeliness about the place.

We'd cut down on the gear considerably, as it was clear the set-up would be something of a tight squeeze; but, taking on board that the facilities were somewhat alien to us, Eddie and his small band of personnel worked tirelessly to help out and make the predicament workable.

I got this place! The park had a charm and ambience that ninety-five per cent of the camps were completely devoid of. It radiated peace with just the tweeting of birds in the background, flying amongst the surrounding tall leafy oak trees, and there were lovingly manicured beds of verdant landscaped shrubs and flowers. Even the avenues of white caravans were pristine and had a hospitable feel about them; and there were no fast-food hangouts here, or an overpriced mini-mart with an aversion to fruit.

The extreme weather had had its say for sure, but this was more akin to the caravan sites I remembered as a kid, and almost implausibly I began thinking there were far worse places to spend a week away than here, but then again I'd had getting on for seven weeks of them!

The annual family holiday should be special, and something everyone looks forward to for weeks, perhaps even months in advance; and when it boils down to it, it should be fourteen or more days of fun-filled relaxation with those nearest and dearest to you.

The average human's perception of a 'dream' holiday is perplexing, with the vast majority of people assuming a semi-deserted Caribbean island would be nothing short of idyllic, or that Disney World is the most exciting place on earth to take the kids; but curiously in my experience these theories don't always follow.

I once spent a week at the seaside town of Southwold in Suffolk – which I hasten to add I was not at all looking forward to – and had a fabulous break tucking into the locally caught fish, and sampling real ales from the Sole Bay Brewery, so much so that I almost had to be dragged away from the place to make the trip back home.

At the other end of the spectrum I took a long-haul holiday to the exotic Seychelles islands in 1982, and got caught up in a military *coup d'état*; this was the one and only time my face was plastered all over the front page of the *Sun* newspaper, with the headline reading 'POP STAR STRANDED IN PARADISE!'

The Seychellois Government had called an indefinite curfew after army mutineers had gone on the rampage, meaning that any hotel employees absent from the site were unable to travel from their homes to their place of work.

The first morning of the coup was scary, when army looters (who had already shot a loud-mouthed South African tourist for his protestations) forebodingly entered our hotel as the guests – myself and my future wife included – were taking breakfast, and rebelliously touted rifles as they walked around the tables giving the terrified residents the evil eye.

Observing that one guerrilla's trouser flies were undone, I bowed my head to conceal my amusement; but within seconds, amidst a chilling silence, I found myself peering down the barrel of an AK-47.

'Why you laugh?' demanded the gunman. Absolutely petrified, I pointed to his colleague's camouflaged britches as my whole life flashed before me. The rebel eyeballed me... and spluttered into hysterical laughter, quickly followed by his rag-tag accomplices, who mercifully found the moment as hilarious as their leader.

With a huge sense of relief that felt like a stay of execution, the guy barked, 'You big joking man, you like beautiful Seychelles?'

'I like very much,' I answered nervously. They began trooping off, taking the rise out of their comrade as he zipped up and chortling all the way out of the hotel.

The coup lasted for a full seven days until the mutiny was squashed, but during the curfew the hotel inmates continued to make merry and enjoyed a special camaraderie, as menial tasks were allotted to one another to keep things up and running. I volunteered for the job of wine waiter, but found myself at one point demonstrating my mechanical know-how, flat on my back beneath a leaking industrial dishwasher with a large rusting spanner at the ready.

Fortuitously there was a French chef holidaying in the hotel, and under his direction we dined under the stars until supplies were exhausted, ironically virtually surviving the final two days living on fresh fruit, which included the most sumptuous pawpaw I'll probably ever taste.

Admittedly it was a privilege to have visited the Seychelles in the first place; but there is something unnerving about being all those miles away from home in the midst of cultural differences, especially when there's an automatic weapon pointing in your direction, which most likely would not have been happening at that precise moment at any similar establishments in Southwold.

Being of relatively sound mind I would never for a moment perceive Britain's caravan parks as being anyone's idea of a 'dream' holiday, when the original purpose was to provide hard-working families with a cheap and cheerful alternative to living beyond their means, prior to the affordable overseas package holiday boom. They are quite simply a means to an end, and the attraction of a supposedly inexpensive seaside break together with adequate facilities to keep the kids occupied makes not only for good housekeeping, but perfect sense too.

Conversely a large proportion of these encampments were slap-happily run, paying little attention to any genuine customer service and forsaking their disgruntled clients' wishes, subsequently leaving them out of pocket and feeling ripped off, returning home incensed that their precious sabbatical had proven more stressful than if they'd put their feet up and stayed at home.

Eddie's operation – albeit on a smaller scale than the majority of the camps – was different. All of the public areas were spotlessly clean, the caravans gleamed in the sunlight as the clouds finally dispersed, and the café boasted a simple yet digestible-sounding menu that actually tempted you into giving it a whirl. Even the chambermaids (attired in Nell Gwynne type regalia) went about their daily chores of cleaning the trailers and providing crisp white bed-linen wearing a happy smile; and the bar staff too were courteous and actually enjoyed engaging in conversation, all helping to create a mood of cheerfulness as the paying guests affably made the most of their time at the park, without the faintest hint of dissatisfaction.

Our well-disposed host had pre-warned Steve that there was a noise-limiting device wired into the ballroom's system; and, as the first chord was struck during the rehearsal, Eddie ran from his office looking slightly alarmed as the power cut out.

'I thought that may happen; is it possible for you to delay the sound-check for half an hour?' he asked.

'Have we got problems?' I posed.

'No, not at all, there's nothing to worry about; but we had a comedy show-group here a few weeks ago, and every time they did a musical number there was a blackout as the RCD box tripped. We had to reset the damn thing half a dozen times, and I don't want any of that nonsense tonight,' he explained. 'I'll call an electrician and try and get it disconnected,' he added.

'No need for that – I know how to do it,' offered a helpful Steve, immediately stepping up to the plate. He followed the dependable Eddie into the back room where the power units were housed and, Bob's your uncle, ten minutes later any potential interruptions during the show had been averted.

Attracting some attention in the foyer was a man clad in a clown's outfit surrounded by a group of young children, with an African grey parrot perched on his gloved hand. The bird was keeping the kids entertained as it mimicked every word the amused sprogs were saying. Danny soon appeared at my side, and as we looked on I mentioned: 'I wonder if that bird's related to your feathered friend in Strabane!'

'He bloody well hadn't better be with all these kids listening in,' Dan retorted.

The incident I'd referred to had occurred in the inhospitable Irish border town a couple of years prior. To avoid a spate of showers the three happy drifters had diverted into a moribund-looking shopping centre on the edge of town, where just three shops were still trading with the remainder boarded up, the most inviting of the trio being a pet shop. With no serious intention of buying anything we pinged the door and entered.

Rod was first to pass inside as a caged, animated African grey to his left perked up 'All right mate?' in a screeching Ulster twang; but curiously as I followed close behind the creature bid me no welcome at all.

Dilly-dallying, Dan was last to enter; and, as he sauntered in, the parrot amazingly chirped out in a clear native accent, 'Wanker!'

Looking at each other with raised eyebrows to check we'd heard the critter correctly, it again peered into Dan's eye-line and this time croaked 'Fuck off!'

Totally flabbergasted as we were, it was impossible to keep a straight face, with the hilarity of the spectacle proving irresistible as we tiptoed through the shelved racks round in a circle which brought us back to Polly's cage.

'Hello Michael,' it voiced towards Rod, tilting its head to one side, but again totally ignored me. Meanwhile Dan, as quiet as a mouse, crept surreptitiously from behind a display of bargain dog-food, closing in on the coop, hoping to pass unnoticed.

'Dickhead,' squawked the canny feathered fiend as it spotted him, to squeals of delight from Rod and myself who'd begun acting like kids, cracking up and wanting more.

Unperturbed and obviously used to this kind of behaviour the staff just let us get on with it, but guiltily I purchased the only humanly consumable item on sale, a bottle of water.

Dan was becoming somewhat perturbed by the cawed insults coming his way, and suggested passing by the parrot in a different order to spare him further abuse, which we agreed to give a go. Taking the lead I received another 'All right mate' greeting; Dan was next in line and sneaked past in complete silence, peeping backwards and respiring in palpable relief... but only until the plumed creature caught his eye and once again uttered, 'Wanker!'

Doubling over at the parrot's superb timing we childishly completed a couple of circuits more before Polly finally lost interest, and turned his back on us.

'You can have it for fifty quid; we're sick to the teeth of being called a wanker and told to fuck off every day,' the proprietor offered.

'I'm not too sure I'd be in the wife's good books if I returned home with him,' I stated, shaking him by the hand and thanking them for their time, before heading back into the wintry gloom.

♪

Under the circumstances the show went well, with the band resorting to a more sophisticated cabaret-style approach, cracking old chestnuts about the weather mixed in with a few other old pro's tricks. The audience reacted warmly and appreciatively, much to the relief of the amiable manager who appeared backstage soon after the show's close, armed with a bottle of celebratory bubbly.

In retrospect Eddie's fine-tuned operation was more along the lines of what I'd had in mind prior to agreeing to the tour; and though the facilities had been far from ideal, the level of professionalism in all quarters had not only made the show possible, but ultimately satisfying for everyone concerned. I pondered to myself: 'Another seven nights like this and it'll be a stroll in the park!'

Breakfast was sensational, with no cold beans or excessive grease present on our plates: simply a pukka, great tasting, old-fashioned fry-up with lean bacon and Lincolnshire sausages. Trevor, however, still managed to find fault when he was served a triple-yolked egg, and complained: 'I only wanted one!'

'It *is* only one, it's just got three yolks you dumbo – it means the hen was having triplets,' interjected Rod.

'Well, it doesn't look normal to me,' said the disgruntled guitarist as he proceeded to smother the offending oddity in tomato ketchup.

As we left the café to check out and collect our things, the African grey and his handler were already on duty; but as three or four of us held back to make the bird's acquaintance, we failed miserably in our efforts to get so much as a peep out of him.

'He sulks when there's no kids around; they're right attention-seekers this breed,' said the clown.

'Are they a little bit moody then?' asked Jeff.

'Not at all, he's as gentle as a pussycat! Could I have a photograph of you all with us both?' the entertainer respectfully asked, calling on a nearby assistant to take the snap.

Stood in a line, arms around each other's shoulders with the bird taking centre stage, the creature looked towards Danny and let out a hair-raising squawk, causing him to jump to the side and out of shot.

The image finally completed, we wished the pair of them well and headed off to bid Eddie a fond farewell, as Dan sneakily looked back at the unpredictable creature and uttered: 'Wanker!'

32

GOD IS A DJ
(PINK)

Thursday 25th August 2005

For varying reasons I've long had an intrinsic dislike for the vast majority of DJs the band have so often had the dubious pleasure of working alongside. Don't get me wrong: in my humble opinion there have been many talented protagonists of the decks over the years such as Emperor Rosko, Tommy Vance, Kid Jensen and more latterly Steve Lamacq, who all share(d) a genuine appreciation for good music and consider their playlists to be infinitely more important than filling the airwaves with inane verbal diarrhoea; but, those apart, in our eons of experience we've shared stages with a whole multitude of egotistical dummies, most of whom bear no responsibility whatever for the tunes blasting out from their mixing consoles and turntables.

One episode in my career of which I'm not particularly proud was back in 1978 when the band was invited to record a song with the high-profile Radio One DJs of the day. The studio was littered with such names as Tony Blackburn, Dave Lee Travis, Noel Edmonds, Diddy David Hamilton, Simon Bates (there was a face for radio if ever I saw one!) and many more; but the session itself was to put it mildly an eye-opener, with the celeb DJs resembling a clan of hyenas released into the wild for the day as they bitched and hen-pecked from the word go.

Such was the unremitting nature of their jawing that at one point I was forced to rudely request they pipe down and concentrate on the task in hand, which was to deliver in unison a football-style chorus that provided the song's monotonous hook and which would be dubbed over the backing track that five of our members had prepared a couple of days earlier.

The record – *New Wave Band*, by Jock Swon and the Metres – was made to mark the frequency change of Radio One from 247 metres to 275 and 285 metres; and, despite receiving a fair amount of airplay, it was a mercy that the band's name remained anonymous, as the awful release justifiably sank without trace.

There is a diverse range when it comes to the differing categories of DJ, both in clubs and on local and national radio; but in an effort to simplify the reasons for my aversion I've compiled a mini-directory that should provide an insight into a large proportion of the species:

a) The Cream of the Crop

This jock is informative, shies away from a high-profile everyday life, and cares wholeheartedly about music, spending hours deliberating over his playlists. He always mentions the song title and artist, and hardly ever talks across the introduction or ending of a record. This genus I hasten to add is extremely uncommon, and in grave danger of extinction.

b) The Safe-as-Houses Operator

This breed specialises in occasional radio slots, knows his stuff, but is obsessed with furthering his career, whatever backside he has to lick. He can regularly be seen performing at the town's most high-profile nightspots which boost his social status, and plays anything from fifties rock and roll all the way through to up-to-the-moment chart tracks, including a smattering of hip-hop. The thought of being upstaged and losing the kudos of his radio show petrifies him.

c) The Poseur

Here is a guy who does well for himself. He owns the most up-to-date decks and gear, and charges well over the odds for live appearances. He would normally drive a convertible sports car, with the soft top down in February. Music is in no way his passion; however, the ladies are, and as he considers himself a local celebrity his main ambitions revolve around notches on bedposts, rather than furthering his career. The paltry financial rewards from radio stations are insufficient to be of any interest.

d) The Blatherskite

This pancake-turner is obsessed by the sound of his own voice, and rarely plays the introduction or closing bars of a recording without babbling something incoherent over the top. He does though spend no little time putting together his own mixes, thus allowing him to boast to all and sundry how creative and talented he is; but in reality he knows precious little about music, and is so far up himself that radio producers wouldn't touch him with a bargepole.

e) The Oily Git

This species is common to the north of England, and possesses strange markings and colourings, generally taking the form of highlights in the hair and an orangey protective layer of fake bake. The variety is known to flaunt gaudily patterned shirts, often unbuttoned to the navel to parade an excess of bling, and is narcissistic in the extreme. By the age of thirty-five he has four failed marriages behind him, and will work anywhere, but particularly enjoys eyeing up the mums at their children's parties.

f) The Honest Joe

As implied this fella is not in it for the money, and owns a small rig, playing predominately at church halls and local charity events for next to nothing. He is always immaculately turned out in his best bib and tucker, buys the majority of his record collection from car-boot sales, with his up-to-date repertoire downloaded from iTunes. He is a music geek and has no other mode of conversation. He is not the outgoing type and his links are often uncomfortable and nerve-jangling, but one thing he does possess is a heart of gold.

g) The Holiday-Camp DJ

This genus enters into a contract during the winter months that guarantees him a residency from May through to October. He considers himself vastly superior to the mundane day-to-day camp staff, but during his summer internship is worked half to death, performing for kids on the day shift and between the night-time 'turns', before closing the evening's entertainment until two a.m. six nights a week. He loathes his job, with the bulk of his playlist consisting of hackneyed 'oldies' (mostly listed below), the choruses of which he either sings over, or pauses to allow the audience to participate. The species is also a control freak, and cuts up rough when bands sharing his platform attempt to steal his glory. He is frighteningly insincere, and basically is an all-round unpleasant piece of work.

Categories *c)* thru *g)* could never be termed as imaginative and innovative exponents of their craft, and during each and every uninspired performance would doubtless include a number of vastly over-played, cast-iron crowd-pleasers that can be heard in tourist resorts the world over. This collection of songs we'll exhibit here as:

THE DJ'S DONE-TO-DEATH DOZEN

1. *Summer Nights* – John Travolta and Olivia Newton-John
2. *Hi Ho Silver Lining* – Jeff Beck
3. *I Am the Music Man* – Black Lace
4. *Hey Baby* – DJ Otzi
5. *Is This the Way to Amarillo* – Tony Christie
6. *Young Hearts Run Free* – Candi Staton
7. *Y.M.C.A.* – Village People

8. *Oops Upside Your Head* – The Gap Band (where everyone sits in a train formation on the filthy floor!)
9. *Saturday Night* – Whigfield
10. *New York, New York* – Frank Sinatra
11. *Macarena* – Los Del Rio; and of course not forgetting:
12. *I Will Survive* – Gloria Gaynor

It was our misfortune to come across a full-blown category *g)* case at the next camp, the location of which was the pleasant Welsh seaside town of Tenby.

It was Groundhog Day for the umpteenth time, and Steve and Stefan had turned up early as per usual to allow plenty of time for the set-up, only to find that the staff at reception had no idea which of the camp's venues the band were scheduled to perform in. Urgent phone calls were made followed by tannoy announcements requesting the presence of the 'Entertainments Team' in the foyer.

Around an hour later the band of musicians arrived and noticed the truck was parked in the reception bay, with a blue-nosed security guard pacing around the wagon and peering inside in search of the owner.

'Do you know who this truck belongs to?' he enquired abruptly. I sussed there must be a problem and, trying to buy a little time, lied: 'Sorry mate, I haven't got a clue,' before joining the rest of the gang as they descended from the bus and strolled inside to the desk.

Steve was standing conspicuously in the adjoining bar with a pint of lager on the go, while a voice perked up to our rear. It was Stef, who was quickly picking up the art of public relations from his crew boss. 'What a fuck up,' he stated bluntly. 'There's nowhere for the band to play; we've been hanging around for ages waiting for someone to make a decision, but nobody seems to know their right hand from the left!'

As he spoke a tubby man in a black open-necked shirt paced into reception, and over-officiously laid into the girl at reception. 'Jean, what the hell is happening? I can't even have my lunch without being disturbed!'

'I'm sorry, Mr Eames, but the band have turned up for tonight's show, and nobody seems to know which room they are supposed to be playing in,' she calmly replied.

Clearly perturbed, Mr Eames raised his voice and looked brazenly towards us. 'In the Vegas Show-Bar of course,' he carped. 'It's a special seventies-themed evening, which is why we've run to the expense of employing these gentlemen!'

The girl reacted a little dumbly, saying, 'I spoke to Geno and he didn't know of any live band playing in the Vegas tonight; he just said he'd brought some lighting over from the Stardust lounge and that he's spent the whole morning decking out the stage!'

With a look of apoplexy the manager lifted the wooden flap and marched into a nearby office, dragging the hapless Jean with him, and listening in we could make out their muffled, heated voices. Soon after, a distorted announcement was made for all to hear: 'Geno Sanchez to reception, immediately!'

Mr Eames reappeared and obsequiously apologised to us all. 'There's not much point putting on a special night with star cabaret if we can't find somewhere for you to play,' he girlishly explained with a nervous high-pitched laugh.

Just as he finished his sentence, a guy dressed from head to toe in white with dyed jet-black hair and sunglasses strode arrogantly into the foyer and made straight for the manager before baying: 'Gerry, I've just heard there's supposed to be some fucking band on in the Vegas tonight. I've gone out of my way to make this night special, and now this; well, I'm not fucking having it!'

'Geno, you will refrain from using that kind of language in a public area – next time, in accordance with house rules, I will fine you. We've gone well over budget to put this act on, so you must clear your stuff from the stage onto the side rostrum,' the ruffled manager countered.

'Impossible! I was told I had full control over this seventies night and I won't be moving a thing. This is my gig, Gerry, not some poxy band's!'

Steve had been keeping tabs from the far side of the reception area, and couldn't resist chipping in: 'Perhaps we'll just have to move your stuff for you,' followed after a short pause with, 'What a big-headed twat!'

The DJ turned on a sixpence, and dangerously put to Steve in true Robert De Niro style: 'Are you talking to me?'

The crew boss instantly fired back: 'No, Humpty Dumpty, you bloody tosser!'

The proverbial shit hit the fan after Steve's comment, with things getting pretty hairy until Gerry intervened, waving his arms around: 'I will not have a pitched battle breaking out in a public area; perhaps this can be resolved in a more gentlemanly fashion?'

'Name your weapon, or better still I'll just give the wanker a good hiding,' Steve carped aggressively.

In an attempt to placate things I touched Geno's arm, and beckoned for him to come outside for a little heart-to-heart.

'We are here to do a gig, and despite what you may think we are going to do it; so I suggest you co-operate or this is going to be a long night – and we wouldn't want any of your precious gear to become accidentally damaged now, would we?' I put to him.

'Are you threatening me? Look, I was asked to put on a Glam Rock show with no mention of a fucking live band,' the idiot disrespectfully exclaimed.

Even I was becoming irritated by him now, and countered, 'Oh I see, so everyone on this camp is getting togged up in their seventies gear especially to see you are they?'

'This is a joke; I don't need this shit,' he ranted, before storming off in his starched white flares.

The band and crew, upon Mr Eames' instructions, drove the short distance to the 'Vegas Show-Bar' where assistance had already arrived to rearrange the stage area. The four lads humping the gear seemed over the moon that we'd got one over on Geno, towards whom there was a clear antipathy.

'He thinks he owns the bloody place,' one of them commented, followed by a remark from another helper:

'I don't know where he got his name from 'cause he ain't Italian, you know – he's from Bury in Lancashire!'

Ninety minutes later with the gear set and our run-through complete, we wandered back to the basic but acceptable caravans. Something was bothering me in the back of my mind, suspecting that Geno's ego would rear its ugly head before the night was out; but little did I know how on the ball my instincts were to prove.

The Lancastrian wop's introduction instantly spelt danger, with a string of carefully chosen words designed to belittle the band in every way possible. In an awful mid-Atlantic drawl he whittled, 'Hey dudes, it's time now for the live band; I'm told these guys had a couple of hits in the seventies, so they must be a little long in the tooth by now, but don't worry people 'cause I'll be back in just one hour with wall-to-wall hits from the real stars of the seventies; anyways here they are... *Showdaddydaddy!*'

A large proportion of the crowd tried with some difficulty to correct him, but he brushed them aside thinking his insult so clever, whilst continuing his waffling for the duration of the band's recorded intro of the wartime classic *The Dambusters March*. The jingoistic piece as always was followed by a rousing instrumental aimed at setting the scene and impressing the audience with a few tricky guitar licks along with a semi-choreographed routine, which in general would include some nifty, but slightly uncoordinated footwork.

Twanging their way through Duane Eddie's *Peter Gunn*, the boys then thrashed into a pseudo-punk version of the Shadows' original *FBI*, demonstrating a sense of urgency that had been lacking in so many of these camps.

To enthusiastic applause Romeo began belting seven bells out of his kit, as I emerged from the wings breaking into, 'Everybody say yeah-yeah,' which the audience raucously mimicked – as, disturbingly, an amplified voice other than my own was heard bellowing 'yeah-yeah' through the PA system. Shrugging it off and peering across at Geno's rostrum with clenched teeth, we closed out the song – *Dancing Party* – only to witness the same interruptive tone loudly hollering, 'Hey folks, Showaddydaddy live in the Vegas Show-Bar,' from the attention-seeking DJ who now evidently considered himself to be part of our act.

Going into my introductory verbal routine as Romeo thumped the bass drum in the background, I yelled, 'It's good to be here! Let's get this party started – everybody clap your hands,' but again the moronic DJ intruded: 'Yeah c'mon people, clap yer hands with Geno and Shoodaddywaddy!'

This was becoming ridiculous, but I figured even he'd have to call it a day before long. To our amazement, however, well into our next song *You Got What It Takes* there he was yelling some other pathetic mispronunciation of the band's name, before singing tunelessly along with me in the chorus.

Enough was enough! The song ended, with the crowd appearing bewildered and distinctly irked by the streaky-haired egotist's interventions.

'We appear to have an uninvited seventh member who's making a helluva nuisance of himself, but he's going to stop now,' I told the punters, shaking my fist towards the podium.

Remarkably during the next couple of numbers he refrained from any further irritating interference, but still retained an air of menace as he boogied for all to see from his position close to the stage.

Finding it impossible to resist for too much longer, during a pause between songs as I chatted to the crowd the temptation proved too great as he suddenly bawled into his microphone, 'Everybody say yeah-yeah,' to startled looks and no response whatever from the holidaymakers, who were fast becoming as angry as the band and gestured their displeasure in no uncertain terms.

It was time to nip this in the bud, once and for all. 'Will you shut the hell up?' I shouted forcefully, to cheers from the supportive crowd who were firmly in the band's corner; but like water from a duck's back he retorted in his irritating drawl:

'Hey man, it's party time, ain't no need to get uppity – let's all enjoy ourselves.'

A chorus of boos rang out from the furious punters, as I spotted Mr Eames rushing over towards the podium; but Steve had already left his mixing position and beaten him to it. Like a man possessed, the roadie ferociously wrestled the microphone from Geno's grasp and proceeded to rip the cable straight from its socket, shearing the lead in the process, soon after which a succession of red lights dimmed as he tore his hand aggressively across the rack of amplifiers, finally silencing the conceited meddler.

There followed a slight scuffle between the moron and the park manager, but a bulky security guard was soon on hand and escorted the deluded DJ from the building to howls of derision. 'Everybody say bye-bye,' I loudly advocated, as close on six hundred hands waved towards the exit, giving the buffoon a fitting send-off. To add insult to injury I satirically screamed, 'Hip-hip hooray!' to which the revitalised crowd's response almost took the roof off, as belatedly in an electrified atmosphere we duly ripped into another song.

The shackles had been well and truly removed, and the band rocked with a renewed vigour of which any up-and-coming young band would've been proud. With the evening temperature continuing to soar, the sticky, perspiring crowd lapped it up; and ultimately, without the aid of any additional support, we enjoyed a great night.

After slipping out of my sweaty things I headed back to the seclusion of the caravan, feeling the need for a little space, on what was one of those rare balmy summer nights which could have been in any Mediterranean resort.

Taking a deckchair from the caravan cupboard I reclined outside beneath the stars with my iPod for company, and scrolled down to the band I've forever associated with warm summer days and nights, namely the Beach Boys; and put on one of my all-time favourite albums – *Pet Sounds*.

Before long it dawned on me that this masterpiece bore none of the sterile trademarks of many twenty-first-century productions, and that in truth music hasn't really moved on one iota. Television is largely culpable as our screens are plagued in the modern age with talent-show this, reality-show that, *Strictly Come Dancing* or some watered-down satellite equivalent, and a plethora of wannabes obsessed with becoming famous by whatever means, as opposed to displaying a unique, God-given talent for the nation's visual pleasure.

God Only Knows played; and I leant back, almost in a trance listening to the evocative harmonies, admiring a quite beautifully constructed piece of music that surely would have had many of the great classical composers quaking in their laced-up boots. I drank in the peace of the moment as the moonlight in a clear night sky created shadows over the grass-topped sand dunes nearby.

When the song ended, removing my in-ear headphones I became aware of a rustling sound to the rear of the trailer, and jumped up to try and find the root of the disturbance. A petty fly-tipper had dumped a black plastic bin-liner full of rubbish and rotting food underneath the neighbouring caravan, and the bag had subsequently been ravaged by a mischief of rats, which were busy demolishing the smelly contents.

I truly despaired: even on a beautiful night such as this, in the haunting dimness beyond the bewitching hour, it was impossible to escape the squalor we'd endured for the best part of two months; and my surreal musical interlude was over for the night, as I scratched restlessly before hitting the sack.

Prior to leaving the following morning, whilst walking across to share a coffee and sort out some fuel bills with Steve, I was waylaid by an anxious-looking couple who had mistaken me for a member of staff, no doubt swayed by the briefcase I was carrying.

'There's not one bleeding Go-Kart working up at that track; it's absolutely disgusting – your company should offer us compensation 'cause our kids are devastated,' ranted the thickset woman.

'I'm sorry, I don't work...'

She cut me straight off. 'What are our boys supposed to do? They set their hearts on using that track; now they're bored to tears! And what's more...'

I was forced into interrupting her, and said firmly: 'I'm trying to tell you I don't work here, or for the company!'

'No need to get funny, mate; are you sure you can't do anything?' she persisted.

'I really wish I could help, but I'm pleased to say I'm only here for the day!' I explained.

'Come on, Madge, let's get loaded up and piss off,' said her disenchanted husband, as I walked on shaking my head yet again in disbelief and muttering to myself, 'Another satisfied customer!'

Retribution can be swift, but – for he who waits – heart-warming; and I couldn't help but notice a look of warm satisfaction in Steve's eyes as I joined him in the coffee-shop by reception.

'Wait until you see this,' he smugly intimated, nodding over to the desk.

Two ostentatiously coloured suitcases stood unattended, and from behind closed doors a muffled fracas was taking place in the manager's office. We shuffled our chairs closer to the adjoining door to eavesdrop on the proceedings.

Geno suddenly appeared – almost swinging the door from its hinges – looking like Johnny Cash clad all in black, and with a face like thunder, followed shortly afterwards by an equally furious Mr Eames. The DJ lifted up the heavy cases and lugged them out of the doors to a waiting souped-up Ford Mondeo. He stowed the items in the boot and leapt into the car, hitting the accelerator like a madman before speeding off with baffles farting like a boy-racer, bumping over the ramps and out of the park.

Steve caught Mr Eames' attention, and as he walked over to join us he gasped, 'Good riddance,' informing me that Geno had been sacked with immediate effect. Punching my fist into the air with a broad smile I offered contentedly: 'I think today is gonna be a great day!'

33

ONCE IN ROYAL DAVID'S CITY *
(TRADITIONAL CHRISTMAS CAROL)

Friday 26th August 2005

The exertions of the previous day had interfered totally with my
aspirations to relax and catch some of the fourth Ashes test match on
TV, but to atone the newspapers were full of it. 'IS CRICKET THE
NEW FOOTBALL?' read one of the headlines; but whatever, there
was no doubting that public interest in the sport was at an all-time
high, with fans unable to obtain tickets, and thousands turning up at
Trent Bridge in Nottingham only to be locked out.

The match itself was evenly poised, with England on two hundred
and twenty-nine for four wickets at the close of play on the opening
day; so I was determined to witness a little bit of history in the making
today, particularly as we only had a five-mile hop to the next camp at
Lydstep. Fifteen minutes after leaving Tenby, whilst driving along an
attractive country lane, we picked up a sign for the camp over to the
left; and three hundred metres further ahead in the centre of the road
stood a red and white barrier next to a cubicle which housed a
uniformed man in what appeared to be a naval officer's cap.

'Can I help you gentlemen?' he courteously asked, to which we
explained the purpose of our visit; but that was in no way sufficient to

---

* Two wonderful versions are featured on Sufjan Stevens' *Songs for Christmas*
album.

allow us a speedy entry, as barking into a walkie-talkie he informed the powers that be that we were waiting at the entrance.

Shortly afterwards the guard manually lifted the barrier and directed us through to weave our way for a further half a mile down a narrow winding lane, where concealed caravans poked their noses from beneath a woodland plantation, giving the initial impression that a degree of privacy was the order of the day at this enterprise.

The park was appealingly small and bucolic, with a river running through its centre, and our hopes were raised as we perceived a similar operation to that of Eddie's place in Burnham-on-Sea.

We finally happened upon civilisation and a smartly dressed man in a navy-blue blazer flagged us down, uttering a garbled message into his personal walkie-talkie. Rod observed: 'Do you remember that road that used to run from the West German border through the east to Berlin, where they timed your journey?'

'I know what you're thinking!' I replied, and we said in accord: 'They just put the clock on us from the gate to here!'

We were promptly distracted, as the dapper man opened the vehicle door and announced in a militaristic tone: 'A very warm welcome, gentlemen; will you please report to reception and check in?'

'What's all this about, it's a bit over the top for a crappy holiday camp innit?' Romeo questioned as we scrambled out.

The well-groomed host picked up on some of our comments as we moved inside and remarked, 'We are aware that you have experienced procedural problems at other centres owned by this company during the past weeks, but rest assured we like to think of Lydstep as being autonomous, and pride ourselves on courtesy and efficiency; so if there's anything we can do to make your stay more comfortable, we are constantly at your service!'

There was no faulting his impeccable manners and sense of chivalry, but Romeo was spot on: this was way over the top for what was basically nothing other than a caravan site.

The genteel receptionist requested we all sign the register, and handed over three large white envelopes bearing the company logo for our safe keeping, which contained the keys to the night's accommodation.

The pastoral lane wound back in the direction of the camp entrance, as we followed the map and took a sharp right turn into a glade that harboured a dozen or so neatly laid-out caravans, with our allocated ones situated on Arboreal Avenue, which was marked by a carved wooden sign. Happily upon inspection the trailers were clean and well-equipped, and would doubtless serve us well for the duration of our stay.

I'd called my wife first thing to wish her a happy wedding anniversary, but she'd understandably been feeling a little low with my being away for yet another celebration (for some coincidental reason we perennially seemed to be on the road when it came to family birthdays and the like) and it saddened me that she was unhappy.

Indeed it takes a special kind of woman to put up with a husband who constantly works unsociable hours, and spends a lot of time away from home, when RSVPs to wedding or party invitations are often returned making excuses for non-attendance, and friendships become strained as weekend soirées occasionally have to be reorganised for a working mid-week day to assure our esteemed presence.

Fortunately for me my good lady is probably the most tolerant woman I've ever met, but that apart it was still a little unfair that she'd be spending the day alone, and I'd just have to – yet again – organise something a little bit special for when I returned home at the weekend.

♫

The lure of the water was too great for Dan to resist, and sure enough within minutes he came banging on the caravan door to ask if we wanted to join him in some maritime pursuits. Rod was champing at the bit, but I declined and switched on the TV hoping to catch up on the day's events at Trent Bridge.

I cursed bitterly as I flicked through the five terrestrial channels to find no sign of twenty-two sportsmen clad in white sweaters and flannels; upmarket as this camp liked to portray itself, there was no satellite TV on which the test match was exclusively live.

I called Rod on his mobile and asked: 'Are you likely to need the Previa in the next few hours?'

'I wouldn't have thought so; why, are you planning to go off somewhere?' he queried.

'Yeah, I'm going to while away the afternoon with a visit to St David's.'

Over the course of the previous thirty-two years I'd travelled to almost every UK city, with the exception of Lichfield, Brechin in Scotland (which was no longer a city) and St David's in Pembrokeshire, so here was an opportunity I couldn't let slip with the ancient settlement being just forty miles north-west of Lydstep.

With regular cricket updates on the radio I drove along a quite stunning stretch of coastline that spanned the westernmost strand of Wales, stopping off to check out the view over St Brides Bay from an elevated locality called Newgale. On a glorious summer's day the uninterrupted panorama was truly breathtaking, and I found it hard to come up with a similar headland in Britain that is so spectacularly unspoilt and beautiful.

I resumed driving onwards to the smallest city in the United Kingdom, and came across a rural neighbourhood that was more akin to a sleepy village, with a sprinkling of art galleries, tea houses and souvenir shops littering the main street.

Parking though was problematical, as I wound to the right down an undulating road, where before my eyes stood the huge cathedral buildings from which the conurbation's city status had been granted during ancient times.

I parked up on a shingle track close to the tourist route, purchased a pay-and-display ticket and went for a wander, firstly checking out the twelfth-century cathedral, and continuing on to the magnificent Bishop's Palace ruins; but after a cultural treat that had lasted all of forty-five minutes I was desperate for some sustenance and made my way up to the quaint shopping street.

In no time at all I found a small establishment full of charm, with an appealing value-for-money lunch menu, but more importantly mounted on the wall was a TV showing live cricket.

With a limited choice I ordered a wholesome light lunch with a pot of tea, and reclined in my chair to take in the afternoon session. An old chap on the next table leaned over and murmured: 'See – it took a proper Welsh boy to come to England's rescue today!'

I turned towards him and commented, 'I didn't realise Freddie Flintoff was a Taff!'

'Naw naw, not 'im, I'm referrin' to the Jones boy – Geraint the yeng wicket-keeper,' the quite clearly local man retorted.

'He's about as Welsh as I am: he was born in Papua New Guinea,' I commented, further winding him up.

To be fair both players were giving the Aussie attack a caning, but the beefcake Lancastrian Flintoff was closing in on his first test ton against the old enemy.

Amidst the calming setting my mobile trilled, and seeing on the screen it was Steve, I whispered, 'Oh no, that's all I need!'

'Dave, where the hell are you? I think you should come and have a look at the gig,' he voiced in a measured tone and without complaint.

'Is there a problem?' I asked, after explaining where I was.

'I'd better let you be the judge of that,' he replied, trying his best to be non-confrontational.

'It'll take me the best part of a couple of hours to get back, so shall we meet at five p.m.?' I suggested, adding: 'I'll see you later.'

'I 'ate those bleddy things, nobody can never get a moment's peace,' whined the old feller.

'I totally agree,' I replied with a smile, adding, 'but I'm in Wales on business, and at least it's allowed me the opportunity to see your lovely little town.'

'*City*,' he was sharp to correct me.

Driving back I considered the tone of Steve's voice when he'd called; it became blatantly obvious that all was not well over at the gig, and that he had most certainly been keeping his cards close to his chest as he spoke.

The one-way traffic system around the county town of Pembroke was at gridlock, so rather than take a look at the famous castle as I'd intended, I surveyed the buzzing hive of activity from the clammy innards of the largely stationary works bus. 'Oh well, I can say I've been,' I mused, feeling slightly under-impressed by the historic place as I finally got moving away from the congested streets and picked up the signs to Tenby.

Jeff was busy chatting to the jobsworth at the barrier as I arrived back, but even so I was given a third-degree grilling by the man, as the bass-player hopped up into the front passenger seat for a lift back down to his trailer.

'Turn right here and take a look at this,' he said, about a hundred metres along the lane, and with my right hand down we pulled into a tucked-away clearing to find a quartet of weather-beaten caravans that looked in need of a good scrub-up.

Parked by the first one was a Japanese four-wheel-drive jeep with a trailer attached, presumably for a boat, with the second algae-covered van appearing to be unoccupied with all the curtains drawn and not a flicker of life. A beat-up old Mini lay alongside a rotting Suzuki jeep that was listing to one side strewn across the forecourts of the third and fourth trailers, where two families were seemingly having difficulty in setting up a joint barbecue venture on a raised decking area that skirted around the caravan entrances in an L-shaped formation.

'What's so special about this?' I asked him, almost lost for words.

'Look in the rear windows of the three inhabited caravans,' he urged, with an incredulous look on his face.

Exactly how I hadn't picked up on what was bothering him, I wasn't sure, but boldly displayed in each double-glazed pane were wooden placards with vivid yellow lettering that read, 'Owners in Residence.'

'Are you with me now?' asked the niggled Jeff, before continuing his tirade, 'Fucking snobs, that's taking it to a new level,' he bleated.

Having enjoyed my chilled-out foray away from the park I found his reaction strangely amusing and began chuckling, but he wasn't finished yet. 'Who in their right mind would want to advertise that they're the proud owners of one of these shit-heaps? That's the most stupid piece of one-upmanship I've ever seen,' he cantankerously ranted on.

To be fair he did have a point, as this was a pretty low-life form of elitism which not only was flabbergasting, but in many ways needless and abstruse.

'Ah well, each to their own, if it rocks your trailer,' I joked dismissively, before attempting to divert him away from the subject and chucking in, 'I think we've got problems at the gig again.'

'Oh, I know that, I've been down there: the place is just a pub!' Jeff informed me.

Looking him directly in the eye, I thought out loud and groaned, 'Shit, here we bloody well go again!'

There was a crowd of thirty or more drinking in the Tavern in the Wood, which doubled as tonight's gig. They roared enthusiastically as Matthew Hoggard was ripping through the Australian batsmen with an inspired spell of swing bowling, on the bar's new flat-screen TV. The cheers of our patriots, however, rang hollow in our eardrums as everyone stood, hands on hips, trying to work out how we could put on a presentable show in such a weirdly shaped and restricted venue.

A lady in a bright red summer frock was trying to catch my attention, as she waved from the double saloon-bar doors at the far end of the room. I mooched towards her to try and make out what she was mouthing.

'Would you be so kind as to have a photo taken with our party? We love your music, especially *Under the Blue Moon* and *Tiger Feet*,' she bade in a nasal tone much to my annoyance.

'Okay, no problem, I'll be with you in a sec,' I politely shouted above the hubbub across to her.

The guys were busy tuning up and making adjustments to the amps, so leaving them to it for a few minutes I sauntered across to the estranged area and was ushered through the saloon doors, where two chunky chromium-plated airport-style stands carrying thick bands of yellow tape prevented all and sundry from entering the exclusive facility without being vetted first.

A large wooden sign was mounted on the wall above the entrance that advised in no uncertain terms, 'OWNERS ONLY – KEEP OUT!'

'Do I need to curtsy as I enter, or will a toastmaster announce my arrival?' I joked facetiously.

'Don't be silly – it's just that we don't take kindly to riff-raff tenants strolling in here as if they own the place,' she prudishly affirmed.

Feeling a trifle agitated at the overblown display of discrimination, I posed a loaded question: 'Maybe that's because you people in here actually *do* own the place?'

Either exceptionally thick-skinned or not at all catching my drift, she haughtily chuckled, 'Ha ha, I never saw it quite like that, but I suppose in a way we do,' and went on: 'We've all worked terribly hard to make this centre far more exclusive than many of the downmarket resorts that this company see fit to put their name to!'

Reining myself in, and needing to make a break for it, I politely asked: 'You wanted me to pose for a photo with you and some of your pals, didn't you?'

'That would be absolutely marvellous darling, and who knows you may even make it into the rogues' gallery behind the bar,' she painfully screeched.

Studying the autographed mug-shots that had pride of place on the wall of shame, I saw Keith Harris and Orville (who had actually signed the photo too), Little and Large, the Black Abbots, and many other less celebrated artists who'd shared the distinction of rubbing shoulders with the elite of the owners in residence.

Once the snapshot had been taken I was offered no thanks, or for that matter hospitality, and was without delay shepherded back to the plebeian side of the yellow-taped boundary, feeling a sense of relief as I trod back to the reality of the sound-check.

The tiny stage could hardly accommodate Romeo's drum kit, and it was decided the band would have to work the floor, which in truth meant we'd be encroaching on the public area by the main bar. The entertainments rep was not at all happy with this state of affairs; as he stressed, 'You won't be able to move a muscle in here tonight.'

'Well, we've got no chance of getting six musicians on that plinth,' I pointed out.

'I understand that, but your speakers will be right in front of the VIP area, and they'll have my guts for garters,' he claimed.

'Are these VIPs the owners in residence?' I enquired.

'Indeed they are, sir,' confirmed the rep.

'I get you. So they'll be slumming it in here for the duration of our show, will they?' I cheekily suggested.

He raised his eyebrows, his expression saying it all, as not another word passed his lips.

The lengthy tour was seriously taking its toll as I struggled hoarsely through the brief sound-check, noticing also that the ubiquitous yellow-taped stands had been moved and repositioned around four rows of chairs to the front right-hand side of the performance area. This presumably had been earmarked as the exclusive VIP pen, which made little sense at all as we recognised that those seated at the end of the tiers would be virtually deafened by the proximity of the PA system. When I pointed it out to Jeff, he carped: 'It serves 'em right for being so far up their own arses!'

However, in reality this venue was not just a tight squeeze, but compared to the twenty-seven we'd already played it was the most unworkable of the lot. Yet with barely two hours to the scheduled performance time, there was little or nothing we could do to change matters.

Under duress the band's performance was better than expected, but on a personal level the gig had been something of an ordeal, with my respiratory system affected badly by the dust and irritating ticks from the nearby harvesting of the region's crops. The air quality, together with my ailing vocal chords from weeks of overuse, had caused an intermittent bout of asthma to kick in, which is every vocalist's worst nightmare; but that said I was left with no alternative but to tough the gig out, use every ounce of professionalism in my bones and put on a brave face.

The VIPs were seated – a few of them with their arms folded – in a kind of judge-and-jury juxtaposition, reminiscent of *The X Factor*, which was a little unsettling for the band; but most of them along with the riff-raff majority were the worse for drink, and gladly the razor blades in my throat came through as incomprehensible and went largely unnoticed.

A royal summons was received for us to 'take drinks in the owners' bar,' which was politely declined. Jeff, still with a bumble-bee in his bonnet, commented: 'I'm glad you said no; I wouldn't have gone anyway, the stuck-up twats!'

The day's events had gotten too much for me; and, desperately in need of a good night's sleep, and some loving care on my anniversary, I sloped off back to Arboreal Avenue.

Rod was up bright and early at eight a.m. the next morning, but without realising the time I promptly vacated my snore-bag to put the kettle on.

Still half-asleep, he seemed to be making a meal of zipping up his waterproof; I asked, 'You off somewhere?'

'Yeah, Dan and I met a guy with a mooring just along the river; he promised to take us out on his boat for the best bacon sandwich anywhere in the world. Do you wanna come? I'm sure he'd have room for one more,' he made out.

Looking at the clock, and still in a daze, I said, 'I hadn't better; I'm gonna rest up and try and grab another hour's kip. I'd like to be on top of things by tonight!'

The decision turned out to be a wise one, as twenty minutes later the rain began hammering down on the caravan roof.

34

(SITTIN' ON) THE DOCK OF THE BAY
(OTIS REDDING)

Saturday 27th August 2005

Dan and Rod arrived back at the caravan shortly after ten-thirty a.m., resembling a pair of drowned rats.

'How was the bacon sarnie?' I asked flippantly.

'Don't ask,' said Dan, leaving Rod to take up the mantle: 'It was choppy as hell out there, and it pissed it down all the way there and back; Dan left his breakfast over the side of the boat!'

'Not to worry; so you won't be up for another trip out to sea later on?' I enquired.

'How do you mean?' asked Rod.

Doing a feeble impression of David Attenborough I bookishly told them about a resident pod of bottlenose dolphins famed for their personal appearances in Cardigan Bay, and particularly just off the coast at New Quay, our next port of call, from where there were regular trips out to study the local marine life, and even swim with the friendly critters.

'There's no way I'll be doing it – my stomach's churning like a washing machine,' said a pale-looking Dan; and Rod agreed that he too had gone through enough bumping around in a boat for one day.

The wagon was loaded up, and we took our leave, bidding farewell to the owners in residence hidden away in their private glade before wishing *bon voyage* to Jeff's security-guard pal at the gate as he liberated us from the complex. Rod then hit the gas as we proceeded towards the Welsh backroads in a northerly direction. Within seconds the verdant fields were abundant with sheep, and the landscape reminded me of some photos I'd studied in a New Zealand tour brochure.

Worn-out jokes about Welsh leisure centres and the locals' sexual preferences soon came springing to mind; but the gang finally settled down into scrutinising the daily rags, as we continued to carve our way through the Dyfed countryside.

Play was under way in the test match, and the media hoo-hah even had the non-converts curious to find out what was going on in Nottingham, where our boys certainly carried the upper hand.

We reached a 'blink and you'll miss it' hamlet, and braked suddenly to make a pit-stop at a garage which could have been mistaken for a tractors' graveyard: rusting old agricultural vehicles and other mechanical debris were cluttered all over the place. I hopped out and asked a florid-faced man for thirty quid's worth, taking into account that the advertised pump prices were too steep to fill her up to the brim.

'It's not a diesel model is it?' enquired the lone proprietor.

'No mate, normal unleaded,' I replied.

'Only I've got a hell of a deal goin' on red diesel – I'm sellin' it at half the price of the other stuff,' he craftily emphasised.

'That's a pity, but this is a petrol engine mate,' I confirmed.

A pregnant pause occurred, as the old boy began pumping the fuel into the bus.

'Hell of a deal I say: half price the usual stuff and it runs every bit as well,' he reiterated.

'Yes, it's a real shame we're not running on diesel or I'd have snapped your hand off,' I agreed, trying to remain polite.

'Well, it's stupid to go throwin' money away when you can get a bargain like that, isn't it?' he blabbed on.

'If I hear of anyone looking for diesel I'll point them in this direction for sure,' I said, with a hint of sternness.

He still rambled on: 'Far too many people throw their money around these days with the silly fuel prices, and I've got diesel here at half price!'

'So you keep saying; look, I tell you what, when we get to New Quay I'll see if there's a mechanic who can convert us over to diesel, then we can make a point of coming back this way tomorrow to get her filled to overflowing,' I beefed satirically.

My sarcasm fell on deaf ears, as he just murmured, 'Okay, that'll be thirty pounds and a penny.'

Not having the time or the inclination to argue the toss over one penny, I took the notes from my pocket and rooted around for some change, but the smallest I had was a twenty-pence piece, which I gave to the man, generously telling him to put the extra coinage into his charity box.

As I turned to walk back to the bus he pulled me up: 'There you go, that's exactly what I was sayin' – just throwin' bloody money away!'

♪

New Quay (not to be confused with Newquay, the Cornish equivalent) is basically an old seaside fishing village perched on a ridge between Cardigan and Aberystwyth in the lesser known county of Ceredigion on the west Wales shoreline. From the perfect angle it possesses an archaic quaintness almost as if time has stood still; but in stark contrast whilst panning around from the harbour the viewer is confronted with a multitude of dowdy-looking off-white caravans that cling to a shabby hillside leading down to a shallow beach on the edge of the small municipality.

New Quay's main claim to fame is that it was home to the legendary playwright and poet Dylan Thomas from 1944 to 1945, when he was said to have frequented its surplus of local hostelries with enormous vigour. My only lasting schoolboy memory of Thomas' work was of a fictional Welsh village called Llareggub (try spelling it backwards) in his celebrated drama *Under Milk Wood*, which made me ponder just how easily the smaller, more mischievous pearls of wisdom spring back to mind from one's formative years; I deliberated whether this may have been the village in question, as there certainly wasn't a lot going on around here!

It was now a month to the day since my Mum's passing, so I left my chums at the site, craving a little solitude to wallow in my thoughts, and took my journals down to a quiet spot by the quay, sitting in the sunshine with my legs dangling over the ramparts, and adding a few notes to my ever-expanding account of the happenings of the past eight weeks.

The peace was broken by a whirl of activity as a bevy of tourists dashed to the water's edge excitedly raising their binoculars, as a pair of dolphins had entered the bay and were performing somersaults to the delight of the onlookers. My melancholia vanished as I watched the captivating creatures entertain the small crowd with an effortless display of synchronised swimming that surely would've lifted anyone's spirits.

Five minutes later they leapt up, nosedived and disappeared from view. A little girl, who was wrapped up as if it were February, screamed and urged her father to get them to come back; but sadly the show was over, with little chance of an encore.

Back up the road at the base camp I entered the venue through the reception area, and became confused as I spotted half a dozen large A2 posters, plastered right by the entrance, advertising a Queen tribute scheduled for August 27th. Not a single soul would have realised that we were also scheduled to perform – at great expense – on the very same night; but an added concern was the amount of space another act would take up: and having thus far encountered cuddly characters, dancing girls, canine guest appearances, along with a host of other weird and wonderful floor-shows, there really was no call for any further intrusive obstacles to encumber our ability to perform.

On the plus side the crew boys Steve and Stefan looked happy enough, perched upon tall stools at the bar relaxing with a pint of lager apiece.

The rig appeared to be set in its entirety on the amply sized platform, and there was no sign of any extra gear belonging to the royally appointed tribute band, other than a banner draped across the top of the stage that read 'We Are The Champions.'

'Do you know what time they're putting this Queen outfit on?' I puzzled to the crew boys.

'Around nine o'clock,' said Steve. 'It's only a playback show with some of this mob here poncing about with wigs on,' he descriptively enlarged.

Dan and Rod arrived to ascertain what time we'd be sound-checking, and as I filled them in I also gave an account of the cetaceans in the bay entertaining the day trippers, before enquiring as to what they'd been up to.

'We just went for a general stroll around; not much here is there?' mumbled Rod.

'We've been watching the cricket since then!' Dan added.

Dumbfounded, I asked where it was on; but Dan, dodging the question, said, 'By the way, the woman in the shop here is dying to meet you; she told us she had your ugly mug on her bedroom wall when she was fourteen!'

'Have they got any of those steak bakes? I'm a bit peckish and maybe she'll give me a discount,' I enquired.

'Oh yeah, they've got just about everything in this one!' Dan affirmed.

We strolled together over to the mini-mart, where I was soon introduced to my middle-aged fan and scrawled a signature on a poster that the lads had given her. I was about to relocate to the grill bar in search of a tasty patty, when disbelievingly I was stopped dead in my tracks.

A wire basket was situated to the side of the counter, and inside it rested an apple, an orange and a banana; virtually lost for words, I croaked, 'Excuse me, but are these for sale?'

Coyly she didn't answer right away, and then began giggling uncontrollably, before gathering herself and gibbering out, 'Why, would you like them?'

'Yes please, how much?' I inquired.

Dan and Rod were beside themselves and sniggering like kids as she replied, 'There'll be no charge for you,' and began tittering again.

Soon cottoning on, I smirked and inferred: 'This is a wind-up, isn't it?'

'I couldn't help myself; there's a little greengrocer's shop in town, and anyway you're getting them for nowt,' Dan explained, in stitches.

'Brilliant!' I complimented them.

The shop assistant finally relaxed and with a look of relief said, 'I thought you might be cross when you found out!'

'Not at all – it's saved me one pound seventy-five for a steak bake,' I chuckled.

'You tight git,' groaned Rod as we fell about all the way up the avenue.

♫

In typical Aussie fashion their countrymen were making a game of the test match, after being to a great extent outplayed; but with England still in the box seat to take a series lead with only one test to go, it would be wonderful to sit and witness the humbling of the Antipodean visitors on a day of rest in the comfort of my living room the next day – especially as on the sporting front my precious football team had fared badly, going down two-nil at home to an unfancied Luton Town side.

Stef had conspicuously been identified sneaking back to his caravan with a skimpily clad young lady for some afternoon high-jinks, as Trevor, passed out on the sofa, made snorting sounds much to Jeff's chagrin. Meanwhile Romeo, surprise surprise, was watching

TV, as he performed a few neat paradiddles on a practice-pad on top of a chair.

Over at the frugal venue Steve had everything up and running; but apathetically, and with the countdown very much under way, we decided against bothering with a sound-check. Instead, Dan suggested: 'Anybody fancy some flapping fresh seaside fish and chips in town?'

'What a great idea!' I smiled.

Arriving back from our battered treat we stumbled upon Steve walking out of the main building.

'Talk about bloody stupid,' he complained.

'What's up squire?' asked Dan.

'I just went to the carvery in the canteen; there's fuck all for vegetarians, so I asked the bloke serving what they had, and he said, "Roast chicken, gammon or *boeuf bourguignon*." So I explained I was a veggie, and guess what the idiot said?'

We looked glumly at him and waited for the pay-off line; it finally came:

'"I'll nip into the back and prepare you a cold-meat salad" – can you bloody believe it?' he griped, before wandering off in a sulk.

'Well, at least he's stopped moaning about the gigs!' I commented.

♫

The Queen tribute was – to put it mildly – outlandish, with the four characters looking more like the Flintstones as opposed to Freddie Mercury and co. What's more the singing and backing harmonies were dreadfully out-of-tune and -synch, with what sounded like third-generation backing tracks, making for a routine that was worse than awful.

On a hot, sticky night the attendees were soon making for the exits, and some much needed fresh air, as through the open dressing-room window we amusingly picked up on some passing comments from a string of disenchanted punters who were voicing their criticisms of the show.

One guy, clearly from the north, commented: 'He sounds more like Freddie Flintoff than Freddie bloody Mercury!'

'They were fookin' shite, that's what,' answered his Manc mate.

Luckily the complainants all returned after a breather, in anticipation of some half-decent live music, and an hour before we were due on stage the clammy room was absolutely heaving.

Each of us must have shed getting on for half a stone that night, as the stultifying heat in the venue was bordering towards unbearable. Fire exits and every window in sight were opened, but the room still got warmer and stickier as the evening pressed on.

Upon returning to the airless dressing-room after a genuine encore, I took off my stage shirt and was able to wring it out into the nearby sink; the rest of the guys sat in a circle within the small confines, also completely exhausted by their efforts, and gasping for some liquid refreshment which annoyingly never arrived.

It seemed something was above us, clambering around in the roof space making sharp hammering noises, as all of a sudden small shards of plaster and dust came raining down followed by a booted foot that clattered through the ceiling. Everyone looked over in Jeff's direction, to witness his shoulders were covered in debris and his hair had turned white. The spontaneous laughter was deafening as he disconsolately sat, head bowed like a slapstick character from a Laurel and Hardy movie, as to everyone's added amusement he chuntered forlornly: 'For fuck's sake!'

♫

With a couple of days between gigs and the next stop barely forty miles away, it had been a toss-up as to whether or not it was worth making the five-hundred-mile round-trip home; but the prospect of a precious Sunday lunch with the family was hard to resist, as was the luxury of sleeping in our own beds.

So it was ironic when the tight-fisted holiday company made the decision for us, by insisting we pay for our accommodation on the free nights; but whatever, the winding Welsh backroads would be far less busy during the small hours, so avarice or not it really was a no-brainer.

I was desperate to see my Dad, as my siblings had advised me that Mum's death had finally sunk in and that over the past couple of weeks he'd become tearful and disorientated. Rod had organised a round of golf with friends, teeing off on the Monday morning; Danny was taking his teenage son Sam fishing; Jeff had arranged to meet up with daughter Natalie for Sunday lunch in a posh pub; and Romeo had two days to catch up with hours of his favourite programmes recorded on VideoPlus.

Trevor, so often the odd one out, was not quite as keen as the majority to return home; and to avoid forty-eight hours of interrogation and hen-pecking decided to move on with the crew boys to the next camp in Pwllheli, where they would bed down in a couple of chalets provided by the caravan company due to a requested early load-in on the Tuesday to accommodate the travelling wrestlers, who once again would be shamming knocking the hell out of each other throughout the afternoon.

Bidding the boys farewell as we prepared to leave, Steve uttered a statement of intent: 'I'm gonna get completely shitfaced tomorrow!'

'Well, make sure your hangover's gone by Tuesday, or you'll be grumpier than ever,' I jested to the delight of the passengers, as we idled away to begin the two-hundred-and-fifty-mile nocturnal trek.

♫

Suffering from sleep deprivation I collected my Dad on the Sunday morning to allow him a much needed change of scene, and a chance to gorge himself on an old-fashioned home-cooked roast.

A pleasant day was spent looking through old family photos, and generally taking his mind off things. The old-timer understandably became a little emotional, in spite of still managing to chip in with a few puckish witticisms; but all told, at the end of an enjoyable day, uncharacteristically he seemed relieved to be returned to his comfort zone, as I dropped him off late on at the more familiar surroundings of the nursing home.

On the Monday morning I paid a visit to the band's office in the less than salubrious town of Corby in Northamptonshire, having a catalogue of things to attend to along with a welcome compensatory cheque to pick up from our current employers.

My day's business almost done, I parked up and walked across the dreary town square in the direction of the bank, almost tripping over a purportedly homeless guy whose legs were covered by a grimy sleeping-bag, as he loafed, hidden away beneath a sheltered part of the paved area. Beside him lay a wistful, lethargic old Labrador cross, with greying fur around his wet nose, wearing a dejected expression as his surprisingly healthy-looking master caught my attention by saying, 'Have you got some spare change mate, my dog's hungry?'

Disappointed at his lack of manners I walked on by, as it seemed did everyone else; but when I came out of the bank strutting in the reverse direction he again implored: 'Ah c'mon man, my poor dog's starving.'

Directly across the square was a butcher's shop, which I purposefully headed for and, after queuing for five minutes, I asked if they had a large bone. The assistant disappeared into the back, returning seconds later with a large osseous feast for the mangy canine.

'Two pounds, please,' said the ruddy-faced trader. A little nonplussed, I passed over the change before ambling back to the mendicant who was now engaged in deep conversation on a stylish mobile phone.

As he looked up I said, 'There you go, this should make his day,' and handed him the plastic bag – to which he reacted by taking the phone from his ear before grousing, 'What the fuck's this, man?'

In a chastening riposte I said, 'You mentioned your dog was hungry; it's a bone, a special treat for him – MAN!'

'What is this shit?' the ungrateful down-and-out snarled, throwing the package aside without so much as retrieving the contents to satiate his sniffling furry friend.

Driving back home, pangs of guilt left me feeling a little mean-spirited, as I pondered whether or not the guy genuinely was homeless; but if – as I doubted – he actually was, then how did he feed the dog, and pay his mobile phone bill?

35

BROTHERS IN ARMS
(DIRE STRAITS)

Tuesday 30th August 2005

On the morning of our departure for Pwllheli on the western side of the Snowdonia National Park, I received an email from an old army friend who had escorted and looked after the band when we'd entertained Her Majesty's troops back in 1998. The message read:

To: Dave B
From: The Batty Boys of Banja Luka
Date: 27:08:2005
Subject: Pwllheli

Hey Dave
Long time no see buddy. It's Nora Batty from Bosnia, I hope you remember me.
Looking after you guys was probably the best assignment I ever had in my time out there, and I'd always hoped that we'd bump into each other again.
I looked on the band's website and couldn't believe that you're playing in Pwllheli on August 30th, as myself and 2 squaddie mates are on our way up to RAF Valley to visit friends tonight (Saturday) and will be going on to Abersoch, which is only 5 miles from where you guys have a show on Tuesday. We've booked day passes so will be there cheering you on.
It would be great if we could meet up for a beer after the show and catch up on the last 7 years.

Let me know if this is possible and look forward to seeing you.
Kind Regards
Batty (Nora)

On a working Tuesday morning the roads were extremely busy, and it was stop-start all the way north on the congested M6 motorway. The guys were delighted that the army lads had been in touch and were coming along to see the show, which stirred a few memories of our experiences as guests of the British armed forces in various troubled corners of the globe.

The hospitality of the military was unerringly – to our knowledge – second to none, and even in remote outposts the food was nutritious and of high quality; plus there would, needless to say, be a bountiful supply of alcoholic refreshments laid on after each gig.

On a tour of the Falklands in March 1998, this was amply demonstrated when we performed a couple of shows at two isolated, vertiginous reconnaissance sites named Mount Alice and Byron Heights, situated on the largely uninhabited West island.

The only means of reaching the bases was to be airlifted by Chinook utility helicopters from the main headquarters at Mount Pleasant, which after forty minutes' flying dropped down directly into the mountainous garrisons.

At first I'd assumed there were just two choppers, i.e. one carrying the band, crew, dancing girls and ushering personnel, with the second one bringing in the equipment for the gig.

Chatting and looking on with the young Captain (nicknamed 'Mainwaring') responsible for the touring party, I spotted a third helicopter preparing to land, and enquired as to what was on board; to which the amiable host reassuringly grinned and explained, 'That, David dear boy, is the supply of beverages for the *après*-show knees-up!'

The Captain's statement more or less summed up the congeniality which the forces afforded their guest performers, amply demonstrated upon our arrival at the main headquarters in the

Falklands where we were all designated basic but comfortable single-occupancy quarters in the vast complex of two and a half thousand military personnel. After settling in we were shown into a restricted area assigned for our rest and relaxation, or 'R & R' in soldierly speak (but not to be confused with its musical equivalent that was the band's speciality), which effectively served as our very own private bar.

By 1998 when we visited the islands the threat of any further hostile action had completely evaporated, with the tyrannical dictatorship in Argentina shamed and long gone; but, dare I say it, as a result the attitude within the stronghold had become enormously laid-back, and even a little undisciplined. During our three-week stay we extended numerous invitations to guests of all ranks, threw impromptu parties, and pretty much had the run of our not-so-hush-hush retreat, after which our visitors soon reciprocated and solicitations were made requesting our presence from various other hidden shebeens that belonged to the many disparate squadrons.

Throughout the first few days, as we familiarised ourselves in the new habitat, band members would regularly be spotted seeking directions whilst attempting to navigate the labyrinth of corridors in search of the next party venue, not to mention the ensuing chaos as we staggered back later to relocate to our quarters; however, in time we found our compass, often returning to find another spontaneous bash in progress at our own hostelry.

In the course of our stay we occasionally dined in style courtesy of the Officers' and Sergeants' Messes, but more frequently were fed and watered in the less highfalutin surroundings of the NAAFI along with the squaddies, who flatteringly treated us all with the utmost respect.

The menu invariably featured curry, which Trevor devoured every single day (sometimes twice); and there were endless supplies of chips to go with everything, leading the entire gang to overindulge themselves big time, with Romeo and myself the only ones to show willing and burn off a few excess calories in the all-singing-and-dancing, impressively equipped gymnasium.

The daylight hours were often spent (other than sobering up and nursing hangovers) going out on organised excursions to former battlegrounds such as Tumbledown, and Goose Green close to where we movingly marched through the same ravine into which Colonel 'H' Jones had led his men, and subsequently lost his life in 1982.

Some of the sightseers picked up half-buried rotting plimsolls that had slipped from the feet of young Argentine conscripts almost sixteen years before, beckoning the obvious question that was put to our guide: 'Why were a group of young soldiers wearing plimsolls in atrociously heavy mud?'

His answer was chilling, surprising and saddening: 'Because the Argie Generals ordered the confiscation of their boots to prevent them all from running away!'

As goosebumps ran up my spine, a couple of the party were admonished for trying to take the tragic items as souvenirs; but the ferocity of the reprimand, together with an order that they were to be left untouched as a mark of respect, caused the petty pilferers to quickly return the articles to their original resting place.

The actual purpose of our extended visit was unquestionably to give the forces a good time, and the gigs were heart-warming, as we played eleven shows to the diverse stationary squadrons and visiting Royal Navy crews who were temporarily stopping over, plus a special one-off performance for the resident Falklanders at Port Stanley Town Hall, the experience of which really was like going back in time but also truly memorable.

As our mission drew to an end, a fitting swansong took place in the form of an impromptu acoustic performance for the guests in what had affectionately become known as 'Waddies Bar'; after which, unavoidably, we all got absolutely smashed.

The islands had left a lasting impression, and the overall feeling was that other than stupid politics, and mineral wealth, the unique territory had been well worth fighting for, and in spite of its geographical position the remote colony is indisputably British soil. Hardly a soul speaks a word of Spanish; and the successful intervention to defend the dependency, love her or loathe her, extolled Margaret Thatcher into a saintly figure in the eyes of each and every Falkland Islander.

♬

Our friendship with Batty (or Nora for obvious reasons) began when he took charge of a small body of men who escorted the band through the trouble-torn countries of Bosnia and Croatia during February 1998.

Although the conflict had largely subsided, there was still an underlying threat from a few fanatical rebels, who basically were opposed to the cessation of hostilities and sought to wreak havoc out of sheer bloody-mindedness. Consequently, as we travelled through the battle-scarred region between military bases, we found ourselves accompanied by a whole cavalcade of armoured vehicles, in similar fashion to that assigned to any visiting dignitaries.

Over fourteen days we were ushered to the far corners of Bosnia and Herzegovina, before ending the stint with an amazing gig in the Croatian city of Split before a crowd of over three thousand exuberant soldiers desperate to let off some steam.

At times we came face to face with how heinous and evil-spirited the human kind can be – even to their close neighbours – whilst masquerading behind a barricade of religious or political beliefs, which made the experience both devastating and at the same time in many ways enlightening, particularly in the Bosnian capital of Sarajevo; but in truth the whole company owed a debt of gratitude to the forces guys, who made the expedition so unforgettable.

Ominously it initially appeared that we'd be in for something of a rough ride, when the whole contingent (i.e. band, comedian and dancers) were airlifted to a distant base close to Sipovo, where we were to spend two nights.

After arriving with little time to prepare, the opening show had gone surprisingly well, with a young and enthusiastic crowd warming to the band and clambering up to join us at regular intervals to perform stage dives, mercifully into the waiting arms of their pals.

The first taste of army hospitality had been warm and top-notch, much as we'd been led to believe, and everything seemed to be hunky-dory, until we were finally shown to our sleeping quarters.

Patches of ice had formed on the window-panes as – in brass-monkey temperatures of ten degrees below – the party were led outside to a storehouse where thick quilted sleeping bags were issued to one and all, before in freezing-fog conditions we were directed up a fire escape to an isolated first-floor room.

Upon entering the makeshift dormitory we were confronted by twenty metallic bunk beds in close proximity to each other within the dismal room, at which point I realised our agreement included the sharing of facilities with any other civilian visitors present on the bases at the same time.

Following a shedload of booze the male species is renowned for making piggish impersonations; and at lights-out this fleapit was no exception, with the cacophony of grunts and wheezes resembling a menagerie, rendering it nigh-on impossible to sleep in the midst of constant sniffles and farts. Tossing and turning and zipping the bedroll above my head, I imagined the bedchamber of Hades to be little different to this set-up.

I climbed down from the bunk, and was joined by a fresh-faced new recruit who was also having difficulty sleeping; and together we tiptoed out of the room dressed only in T-shirts and briefs to try and find someone on duty who could find us a pair of earplugs.

'There's a store cupboard in the next wing – I was over there yesterday,' said the lad.

'Okay, come on, let's get a move on or it'll be a severe case of frostbite and not insomnia that we suffer from tonight,' I urged.

We dashed across an icy quadrangle, making for a door at the corner of the adjoining block; but as the rookie tried the handle he found it was bolted from the inside.

Now shivering uncontrollably from the vicious cold, we urgently needed to get back inside the same way we'd exited – but nightmarishly the latch on the door had clicked shut and locked itself, leaving the both of us stranded on the forecourt seriously at risk from exposure.

Half frozen we hurried around the building's perimeter looking for another way in, or just the olive branch of an open window; but soon found ourselves on the main thoroughfare that ran through the camp.

Shuddering with chattering teeth, we were high and dry, clueless as to which way we should go, when a sudden mass of blinding floodlights illuminated the middle of the muddy highway where we tremulously stood, and a deafening tannoy distortedly belted out: 'Random civilians in Sector B!'

Literally frozen on the spot, within seconds the pair of us were surrounded by troops, who escorted us at gunpoint into a private office where a sleepy-eyed Sergeant scratched his forehead and screamed apoplectically: 'What the fucking hell do you idiots think you're doing?'

As we nervously explained and awaited our fate, the military man seemed largely uninterested as he burst into an uncontrollable smoker's cackle, to be ably assisted by his chortling sycophantic underling, who rose from his desk to pat the officer's back.

'Is that the only reason you pair of dorks are out here freezing your bollocks off: for some fucking earplugs?' he barked.

The small foam sound-buffers issued that night became an important part of my kit for the next fortnight, but nothing could cushion me from the piss-taking squaddies once they got wind of the foolish escapade; however, in hindsight I suppose the incident – almost literally – helped to break the ice!

Midway through the tour, Nora and the boys drove us into the devastated city of Sarajevo, where the horror of the past years soon became patently evident.

On the way through an area of bullet-torn tenement blocks, one of the guards pointed out a square of patchy grass, with a couple of rusting, dilapidated swings and see-saws, where the local children had once frolicked together; but to our sadness and disgust, in the midst of the atrocities this playground had become a place of target practice for malicious and cowardly snipers who lay on the rooftops of neighbouring apartments picking off innocent young kids to entice their horrified parents into view, only for them to suffer a similar fate.

On a tour of the city organised by the United Nations there was an enormous amount that would leave a lasting impression, even on the most cynical of souls. A football field, where once youngsters of differing religious beliefs had happily kicked a ball around as friends, had become a burial ground littered with exposed earth-covered tombs, some of which upsettingly outlined the tiny caskets of unsuspecting tots who in their short lives bore no malice.

The locals went about their daily business as normal, toing and froing in what had clearly once been a conglomeration of disparate cultures that somehow had merged into one bustling but characterful metropolis. Random patches of red cement were scattered throughout the crazy-paved streets in the centre of town, some in giant formless shapes as if on an oversized artist's palette, and known as 'Sarajevo Roses', symbolising a mark of respect to the many blameless victims tragically murdered by indiscriminate mortar bombardment whilst out doing their daily shopping.

The most catastrophic of these atrocities, which still sticks in my craw today, was the Markale massacre of February 1994, when a deadly attack on the crowded marketplace took sixty-eight lives, and wounded a hundred and forty-four harmless souls as they queued for bread, vegetables and other provisions.

The thoughtlessness and futility of it all was utterly numbing, and having once taken a holiday in the former Yugoslavia I found it impossible to get my head around how these contrasting races had ostensibly been united with little bloodshed under the leadership of Marshal Tito until 1980.

The Winter Olympics had even been staged in Sarajevo as recently as 1984; and the camouflaged jeeps carried the sightseers all the way to the top of the bobsleigh run, from where there was an uninterrupted bird's-eye view of the woebegone city.

On a bitterly cold February day, with the snow piled high at the roadsides, in an effort to lighten the slightly doleful spirits a couple of the band chucked snowballs in the direction of the army escorts, which soon led to a full-scale pitched battle between musicians and squaddies.

Ultimately victorious, the rock-and-rollers posed for a team photo, beaming with pride as our undisciplined gutter tactics overcame the so-called precise military combat skills of our hosts, the subject of which wasn't dropped until close to the tour's end.

We left 'the Jerusalem of the Balkans' after three never-to-be-forgotten days; and although we'd learnt much during the visit, the sheer forcefulness of the bitter hatred that fellow human beings were capable of in that region between 1992 and 1995 still from time to time causes me to shake my head in disbelief.

♫

Arrangements had been made to meet up with our army mates in the small town of Criccieth, not too far from the next gig, with the intention of catching up and grabbing a bite to eat.

I'd heard a few stories about the pubs in North Wales, but had taken them all with a pinch of salt; and as we entered the cosy-looking bar, the local 'early doors' customers were happily chatting away in accentuated English.

Incredibly, as we began ordering up our drinks a few heads turned towards us, and the hubbub instantly adjusted to the Welsh native tongue.

Danny had long possessed a keen knack of expressing himself in sentences that contained snippets of Russian, Polish, and Spanish, and would often perform an amusing lingual mix in a kind of Jabberwocky fashion; which, to further confuse matters, he decided to do, coming out with something along the lines of: 'Pushkini como 'esta nastrovichi para quatro bebidas,' which he aimed in the barman's direction.

Hilariously the attendant reached into a cooler and offered up two different brands of Polish beer, and asked: 'Is that what you mean, boyo?'

Dan guffawed and cheerily replied, 'No thanks, guv'nor, I'll just have a mug of tea and a menu please.'

'Oh, you're not one of them then? We've been getting a lot of Estonians in 'eure we have lately,' stated the man.

At precisely the same moment the door crashed open and Nora and the boys arrived, looking like PT instructors in their vests and tracksuit bottoms; and after we'd given our old pal an affectionate man-hug, he introduced us to his mates Graham and Julian. A small culinary feast of steak-and-ale pies and home-made burgers was ordered up, and as we waited we recalled a few ripping yarns from our Bosnian adventure seven years earlier.

There is no doubt in my cranky mind that the armed forces can knock out the youthful restlessness that so often manifests itself into differing degrees of hooliganism, even in the cases of the most unruly of characters; and none more so than Batty's friend Julian. His father was a wealthy and much travelled oil tycoon, who'd as good as abandoned his bright son to the supposedly character-building confines of boarding school from the age of seven; but being a precocious kid Julian had earned his love-shy family the kudos of a son attending Harrow by the age of thirteen. His formative academic years showed great promise; but it saddened him greatly that he only met up with his parents at Christmas time, or on Speech Day, which would always be held in the school's famous gardens.

'I used to hate all that self-congratulatory back-slapping crap, and went out of my way to fluff my exams so as not to be awarded a prize, which my toffee-nosed old man would've lapped up! I became a massive disappointment to them, and my visits home all but dried up; and then I disgraced the family by dropping out at the age of seventeen before my finals, and buggered off to live on a kibbutz in Israel for nine months, where I spent the whole time stoned,' he enlightened us, pausing for breath and shaking his head. 'I didn't speak to my folks for almost eighteen months after that,' he continued with an educated plum in his mouth.

Returning to the UK, Julian had become disillusioned with life, and was basically nothing more than a crack-head; when one afternoon, whilst bumming around town in Brighton and without any outside encouragement, he walked into an army recruitment centre and signed on for five years. 'I figured the old man would be pleased; but he was still pissed off, and wanted to pull some strings to get me into Sandhurst.'

Six years on and here he was, a once homeless drug addict who had admirably worked his way through the ranks and was now a Sergeant, with the prospect of greater things on the horizon, purely by his own sterling efforts.

'The great thing is I finally patched it up with my parents, and thankfully now things are pretty good,' he told us.

'You want to see his old boy's yacht,' said Nora excitedly, as Graham chipped in with a strong Scottish twang: 'It looks like it belongs to that Russki who owns Chelsea, "Asonofabitch" – the bloody thing's massive!'

'We're having a couple of days out at sea on it starting tomorrow,' said Nora.

'Two of the crew are female, and well stacked and very tidy,' Julian informed us, before asking: 'Why don't you come on board for brunch tomorrow before we set sail; we're meeting the skipper at eleven in the morning?'

'Ooh, brunch, how absolutely spiffing,' chorused Batty and Graham, shaking a limp wrist and taking the mickey out their well-spoken pal.

Regrettably we were left with no choice but to decline the invitation, since the park manager had politely requested that we vacate our chalets by midday on the Wednesday as there would be a fresh influx of punters arriving for the North Wales heats of TV's *The X Factor*; and, with Abersoch further along the coast in the opposite direction, we'd have had little time to indulge in a taste of luxury on the opulent yacht.

'That's the bloody talent show with all those nutters on, isn't it?' queried Graham.

Nora put in his pennyworth: 'I hate that fucking programme, it's a bloody fix; there's no way that bin man should've won it last year, he was absolutely crap, and he'll be back on that dumper truck in no time!'

Whatever the nation's opinions, in 2005 the show regularly seemed to crop up as a topic of conversation wherever you went, and even some of the multi-lingual locals, who had earlier ignored us, turned back to English to express an opinion.

A short sound-check had been organised for seven p.m., just prior to the doors opening thirty minutes later; and sadly we were forced to make a move, and bid the guys goodbye.

'We'll give you a name-check during the show,' I promised as we shook hands and headed for the door, where prior to disappearing onto the street Danny stood, arms aloft, and shouted towards the local throng, '*Hwyl fawr*' everybody!' to which the entire huddle in

---

* Pronounced 'hoowill vour'.

the pub turned around, looking completely stunned, as we silently made our exit.

'What the bloody hell did you say?' I asked, descending the steps.

'I just said "turrah" to them in Welsh,' was Dan's reply.

♫

With a spacious stage and a more familiar feel to the place, we felt at home and put on a polished performance, with the crowd up dancing, and throwing requests scrawled on junk-food menus up onto the stage.

At one point a young woman in a wheelchair propelled herself to the brow of the platform and passed me a red rose; my heart fluttered at the gesture, until I caught what was written on the attached card.

'All my love to Romeo forever,' it read.

My pride wounded, I placed the flower on the top of his bass-drum, whilst ruminating: 'Well, I couldn't not give it to him, could I?'

36

NELLIE THE ELEPHANT
(TOY DOLLS / MANDY MILLER)

Wednesday 31st August 2005

Breakfast was nightmarish as we queued patiently at the busy buffet-bar while the inmates profligately piled their plates high with stuff they knew darned well they'd never finish, thinking, 'What the hell, it's all-inclusive, and paid for.' In the background a collection of po-faced girls wearing plastic gloves heaped the plentiful leftovers into black bin-liners, the contents of which could have fed a poverty-stricken banana republic for a week.

As we stood kicking our heels it eventually came round to our turn. Trev received a rollicking from an assistant for sampling the vat of baked beans with a spoon, before apologising as on this occasion they were piping hot; but then, not to be outdone, he followed the example set by the other captives and grabbed an extra plate before shovelling a huge portion over his double platter.

After hoovering down the greasy fare the three adventurers announced that we'd prefer to make an early start and leave promptly for Porthmadog, barely thirty miles along the coast, to allow us a good few hours to explore the nearby Italianate village of Portmeirion.

The band had travelled this laborious route in both directions a number of times in recent years, when we'd played a series of Sunday dates during the peak season at a Butlin's resort situated just outside of Pwllheli, and knew first hand of the notorious traffic congestion for which Porthmadog had long been renowned.

On more than one occasion we'd attempted to cross the old toll road called The Cob to gain entry to the small town, and had been delayed for as long as an hour, which was all the more remarkable for the fact that the queuing transport paid the princely sum of just five pence upon reaching the tiny booth. During one such delay Jeff had used a calculator to estimate that the toll grossed around five hundred pounds per day in high season, but barely a hundred pounds at off-peak times, which we figured was scarcely enough to cover the maintenance costs; but not wishing to help matters the locals amusingly just raised their hands, and were waved through free of charge by the gateman.

Thinking ourselves smart, during one passage we decided to chance our arm and attempted the same trick, only to be severely reprimanded and put in our place by the screaming official.

Somewhat sentimentally the booth was no more, and had been abolished in 2003; as Rod commented, 'What a shame, but there's progress for you, even in this backwater,' as we sailed on through without delay.

Jeff, who was renowned for 'throwing a deaf 'un' with his rock-and-roll-battered ears, harped up from the back seat: 'Thank fuck that old toll booth's not there any longer – we'd have been waiting half the day!'

There was no doubting the facilities at the last few camps had taken a turn for the better; but the general consensus upon arriving at the Porthmadog camp was that – taking a leaf from Steve's vocabulary – the place was a shithole!

To make matters worse, it was back to the unfriendly, unhelpful and agitated staff that had made the past couple of months seem interminable, and predictably the caravans provided were – at best – basic, though perhaps not quite as rancid as some we'd put up with.

The old (and now familiar) feeling of dissatisfaction amongst the paying customers was once again in evidence, as they wandered around grim-faced and unhappy; but hardened to it all we simply took it in our stride and without complaining laid claim to our beds, and needing no persuasion got the hell out of the place as quickly as our legs (and the bus) would carry us.

I'd heard from friends that Portmeirion was unique, and the weather apart (it was one of those irritating drizzly days, when the elements couldn't make up their mind what to do) without any question the place lived up to its billing, possessing the ambience of a Mediterranean resort, rather than a remote bay in North Wales; for three or four hours it seemed the perfect antidote to the bleak and hostile environs of the camp.

That said, the excursion didn't begin well as we reached the drive leading to the area marked 'Cars' to find a phalanx of waiting traffic, and further on ahead two police vehicles blocking the entrance, with the day-trippers being questioned by the officers prior to being ushered to a parking space by a scurrying attendant.

It transpired that an hour previously a large uniformed man (thought to be of eastern European origin) had set up his own road-block, and had been charging unsuspecting customers five pounds for entry into the *free* car park; but when an official member of staff had intervened, the con man had cut up rough and assaulted him, leaving him battered and bruised and receiving medical attention in a wooden hut next to the turnstiles where the public were admitted.

'We reckon there must've been fifty cars come in 'ere that bunged 'im a fiver before he was sussed,' explained the bobby in a delightfully lilting Welsh tone.

'What a fackin' liberty,' voiced Dan, imitating the foul-mouthed Nan from the Catherine Tate show, as we idled into a muddy glen full of stationary vehicles.

Portmeirion, undeniably, is mostly renowned as the location of the legendary late-sixties *The Prisoner* TV series, which just about everyone above the age of fifty would have viewed at some point in their history. Without wishing to babble excessively about the one-off place's history, the village was the vision of Sir Clough Williams-Ellis, and took fully fifty years to complete from its initial construction way back in 1925.

Naturally we (along with the majority of tourists) were intrigued to see the villa of Number Six, i.e. Patrick McGoohan, but became a little downcast to find it was used as a themed *Prisoner* souvenir shop, with many tacky and vastly overpriced items on display.

Nonetheless there was absolutely no doubt that the picturesque tourist-trap possessed an unprecedented charm, with the eye-catching Central Plaza and small winding lanes speckled with quaint tea-houses, shops, and other attractive buildings that were externally unchanged from the iconic TV series that adorned our black-and-white screens forty years before.

In addition to the distinctive architecture of Portmeirion, there was the added bonus of the surrounding woods, which made for an uplifting walk as we passed through the mysterious exotic gardens, before trudging on in search of the sandy bay where Number Six was regularly confronted by giant white balloons (affectionately known as Rover) that stood between McGoohan's anonymous character and his freedom.

'Wouldn't this be a brilliant place to film a pop video?' Rod suggested, only to be pulled up instantly by Dan:

'It's already been done – Siouxsie and the Banshees did one here and so did Supergrass with their *Alright* single!'

We skipped through the trees like Frodo and Sam in *The Lord of the Rings*, humming and singing the Brighton boys' catchy tune, as the sun finally put his hat on just before we reached the sands.

The beach was expansive, fabulous and largely deserted, apart from an oddball old guy who was strapped into what looked like a home-made beach buggy, and appeared to be getting up a head of steam going back and forth along the firmer sand closer to the water's edge.

Dan moved closer to take a snap of him, which he seemed perfectly happy with as he noisily motored a little way towards us and drew to a halt before clambering out of the contraption with some difficulty, covered in soot.

Rod murmured in my ear, 'Bloody hell, I thought it was Trev for a minute,' at which I almost choked laughing, knowing exactly where he was coming from.

'It's my first time out; I've been building her for over nine months. I'm eighty-eight, you know,' the old fossil stressed.

One thing the whole band had always had in common was a love of eccentrics, and this guy plainly fell into that category, as we chatted to him in complimentary style about his achievement.

'Oh well, I can't stand around chewing the fat all day; I'd better give her another spin,' he enthused, struggling back into the singular vehicle which spluttered into life and accelerated away; but alas, whilst bumping through the sandy hillocks, the Rube Goldberg device collapsed into a heap of scrap metal wrapped around the man's body.

'Oh shit,' said a concerned Dan, with the three of us grimacing and holding our breath, as finding it hard to conceal his disappointment the old boy looked up towards us and bawled: 'Oh well, you can't win 'em all – looks like it's back to the fucking drawing board!'

Feeling a twinge of sympathy for the senior citizen, we smiled and waved goodbye before continuing on to the end of the bay, agreeing as we walked that at least he had something to occupy his time in the autumn of his life!

Being in Portmeirion was similar to treading a primrose path, and it would've been easy to while away a few more hours in the charming village; but the oldest of enemies was creeping on, and after a pricey but tasty jacket-potato snack, with our shoulders slumped it was back to the dispiriting confines of the camp.

Steve really had it on him as we arrived back for the run-through, but was determined not to make a scene, after our exchange barely ten days prior.

'Are they giving you a hard time?' I asked my glum-looking colleague.

'I'm getting used to it; they haven't got a fucking clue – I was gonna put some extra lights in, but when I asked if they'd got three-phase* the idiot entertainment manager said, "Well, the sockets all have three pins, if that's what you mean;" what a bloody joke!'

I almost spat out my gum as he told me this, and after having a good laugh replied, 'Ah well, grin and bear it – there's not long to go now,' in an effort to console him.

'I only wish tonight was the last one – I've had enough,' he answered disconsolately, without quite knowing what he'd said.

On a brighter note the natives were restless, and had formed a long queue stretching into the car park, waiting for the sound-check to end so that they could lay claim to their tables in readiness for our performance later on.

As I made my way through the rear stage-door, a grim-faced uniformed man uttered a totally unnecessary snide comment under his breath for my benefit: 'I don't know what all the fuss is about – they've not had a fuckin' hit in donkey's years!'

Seeing Steve so downhearted had bothered me, and this time instead of biting my lip I turned towards the stocky ignoramus and stated, 'More's the pity we haven't, or we wouldn't be playing in a cesspit like this, would we now boyo?'

I stormed off before he had time to react, but my mood was buoyed as the people filing into the gig waved over, gesticulating in high-pitched voices saying how much they were looking forward to the show, and with a rejuvenated spring in my step I continued on

---

* Three-phase is a form of electrical power that is often required when running non-domestic energy-sapping devices.

through the grid of repetitious dull-green and cream dwellings, until I came to our caravan.

'The pissing shower doesn't work, it's just a trickle,' groaned Rod as I entered the spartan trailer.

'You sound surprised,' I answered facetiously.

'There's no soap, no bog rolls, nothing, apart from a little drop of Fairy Liquid in a bottle that I found under the sink,' he protested.

'Have they left us any towels?' I asked him.

'You must be joking, there's bugger all,' he further complained.

Turning tail I sped off back to reception to try and find some toiletries and bath towels, but once again met with a grudging welcome from a large-bodied, apathetic woman, who was painting her fingernails.

'We have no welcome packs in our caravans, and would very much like to shower and freshen ourselves up before entertaining your esteemed customers,' I stated.

'We ain't got none left,' she informed me in a couldn't-care-less tone.

'Okay, in that case would you fetch the manager,' I urged firmly.

'Oh, 'e ain't 'ere, 'e's over in the Show-Bar,' the slovenly woman retorted.

'So that means you're 'oldin' the fort does it, well God 'elp us!' I snapped in a sarcastic tone, emphasising the missing aitches.

'Are you tryin' to be funny?' she posed, sneering at me.

'Oh, quite the reverse actually; I just want some towels and soap so that I can wash and freshen up – is that really too much to ask?' I said agitatedly.

Completely ignoring me, she picked up the phone, and I overheard her say: 'Pippa, can you gerrover 'ere right now, I've got one of that bleedin' band kickin' off!'

I was livid, and began ranting, 'You call this kicking off?' but as I was about to launch into a tirade about her skills as a receptionist, a smart, well-groomed woman in a trouser suit hurriedly arrived on the scene to attempt to save the day.

'Can I help you sir, I gather there's a problem?' she asked with extreme politeness.

'I'm afraid we have no toiletries or towels to get cleaned up with in our caravans, and your colleague rather unhelpfully informed me that you have run out,' I put to her.

'Oh that's Dorothy, I'm afraid she's not much of a people person; how many packs would you like?' she asked.

Flabbergasted, I answered: 'Four will be fine please.'

Incredibly she reached underneath the inside of the desk and down towards the feet of the immovable Dorothy, who remained glued to her seat, and produced a cardboard box that contained several clingfilm-wrapped packages, full of everything we needed.

'Will these be okay? They're our emergency supply,' she clarified.

'Thank you, they'll do just fine,' I uttered incredulously.

I received what almost amounted to a hero's welcome as I called in at the other caravans to drop off the goodies, before suddenly twigging what Rod had said about the shower; but undeterred when I reached our trailer I revitalised myself in the stainless-steel sink, using washing-up liquid for shampoo, and making use of the heavily starched welcome pack.

A few minutes later, refreshed and ready, Rod clenched his fist and said, 'Just two to go after this one,' as we prepared to thrust into action before our waiting admirers over in the Show-Bar.

Peeping out from the wings we could see that the place was heaving, with the atmosphere energised and buzzing, as backstage Jeff and Stefan kept busy trying on the heads of the redundant cuddly characters, with Dan happily snapping his camera at the pranksters. Trevor, though, was having none of it, and stayed well out of the way, strumming nervously at his guitar as the threat loomed large of a disturbance to his carefully coiffured barnet.

It was crystal clear from the outset that the crowd were in big-time party mode, as in the aisles between the tables the high-spirited revellers jigged happily, many keeping their sprogs entertained at the same time with their embarrassing antics. As the minute hand ticked well past eleven p.m. I thought it unusual how many tiny youngsters were in the room, noticeably exhausted from the day's excitement, when by now they should be safely tucked up in their beds, as the whooping and hollering merrymakers danced around them, bumping into glass-laden tables with no hint of aggravation at all. The day had been dull and drizzly, but spirits were in no way dampened here, and these folks were determined to let themselves go, giving our performance an auspicious start.

We came to the point in the show when the more exhibitionist types lined up to leap acrobatically and spread themselves around my wearied midriff, with the blue-blooded males roaring their approval when an attractive teenage blonde girl revealed a set of stockings and suspenders as her skimpy outfit rode up when her shapely legs enveloped me.

The bacchanalians aided and abetted by myself belted out *Under the Moon of Love* tunelessly into the offered microphone, while others imitated the band performing somersaults of their own, and the joint was well and truly rocking.

'Hey rock and roll, bring it to town let's stroll,' roared the crowd, as we came to the closing bars of our set. Out of thirty-one dates we'd had only three or four that could be termed good gigs; but here on this night it was resuscitating to feel the adrenaline pumping as we stood backstage listening to the chants of 'more, more'; a rare glow beamed from the face of each band member, whilst the compere did his best to contain the ebullient crowd.

The guys trooped back on one by one before crashing into a rousing, drum-pounding intro as, still catching my breath, I readied myself to join them.

Out of the corner of my eye I saw the large head of the pink elephant called Nellie, and mischievously pondered: 'Should I, shouldn't I, what if?' before deciding in my wisdom, 'What the hell, there's a party going on,' and picked up the prop, placing it over my own bonce in a twisting motion to secure it to my perspiring torso.

In fits beneath the furry noodle I bounced vibrantly onto the stage in my new guise, to a wild reception from the inebriated punters, and peeping through the eye-holes could see that the band were hopelessly cracking up, as were many of the crowd who were literally rolling in the aisles.

The grim-faced staff, however, had failed to see the funny side and had become very animated as in a mad panic they came rushing towards the brow of the stage.

Stefan suddenly appeared at my side and did his level best to yank Nellie's head from my body in one swift movement, without comprehending that a simple twist to the left would do the trick.

'The staff are going ape-shit and the manager's fast losing the plot – we've got to get the bloody thing off now,' he flapped, as tugging mercilessly at the fluffy character he almost took my head off in the process.

'Twist the fucking thing round,' I cried in anguish; and, as he quickly obliged, at long last the elephant's dome broke free.

Feeling slightly nauseous from the mounting chaos I carried on performing the encore song *Mony Mony*, but could almost taste the displeasure in the eyes of the camp personnel, who were observing me like hawks from the side of the stage.

The band hit the final bars of the song, and after a crescendo of sound ended in style to rapturous cheers and further calls for more; but with an overwhelming atmosphere of disapproval emanating from the members of staff, we figured enough was enough and sloped away to the sanctuary of the cramped and fusty dressing-room.

Steve came in, cynically guffawing in his own inimitable way, but was most complimentary: 'That was fucking brilliant; all those twats out there are spitting their dummies out – what a bunch of fucking drama queens!'

Having metamorphosed he was strangely full of it, and was lapping up the fact that the prank had enraged the very people who had caused him so many difficulties throughout the day.

'That jumped-up tosser of an entertainments manager says you should be ashamed of yourself,' he added, chuckling and looking in my direction.

'What a bloody humourless pit this place is,' I dolefully responded.

'Don't worry about that wanker: you went down a storm out there,' commented Steve reassuringly, before reminding me, 'Don't forget I need some float for fuel before we leave in the morning.'

'Didn't you know elephants never forget!' Romeo wittily quipped from his stool in the corner.

Good gig or not, there was something profoundly discomfiting in the air, so I decided against joining the guys for a nightcap back at the bar that adjoined the venue, to avoid even the slightest risk of confrontation.

Wearing only a bath towel I reclined on the caravan's sofa bed, with a kind of self-satisfied glow: not only because we'd wowed the audience, but because – with just two more shows to go in these parks – the end was almost in sight.

From underneath the glass coffee-table I removed a small pile of journals, selected a worldwide holiday brochure that incongruously lay between two well-worn copies of *Heat* magazine and began flicking through the pages.

'The Kruger National Park in South Africa – Number One for Elephant Sightings,' read the pull-out supplement.

'Mm, I quite fancy that,' I thought, before turning out the lights and stumbling into my cot.

Roughly forty-five minutes later Rod arrived back, bumping clumsily up the metallic steps, not exactly appearing too happy with life as he checked to see if I was still awake.

'What's up?' I asked.

'I just don't get these people; some half-pissed woman with a high opinion of herself said we'll never work for this company again, and when Dan said, "What a hardship that'll be," one of the hard-case bouncers tried to pick a fight with him,' he lamented.

'I wondered what had brought you back so soon,' I answered.

'The punters were coming up to us saying what a great night they'd had, but there was no pleasing the bigots that work here.' He went silent for a moment, before softly pleading, 'Dave, will you promise not to book any more of these rat-holes ever again?'

'It sounds as if the decision may already have been made for us,' I retorted, adding, 'Two more and it'll all be forgotten.' It was time for bed.

37

THE END OF THE ROAD
(BOYZ II MEN)

Thursday 1st September 2005

The morning was cloudy and blustery and sleep had not come easily, as Rod and I traipsed down to the cafeteria for the penultimate fry-up.

Bands being the odd creatures they are, only a few days before we'd been discussing the dangers of high cholesterol, and argued that perhaps we'd been overdoing it a little on the greasy-food front; but the negative attitude had soon been reversed after Jamie Oliver appeared on TV only that week, banging on about the merits of a good old-fashioned English breakfast – though we seriously doubted that his sumptuous morning feast would be quite as steeped in cooking-oil as the fare served up on the dishes before us.

The remnants of the gang were still tucked up in their caravans, and clearly hadn't been suffering the same restlessness that had afflicted Rod and my good self; but it was cheering to see a handful of resident holidaymakers passing by smiling and giving the thumbs-up for our efforts of the previous night, as they went about planning their activities for the day ahead.

As we scoffed down our brekkie and mopped up the juices to clear the plates, Trevor arrived on the scene resembling a hobo, sporting a moth-eaten Rio de Janeiro* T-shirt that he'd presumably purchased

---

* *Rio de Janerio* – see 'Trevisms'.

on the band's one and only trip to Latin America in 1979, and a tiny pair of black football shorts (also reminiscent of the 1970s) which revealed one of his overburdened testicles as he stretched over to retrieve a mug from a plastic tray positioned next to the self-service tea and coffee machine.

'You can see your bollocks when you move in those shorts,' I critically pointed out when he joined us at the table.

Rod huffed and admonished, 'There's young children in here, and you look like a bloody kiddie-fiddler!'

'For fuck's sake,' groaned a dismayed Trevor, picking up his plate and mug and moving to a table well away from the cantankerous duo.

Our palates replete, the pair of us ambled through a room full of hi-tech fruit machines and noisy games, and though the time was only just after nine a scattering of eager punters were already pumping piles of coins into the one-armed bandits.

With a couple of hours to kill before the planned departure time, we opted to pick up a daily newspaper apiece, diverting away from the dismal route to the caravan to pass by the mini-mart. En route we came across a small boy who was stood urinating into a paddling pool where another couple of goose-pimpled youngsters played with a radio-controlled boat.

'Look at that guy over there: talk about lack of discipline – he doesn't give a shit,' said Rod, pointing towards the boy's guardian who nonchalantly looked on as if his ward's behaviour was simply an everyday occurrence.

Back at the van I switched on the TV, and we chilled out watching a shell-suited guy on *The Jeremy Kyle Show* with the distinction of fathering nine children – each with a different woman – who I swore blind I'd seen hanging around at one of these parks earlier on in the tour.

Seemingly proud of his record, the miscreant put his shameful notoriety down to a high sperm-count, which enraged the host who theatrically raised his voice; but five minutes of the ranting, holierthan-thou Mr Kyle was more than enough, so I hit the red button on the remote and flicked through the channels until we settled on catching up with the day's news.

Half an hour later a rhythmical tap-tapping sound rattled the caravan door, and uncertain as to whom it may be I trundled over to find Danny stood on the metallic access-ramp.

'Morning guv'nor; chilly, isn't it?' he bid me.

'The top of the morning to ya,' I responded, putting on an Irish accent for no particular reason at all, and a second or two later offering, 'Come on in, I'll get the kettle on.'

'I don't think there's enough time for a cup of tea,' he replied, stepping inside looking scared half to death.

'What the bloody hell's wrong; is there an elephant in the room? Come on, out with it man,' I urged as he stood sighing.

'Mm, funny you should say that; the thing is, I've got some really bad news,' he said falteringly before finally opening up. 'The manager and one of those burly security men just came over and barged their way into our caravan.'

'And?' I pushed him.

'They said they want us all to leave the camp with immediate effect,' he glumly replied.

'What's the rush? We're going in an hour anyway,' I answered.

'No, you're not with me; the manager said we're to leave right now. The company insist we're in breach of contract; the tour is over – we've been *sacked*!' he stressed.

I stood motionless, exhaling and completely dumbfounded for a moment, until the information sank in, at which point I retorted: 'I thought you said it was bad news? This is the best thing that's happened in weeks – that's incredible!'

'Bloody hell – I thought you'd go potty! So you're not bothered then?' he asked, totally bewildered.

'Not at all, in fact I'm overjoyed! We've played about twenty too many of these dives. Have you broken the news to anyone else?' I asked.

'Romeo knows – he was there when the powers that be arrived; but I thought I'd better tell you before letting everybody else know,' he responded, still a little uncertain.

'Okay, you tell Statler and Waldorf,' (Jeff and Trevor) 'I'll get hold of Steve, and let's get the hell out of Dodge!' I urged excitedly.

Dan began laughing, and brightened up considerably. 'You know, you're right: it's great isn't it? I'll come straight over with the Previa when we've packed up our stuff.'

I immediately called Steve, whose line was crackly with an awful signal, but nonetheless he sounded strangely upbeat.

'You've heard then?' he chuckled.

'Yes indeed, it's obviously the world's worst-kept secret; where are you?' I asked, feeling chirpier by the second.

'We've already hit the road home. I went over to check the dressing rooms earlier and that twat the compere took great pleasure in telling me, saying the manager was on his way over to let you know, so I couldn't see the point of hanging around in that shithole any longer than need be,' he elaborated, full of beans.

'Okay, safe journey back – I'll sort the bills out with you later in the week,' I said, preparing to sign off, when in an uncharacteristically sincere tone he offered:

'Oh, by the way, Dave – thanks!'

'Thanks for what?' I asked with a puzzled frown.

He coughed and cleared his throat before replying: 'For putting that bloody stupid elephant's head on last night; I ain't gonna forget that in a hurry!'

The harmonious band of men loaded up the bus for the final time of this never-to-be-forgotten ordeal, with the guys springing into their seats like a bunch of school kids on the last day of term.

The prevailing air of despondency that had followed us for so long had been replaced by one of elation, and the journey home flew by with all and sundry in high spirits, joyfully looking forward to the sanity of a return to normality.

My wife was waiting intently as I arrived back at the house, and after a long hug we jigged around the kitchen like a couple of demented children in what seemed like a mood of celebration, which was further confirmed as the good lady informed me that one of my favourites, beef Wellington, was on the menu that coming evening.

Searching through my wine rack for a bottle of something special to accompany the lip-smacking fare, I figured 'what the hell' and put a bottle of bubbly on ice as well as decanting a fine red; after all, it had been an unforgettable day, and for that matter tour!

The evening passed in a kind of blissful surrealism, abetted by the calming influence of the unrestrained alcohol; and as the small hours approached it felt truly like heaven to snuggle up between the crisp white sheets of my own bed, and crash out ecstatically into a sound night's sleep.

38

A LEGAL MATTER
(THE WHO)

Friday 2nd September 2005

Patently aware that the state of nirvana experienced the previous evening couldn't last, I ate a breakfast of toast, honey and yoghurt, together with a squeaky-clean unchipped mug of tea.

Fry-ups would now be banished ('You have to be careful when you reach middle age,' my wife had warned) for the foreseeable future – probably until the band's next overnight stay – but it was also time to do some catching up, and to make the effort and get back into shape.

I'd expected there would be some repercussions, and perhaps a stern email from the caravan company forwarded on to me from the office; but was straightaway alerted by two dismaying messages of complaint from followers who had basically arranged their holidays to coincide with the band's performance that had been scheduled to take place on the previous night in Prestatyn.

What really rubbed salt into the wound was that the explanation they had been given by the holiday company was that the band had failed to show up, which was simply unacceptable and needed to be addressed without further delay; after all, what right had they to hold ourselves responsible for the enforced non-appearance?

Incensed, I set the wheels of apoplexy into motion.

Not surprisingly the company's head office was 'unavailable for comment' when grilled by our secretary about their dubious interpretation of events, which kicked off a flurry of emails flying back and forth to the complainants, and an announcement posted on the band's website clarifying that our absence was due to the unforeseen termination of our contract, adding that we were furthermore utterly disgusted that the holiday company had seen fit to bring the band's good reputation into question by holding us culpable for the non-appearance.

The day happily passed without further incident, until around six p.m. when a freelance journalist who was writing a piece for a northern Welsh rag called *The Visitor* phoned me, having somehow tracked down my mobile number. In a strong 'Gog' accent he asked to talk to someone about Show-eddy-weddy's failure to turn up for a show in Prestatyn the previous night, and went on to explain that a lady and her partner had made a six-hundred-mile round trip all the way from Thurso in the Scottish highlands to stay at the park for a week, the highlight of which would be the performance of their heroes on the Thursday night.

'They were disgusted when they didn't show up, and have consulted a solicitor,' he continued a trifle effeminately.

After filling him in with the exact details of the story, and asking him to pass on our regrets to the well-travelled couple, I was even more determined to exact some revenge on the deceitful and totally misleading holiday organisation, whose version of events greatly and disingenuously differed from the actual facts.

The very same evening my wife and I were joined for a bite to eat by our close friends Yasmin and Richard, and after filling them in (along with their wine glasses) with the crazy details of the tour's grand finale and the hilarious saga of the elephant's head, I delved into the deviousness of the company's pathetic excuse at the expense of their customers who had journeyed hundreds of miles to see the show, only to be massively disappointed.

'Where were you supposed to be tonight?' asked Richard.

'Fleetwood, in Lancashire,' I answered.

'Well, let's give them a call and find out if you're still advertised as being on,' he suggested.

'That'll be interesting, why not!' I agreed.

Leaning over the computer we Googled the details of the Fleetwood camp and navigated through an illusory website that more resembled an idyllic Caribbean hideaway than a Lancastrian caravan site. Tucked away at the bottom of the screen a barely legible contact number was located, and so putting on a gormless northern accent Richard telephoned the camp.

'Hello there, my name's Brown; we were over at our caravan a few weeks ago and made a mental note that the original Showaddywaddy group were coming to the site sometime this week – is it tonight they're on?' he enquired.

With the call on speaker-phone we shushed each other, giggling like naughty kids awaiting the outcome of a foolish prank, until a high-and-mighty man's voice came on the line saying, 'I understand you have an enquiry about tonight's programme of entertainment?'

'Yes indeed; we're owners you see, and we're just checking that the Showaddywaddy band will still be performing at the centre before we set off for the weekend.'

His response was staggering: 'Yes, that's perfectly correct – they will be on in the Show-Lounge at eleven p.m. tonight!'

'Now, you're quite sure? I've heard a rumour they've failed to turn up at some of the dates,' he asked as the wind-up continued in earnest.

'As far as I know everything is going ahead as planned,' the man fibbed.

'I don't suppose there's any chance of meeting them after the show? I love that group,' Richard requested to our delight.

'I'm not so sure about that, sir, but we can always ask,' said the guy, lying through his teeth.

'Let me take your name: I'll recommend you for the employee of the month award – you've been so helpful,' my pal urged.

'Mark,' he replied.

'Mark who – what's your surname? I want to be sure I put in a good word for you,' Richard promised.

'Oh, it's all first-name terms around here sir,' he replied, with the first hint of caginess.

Richard kept pushing: 'Isn't the guy at the swimming pool called Mark? I don't want to recommend the wrong person.'

The man was having none of it, as if he was on to us, and clearly unwilling to offer his surname came back with, 'I'm pretty sure there's no one called Mark down there; as far as I know I'm the only person with that name at this centre.'

'Oh, I must be mistaken; anyway, maybe we'll see you later – in fact I'll make a point of buying you a drink for your kind assistance,' Richard fictitiously proposed.

'Very kind of you sir, but I don't drink when I'm on duty,' the falsifier closed with, sounding just like a policeman.

'The lying bastards,' pronounced Richard coming off the blower.

'Oh well, if nothing else we've got it from the horse's mouth now; surname or not he specifically said we'd be performing, and we most certainly won't be!' I said excitedly, weighing up my next move in the back of my mind.

♫

On the Saturday morning I took a trip over to my office to do a little catching up on the admin backlog in the peace and quiet of an empty building with only the caretaker for company.

Around a dozen items of mail lay in the company's pigeonhole, which I anxiously retrieved before heading upstairs to my desk.

Predictably a couple of the communications were bills along with some junk mail, but at the bottom of the pile was an ivory vellum envelope marked 'Private and Confidential', bearing the logo of the company which had hired the band's services for the previous ten weeks, which I immediately opened.

Unfolding the quality notepaper and talking to myself I muttered, 'Okay, here we go… this is where the fun starts!'

The correspondence read:

1st September 2005

Dear Sirs

RE: CONTRACT NO: 196181

This company has exercised its right to terminate the above contract forthwith due to the breech of clauses 9, 11 and 12.

We furthermore confirm non-payment for the performance in Porthmadoc on Wednesday 31st August 2005, and the cancellation without payment of the last two dates of the tour i.e. Thursday 1st September 2005 – Prestatyn, and Friday 2nd September 2005 – Fleetwood.

The sole reason for this drastic action is the gross misconduct on stage in Porthmadoc on Wednesday night reference Showaddywaddy lead singer coming on stage with the head of one of our skin characters on.

This disgraceful behaviour has not been taken lightly by our company, who pride ourselves on our programme of entertainment, especially for our younger guests, and we feel that a full written apology from the artist himself would be in order to prevent any on-going legal action.

I must further stress that the performers conduct is regarded as most serious as it may have caused distress to the young children present in the Show Lounge during the show, as in stripping them of their innocence, rather like telling them that Santa Claus had passed away.

I cannot overstate that the number of complaints that may be received to our organisation as a result of this incident may effect our good name, and that any such correspondance will be passed on for your explanation to soften the blow caused to the unfortunate children, many of whom I am tolled were seen leaving in tears, and there parents.

Yours Sincerely

(name withheld)

Head of Entertainment

To say I was gobsmacked would have been a major understatement. Stripping children of their innocence? Santa Claus dead? The person who'd composed the letter wasn't even capable of spelling correctly.

I read it through again, and in a strange way found the letter amusing; but the most worrying aspect was the company's refusal to cough up, as the termination was allegedly due to a 'breech' of the agreement.

What was certain was that the impending deadlock would need careful handling, and maybe even some legal advice; so rather than rush a furious response I took the decision to mull things over and sleep on it for the remainder of the weekend.

News travels fast in the rock-and-roll industry, and during the course of the Saturday afternoon I received a handful of texts, along with a few emails from mates in various bands.

A message from Sweet guitarist Andy Scott read: 'Fantastic stunt, I wish I'd been a fly on the wall, you're my hero, hope to see you soon,' while another well-wisher was quoted as saying: 'You're a star but don't go losing your head over it!'

It seemed as if my childish prank had been well received by my peers and that I was destined to go down in the annals of musical mischief for my potentially costly antics; but whatever celebrity the deed had afforded me, what was done was done, and a harmless bit of fun had undoubtedly backfired. That said I was in no mood to be taken to the cleaners and any further developments would have to be dealt with when the office reopened for business on the Monday morning.

Still overwhelmed by the wording of the initial communication, I continued studying the outrageous text on the Sunday in preparation for my intended response, and having just about memorised every line showed up at the office bright and early the next day champing at the bit in anticipation of what would doubtless be a challenging week ahead.

Turning the key in the lock I was greeted in the corridor by a suspicious-looking character who, uncannily, was the image of Swiss Toni from the TV comedy *The Fast Show*.

Giving an initial impression of shadiness, the individual stealthily introduced himself as Daryl Smith from DMS Legal, before launching into an energetic pitch from which there seemed no stopping him as, getting into his stride, he explained the variety of expert services his go-ahead company could provide, all at specially discounted and affordable rates.

Within seconds it became increasingly clear that he was no more a lawyer than I was, but there was something curiously eccentric about the man that persuaded me to allow him in to suss out whether or not he was for real.

'Do you know anything about the entertainment industry?' was my first question.

'Ah, as luck would have it we represent a number of clients from the world of television, the music business, and indeed all walks of life,' he bilged through his romanticising lips.

'So,' I put to him, 'if I was to explain an awkward situation we have with one of our bands, you may be able to advise us accordingly?'

'Undoubtedly, dear chap,' he responded, before going off on one about his experiences as a mentor to the Rolling Stones.

'Never mind all that,' I blurted, in no mood for fantasising, and began filling him in on the circumstances that had led to the premature cancellation.

Without even considering the matter he energetically offered, 'I'll take the case: five hundred pounds deposit now, pending my investigation, and then…'

I butted in: 'Whoa, hold on a sec, slow down, you've nowhere near convinced me that I should hire you!'

'Listen, buddy, I'm your man. Children in a den of iniquity such as that, after midnight? They haven't got a leg to stand on; you've got 'em by the balls good and proper,' he countered in a flash.

As he excitedly reached the end of the sentence there was a knock at the door, and the office block's security man Fred poked his head in.

'Sorry to bother you sir, but we've had a number of complaints about the gentleman you have with you from female staff to whom he's been making lewd gestures and suggestions; I've been searching for him everywhere. He's not a client of yours, is he sir?'

'No, Fred, he most certainly isn't; in fact he was just leaving!' I confirmed.

'Would you like me to escort him from the premises, sir?' asked Fred.

'I beg your pardon, but what about my fee? I was just in the process of advising a prospective client on some important business,' the scammer ranted in an angry tone.

'I think that may be helpful, Fred, especially as he's begun raising his voice,' I urged.

Swiss Toni looked at me, giving me the evil eye, and voiced, 'You bastard,' as Fred called for assistance on his radio device and gripped the man's arm firmly before ushering him away and eventually out of the door, which thudded shut.

Though the guy had undeniably been of dubious character, something he'd said struck a chord with me when he'd broached the subject of young kids in a drinking establishment full of intoxicated adults.

His parting comment stressing we'd got them by the short and curlies sounded almost informed, as if he actually had been there before and was on to something; and, for all his shifty blather and improper behaviour, there may just have been a speck of truth in what he'd said.

'Who was that creep they were just dragging out?' asked the office girl as she arrived for work.

'Oh him – he's my new lawyer!' I quipped, smirking from ear to ear.

Over the next two or more hours I went through the original contract with a fine-tooth comb, paying particular attention to the clauses that were said to have been infringed.

My response came out as follows:

6th September 2005

WITHOUT PREJUDICE

Dear Sirs

RE: CONTRACT NO. 196181 (Hereinafter called the agreement)

I am in receipt of your letter dated 01.09.2005, the content of which is largely inaccurate and erroneous!

I write to inform you that as a result of your intransigence in this matter, that should the terms of the contractual agreement dated 25.01.2005 fail to be adhered to, and all outstanding monies fail to be received to this company within 30 days, court proceedings will follow forthwith.

My response to the clauses that have allegedly been breached is as follows:

CLAUSE 9

There are clearly no grounds for breach here, as the violation in question occurred after the contracted minimum performance time of 60 minutes had been fulfilled.

To be more precise the band began their performance at 10.50pm,with the contentious incident occurring at 12.05am.

CLAUSE 11

The performance was at all times conducted as is quoted 'decently and in good taste!' Quite how parading in a fantasy character's head is in any way offensive is abstruse and ridiculous. Furthermore there was no angry response from the audience at the time, in fact quite the reverse! The only people present who appeared to take offence were the rather overzealous members of staff.

CLAUSE 12

Your assertions that our client's actions were far from courteous and respectful is ludicrous and incorrect and I reiterate that no kind of offence was caused to any audience member present.

The band and crew personnel were both professional and courteous to all the staff throughout the day, and insofar as the paying customers were concerned received numerous compliments about their show, upon returning to the Show Lounge post-performance.

The band were at the time of the alleged violation performing their second encore which would suggest that the reception received was most satisfactory, with the positive reaction continuing well after the incident, and in no way deterring the adults or children from dancing and showing their extreme appreciation right through to the end of the show.

The Show Lounge was heaving with people, i.e. the terminology used by a senior member of staff was 'one in, one out' which would suggest a very profitable night's bar takings, particularly as many of the customers were severely under the influence of alcohol, which frankly in the presence of many young children is distasteful in the extreme, and far more likely to cause them distress than a prank with a character's head!

Your company has no legal right to withhold payment for the final three performances by attempting to over dramatize this frankly laughable and trivial stunt, and in addition a considerable amount of PA and back line equipment had been set up over a four hour period during the day, at great cost to our company.

Not a single letter or indeed evidence of any complaints from customers have been as you stated forwarded to support your lame assertions.

On a more serious note it has also been brought to my attention in the last few days that your company persisted in advertising that the band were appearing at the two sites i.e. Prestatyn and Fleetwood, where dates had been cancelled after the termination of their services.

We have correspondence to support this from a number of disappointed caravanners who planned their holidays around our artist's performance. This once again I would consider to be far more distressing to your clients than a foolish prank, and the negligence displayed in allowing this to happen shows a total disregard for your paying customers which I personally find utterly disgraceful. I would seek as a matter of urgency a full explanation as to how and why the general public were not in any way kept informed as to the artist's non-appearance.

In summarising: NO small children, as has been suggested, were seen leaving the Show Lounge 'distressed and in tears', indeed there were by the time of the encore very few young ones present or awake.

Subsequently the remarks about 'stripping them of their innocence, and Santa Claus' demise' are to be blunt, utterly pathetic!

I reiterate that young children attending a show in the company of inebriated adults well past midnight is a vastly more affecting and serious matter.

This scandalous inattention should immediately be addressed or these poor unfortunate issues will indeed be prematurely robbed of their innocence, which could lead to extremely damaging press coverage to what can only be described as a neglectful company.

I await your reply prior to the issuing of court proceedings.

Yours Sincerely

All I could do now was await their ensuing response, and keep my fingers crossed that matters could be kept in check without any further nastiness – which would mean the involvement of real lawyers, at yet more exorbitant cost.

39

FAMILY AFFAIR
(SLY AND THE FAMILY STONE)

Thursday 8th September 2005

Business had been brisk since the curtailment of the ill-fated tour, and in spite of the impending threatened loss of earnings, things were looking rosy way into 2006.

I was desperate for a break to recharge the batteries, but there were a number of family issues that needed attending to before there was any chance of getting away.

Dad had now been allotted a single room, which at first unsettled him; but in true indomitable style he was coping admirably, as any old trooper would.

I'd brought him a blown-up colour picture I'd printed off that Danny had taken, of myself posing outside a pet-supplies shop that doubled as a hardware store in the Suffolk town of Beccles, where we'd stopped over during our recent travels.

The retailer's name read 'BARTRAM'S', which not being the most common of surnames was a photo opportunity not to be missed.

Dad was thrilled with it, so much so that on my next visit the carers had been out and had it framed, and informed me I should be honoured it had taken pride of place on the day-room's mantelpiece.

I'd arranged to meet up with my brother to discuss a few legal matters that needed tidying up and had been overlooked in my absence, and when I arrived my sister-in-law Chris mentioned how tired and drawn I was looking.

After shuffling through a wad of documents I gave them an abridged account of the previous week's events, to which their reaction was strangely subdued as if they had no sympathy whatever for my juvenile foolishness.

Over coffee my brother, seeing I was in need of some quality time away, explained that our sister Pat and her partner Rob were joining them for a long weekend's caravanning beginning on the Friday at a site located just outside the former seaport of Blakeney in Norfolk.

'If you've not got anything planned, why don't you come and join us?' he caringly asked.

I folded my arms, smiled and looked to the ceiling, shaking my head, and asked: 'What, you're expecting me to pack up my trunk and say goodbye to the rock-and-roll circus?'

'I suppose you could put it that way, yes,' he said somewhat mystified, as I rose from my chair and delivered a response that was short and to the point.

'NOT ON YOUR NELLIE!'

THE END

EPILOGUE

ENDGAME
(R.E.M.)

1. Trevor Oakes and Jeff Betts (stage name Al James) retired from the band at the end of 2008. We are still constantly in touch.

2. Steve the sound man parted company with Showaddywaddy in 2006, as did his assistant Stefan. Steve has since battled bravely with a life-threatening bout of cancer. Remarkably he responded positively to extensive treatment, and I was recently informed by a reliable source that he is now happily back to his old cantankerous self.

3. England regained the Ashes, beating Australia two-one for the first series win in eighteen years, in what is now referred to as 'the greatest ever series'.

4. Danny Willson left the band after fourteen years in 2009, when he was offered a permanent position with Martin Turner's Wishbone Ash. He'd been a huge fan of 'the Ash' during his early guitar-playing days; and, although it was a wrench for him to go, he found the opportunity too tempting to resist.

5. Sadly there has been no further contact with Laura or her family since August 2005 when she finally attended one of the band's live performances.

6. Connie Comedienne – as far as we know – is still treading the boards. She is now well into her sixties. Her reunion with her father was brief as he passed away in February 2006.

7. A man named Daryl Smith was arrested by Corby Police in Northamptonshire for indecent exposure, after being reported by a young woman working in an office block in the town. The mug shot plastered over the front page of the local newspaper was unmistakably the face of my one-time (albeit only for five minutes) legal advisor.

8. My beloved football team Leicester City had a disappointing season, finishing in sixteenth place after dicing with relegation for much of the 2005/2006 campaign.

9. I had a small (but painful) operation to 'band' my haemorrhoids in 2008. Subsequently long distance travel has become immensely more pleasurable.

10. Between the summer of 2005 and 2011 the band performed at just two caravan parks, both of which were different companies. Each of the camps boasted vastly superior facilities to those of ninety-five per cent of the chain featured in this manuscript. There was, however, one further gig in August 2011 that I have mentioned in the footnote.

11. After a ten-day holiday in Portugal, I returned to find another buff vellum envelope, once again marked 'Private and Confidential'. To my relief the caravan company had caved in, and had agreed to settle in full, thus honouring all of their contractual obligations. The bogus legal expert had been proved right, and the cocktail of children and alcohol in an adult environment the wrong side of the bewitching hour together with the threat of bad press had undoubtedly proved too potent a mix, and would have made for a powerful defence in any court of law. I was, however, forced into signing a disclaimer, confirming I would seek no further redress in terms of adverse publicity, or any form of public bad-mouthing. The matter was now closed, and a cheque was on its way.

12. An incredibly loyal legion of fans continue to support the band through changes in personnel, and basically thick and thin. To

335

each and every one of them I pass on my heartfelt gratitude. Quite what we'd have done without you I'll never know!

FOOTNOTE

THE PARTY'S OVER
(LONNIE DONEGAN)

Saturday 27th August 2011

You'd have thought after thirty-eight years in this game that the prattling sales patter of entertainment agents would wash over my head by now, but caught unawares I allowed a booking at a holiday park to slip through the net into the band's diary, during the early part of 2011.

Perhaps I should have heeded Rod's plea in Porthmadog six years prior and simply said 'no thanks', but the fact remains: I was once again swayed.

After a summer playing a handful of extremely successful and massively enjoyable festival performances, the boys were on a high, but there was a realisation that we may be brought back down to earth with a resounding crash as we all piled into the bus for the journey north to the resort of Rhyl in North Wales.

There were already palpable rumblings of discontent as we hit the M6 motorway and began recounting tales of woe from the summer of 2005, which in truth didn't bode well at all for what lay in wait.

Without entering into too much detail, the camp was an ill-equipped caravan park that any artist(s) with a modicum of self-pride wouldn't have been seen dead in. Yet again we'd become the victims of misinformation, and upon arrival at five p.m. just wanted to turn around and head back home.

The show was quite simply a living nightmare, the stress of which caused me a frightful asthma attack, which visibly didn't help matters at all.

In thirty-eight years on the road, never once had I hated every single minute of a performance with such a passion; this was indeed a first.

Midway through our set something inside of me snapped, and in a brown study I contemplated: 'I honestly don't want to do this any more!'

Arriving home that night totally inconsolable, I thought things over for a couple of days, but was unmoved and resolved that the time was right to bring down the curtain on an illustrious and rewarding career at the end of 2011.

The party was indeed over, and insofar as I was concerned so were the days spent visiting drizzly coastal resorts and dreaded caravan parks.

I played my final show with the band in Ilkley, West Yorkshire on Saturday December 3rd 2011, on an emotional night before an audience of eight hundred people in a wonderful old theatre called The King's Hall.

Dave Bartram
February 2012

ACKNOWLEDGMENTS

FOR THE PRICELESS patience, insight, friendship and help given during the writing of this book, my heartfelt thanks go to:

Cathy Bartram, Holly Bartram, Rod Deas, Romeo Challenger, Trevor Oakes, Jeff Betts, Danny Willson, Steve Beale, Stefan Radymski, Paul Dixon, David Graham, Ollie Petch, Richard 'Bison' Krzyzanowski and any other musicians or crew who survived the calamitous events of the summer of 2005.

Sincere thanks also go out to:

Dexter O'Neill and Paul Ballard at Fantom Publishing, Phil Reynolds for proofreading and typesetting, Ian Dickerson, Theresa Cutts, and to Paul Needham at Mohawk Visuals and Andrew Ball for photography, Alison Griffin and of course the lovely Amanda Holden.